SOUTHEAST ASIA (c. 1971)

500 MILES

CHINA — Hong Kong (U.K.)

N. VIETNAM ⊛ Hanoi

LAOS

Hainan (China)

Vientiane ⊛

Savannakhet ● ⬛ Area enlarged

THAILAND

S. VIETNAM

CAMBODIA

Phnom Penh ⊛ ⊛ Saigon

Gulf of Thailand

SOUTH CHINA SEA

MALAYSIA ⊛ Kuala Lumpur

INDONESIA ● Singapore

25 MILES

NORTH VIETNAM — 1

Gulf of Tonkin

DEMILITARIZED ZONE

LAOS

23

Area enlarged below

Khe Sanh

Dong Ha

9

9

Xepon

SOUTH VIETNAM

1

Hue

92

23

LAOS

N

Ban Dong, a crossroads settlement that in 1971 was Fire Support Base A Loui

200 m

300 m

92

9

200 m

200 m

BRIDGE

300 m

92

9

400 m

500 m

Z PZ Sofia

600 m

Z

X X

V

Xepon

200 m

FSB Delta 1

Z

Ban Satum, whose elders told a U.S. team about Mr. Talin's souvenir

V

V

Ban Chen, where villagers told searchers that they knew of two crash sites in the vicinity

92

Ban Satum Gnai, home to Mr. Talin – and the helmet that has prompted Gwen Haugen's dig

400 m

D0953319

Where They Lay

Where
They Lay

SEARCHING FOR AMERICA'S

LOST SOLDIERS

■

Earl Swift

Houghton Mifflin Company

BOSTON • NEW YORK

2003

For information about permission to reproduce selections from
this book, write to Permissions, Houghton Mifflin Company,
215 Park Avenue South, New York, New York 10003.

Visit our Web site: www.houghtonmifflinbooks.com.

Library of Congress Cataloging-in-Publication Data
Swift, Earl, date.
Where they lay : searching for America's lost
soldiers / Earl Swift.
p.   cm.
Includes bibliographical references.
ISBN 0-618-16820-6
1. Vietnamese conflict, 1961–1975 — Missing in action —
United States. 2. Vietnamese conflict, 1961–1975 —
Campaigns — Laos. 3. Barker, Jack.   I. Title.
DS559.8.M5S95 2003
959.704'38 — dc21   2003041717

Printed in the United States of America

Book design by Robert Overholtzer
Maps and diagrams by Robert D. Voros

QUM 10 9 8 7 6 5 4 3 2 1

FOR MY DAD

CONTENTS

PART ONE

In the Land
of the Lost

■

Ban Alang Base Camp

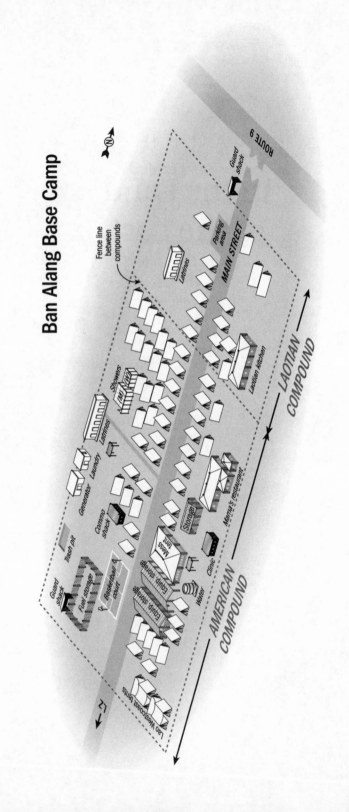

Fence line between compounds

N

Latrines

ROUTE 9

Guard shack

Parking area

MAIN STREET

Showers

Latrines

Generator Laundry Latrines

Trash pit

Laotian kitchen

Commo shack

LAOTIAN COMPOUND

Guard shack

Fuel storage

Basketball court

Storage

Equip storage

Mama's restaurant

Mess tent

Water

Clinic

AMERICAN COMPOUND

Equip storage

L30 Misecoast tents

N

1

THEIR BUDDIES called it suicide, and maybe it was.

They climbed aboard the Huey knowing the enemy expected them. They did it knowing their guns were no match for the cannons that waited. They knew they'd be lucky beyond hope to get past them, and luckier still to get back. They climbed aboard the Huey just the same.

Time was short. Just over the border, their allies were surrounded and outnumbered and taking heavy fire. They depended on the four aboard the helicopter to get them out.

So on a Saturday in March 1971, the Huey skimmed over the mountains into the wide, wild valley beyond, following a rutted, two-lane highway into Laos. The country below was a tangle of splintered hardwoods and sheared bamboo, the jungle's floor laid bare in wounds that stood fresh and red against the green. Off to starboard, a chain of low hills marked the northern edge of the Xepon River's flood plain. Looming ahead was its southern boundary, an escarpment a thousand feet high that showed its bones in cliffs streaked pink and gray. Worn into the rock was a notch a kilometer wide. In it was the pickup zone.

The flak started miles out. The Huey's pilots slalomed the bird among arcing yellow tracers and blooms of brown smoke as it dropped toward the target. Its gunners opened fire with their M-60s, sweeping the trees on the helicopter's final approach.

The reply was overwhelming: Bullets raked the chopper's thin metal skin, whistled into the cabin, tore into man and machine. Then came something worse — a blur, rising from the trees, a telltale plume — and a flash. Fire swallowed the Huey. It hit the ground in pieces.

Other choppers circled low over the burning wreckage, crews marking the spot on their charts. None landed. North Vietnamese soldiers swarmed the bamboo thickets and forest around the smashed chopper, too many to risk a recovery mission. America was forced to leave the Huey, and the four, where they lay.

Which is what brings me, on a gray summer morning thirty years later, to a vibrating seat in the cabin of a Russian-built Mi-17 helicopter. And why its course takes me from a former American air base beside the Mekong River into the same valley, toward the same rampart of cliffs, in the battered highlands along the Vietnam-Laos border.

Somewhere down there is what's left of Jack Barker, John Dugan, Billy Dillender, and John Chubb. For two generations their remains have lain in a remote corner of this remote land, as bamboo and hardwood saplings erupted into new jungle around them, as monsoon rains scoured the red-clay earth and swooning heat baked it dry. Their comrades have grown old. Their children have had children of their own. Today, finally, their countrymen have arrived to take them home.

Sitting beside me are the soldiers and scientists, most too young to remember the war, who will search for the Huey's crew, men and women who for the next four weeks will live in a camp of canvas and nylon and lashed bamboo in the Laotian back country, and who will pass their days on an archaeological dig carved into the wilderness.

They will commute to work in craft all too similar to the ruined machine they seek, and face a host of dangers once they land — steep terrain, triple-digit temperatures, withering humidity, and thickets aswarm with scorpions, foot-long centipedes, and bright green vipers so venomous their nickname is "Jake Two-Steps," said to be how far their victims get before dropping.

The mosquitoes carry malaria, and dengue fever, and God knows what else. Tigers patrol the jungle. And if this weren't worry enough, the ground is laced with unexploded ordnance, leftovers of the fighting that claimed Jack Barker and his crew — half-buried bombs and anti-tank mines and rockets and grenades and baseball-sized bomblets that, jostled the slightest bit, can all these years later turn an arm or leg into a puff of pink smoke.

The Mi-17 is short on frills. The cabin smells of exhaust. The sound of the rotor varies from deafening whine to bone-jolting bass chord.

Hot wind buffets in through open portholes. The floor is plywood; the bare-metal bulkheads are stenciled with instructions in Cyrillic. It has the look and ambiance of an old and neglected school bus.

Only school buses don't yaw sickeningly as they travel. They don't boast clamshell doors like the big pair forming the cabin's back end, doors between which I can see a thin but significant stripe of bright Asian airspace. I watch the gap for a while, see that its width keeps time with the Mi-17's shivers, which course through the frame like a dog shaking dry.

School buses aren't typically driven by committee either. The helicopter's cockpit is crowded with Laotian military men. I can see four of them from where I sit, all speaking and pointing past a pair of jerky windshield wipers into the sky ahead. All are in bits and pieces of uniform. The pilot is a skinny guy in a bright yellow T-shirt. His left hand is pressed against his headset, as if he can't hear over the chatter around him.

There are a couple dozen of us aboard, squeezed into troop seats that line the cabin's sides. My view of those on the far side is blocked by luggage stacked four feet high down the length of the wide aisle. None of it is tied down. The pile — backpacks and suitcases, hard-cased gear and tools — teeters with each banking turn the big chopper makes. Somewhere behind us, another Mi-17 carries a similar load of people and equipment, and sprinkled elsewhere in the sky are four smaller Eurocopter Squirrels, carrying a handful of people apiece.

In all, fifty Americans are in the air. Most work for the U.S. Army's Central Identification Laboratory, where thirty civilian anthropologists and more than one hundred military specialists perform forensic detective work under the microscope and in the wildest of wilds, all aimed at bringing home those lost in America's wars. Others are with Joint Task Force–Full Accounting, a puree of the different services that manage the lab's visits to Southeast Asia and conduct the research that pinpoints where its teams should dig.

Beyond the rain-streaked porthole behind me, wispy clouds race past. I push my forehead against the glass to see the ground below, catch a glimpse of squares and trapezoids and narrow rectangles of bright green, a quiltwork of rice paddies stitched together with dikes that follow the land's irregular contours. A cloud interrupts the view. Then another. A moment later we fly through a bigger, thicker mat of vapor, and then there's nothing but white out there.

Up in the cockpit, water drips from the ceiling, and the three guys assisting the pilot are gesticulating more than ever. The pilot is half out of his seat, squinting. The windshield looks painted over. Some of my fellow passengers shift nervously in their seats. They know the lay of the land, that with every minute we're in the air, the terrain below gets taller and steeper and rockier, that the bottomland from which we took off gives way to a jumble of mountains and solitary karsts, pinnacles of limestone that jut skyward like the teeth of some enormous buried dragon. They know, far better than I, the Mi-17's limitations. Among them: This machine lacks ground-reading radar. We're flying blind.

A big fellow to my right rests his arm on the luggage in front of us and lowers his head into the crook of his elbow. He's been resting that way for a long minute when we burst into the light. Everyone in the cabin seems to take a deep breath at once; even the chopper's crew chief, a sturdy, sullen-looking Laotian soldier in camouflage fatigues, grins for an instant as we speed eastward, the clouds now below us.

The mood doesn't last. Eventually we'll have to descend back through the clouds.

When Saigon fell in April 1975, ending America's thirteen years of open war in Southeast Asia, 2,583 U.S. servicemen were unaccounted for. That might seem a modest number next to the legions lost in the country's earlier conflicts. Tens of thousands of soldiers died nameless in the War Between the States, after all; national cemeteries are crowded with them, Yankee and Reb who died in battle and were buried close to where they fell — dozens to a grave at Richmond, beneath acres at Gettysburg and Petersburg, a thousand miles from home in the desert of New Mexico. Another 78,000 American bodies were never recovered from World War II, from planes lost in the mountains of New Guinea and from island beaches seized by landing marines, from ships sunk a mile deep, from the blood-nourished fields of Normandy.

Half a century on, there's been no sign of 8,000 men who fought in North Korea. Most probably died on the rimy shore of the Chosin Reservoir, or in smaller firefights that never earned titles. Others simply vanished on battlefields their country did not win and could not search.

But Vietnam, more than any of those costlier conflicts, proved to be a slow-healing wound in the American heart, and those who never came home a source of gnawing unease. Many vets had friends whom they'd fought beside, whom they'd seen or spoken with moments before they vanished, and whose fate was uncertain. Thousands of families lacked proof that a husband, a father, a son was gone. All yearned for answers.

So, since the mid-eighties, the U.S. government has been embarked on a mission unprecedented in recorded history: To return to the places where planes went down, ambushed patrols left people behind, men simply disappeared. To find the remains of the missing. To send home all they find. To put a name, the right name, on each of their headstones.

It sends an expedition into Southeast Asia ten times each year. One trip is to Cambodia, where the fates of almost 60 Americans remain unresolved. Four of the trips, or "joint field activities," are to Vietnam, from which more than 1,400 men have yet to return; on each, five or six recovery teams fan out through the countryside, so that over the course of a typical year, Americans excavate better than twenty sites there. And half of the trips are made to the Lao People's Democratic Republic — to this landlocked, xenophobic throwback of stone-simple villages and roadless jungle, where nearly 400 soldiers, sailors, airmen, and marines remain unfound.

Five times a year, American recovery teams fly here on U.S. Air Force cargo planes. The Laotian government permits only fifty people per joint field activity and monitors their movements closely. They land at Vientiane, the capital, where their visas are processed. From there they fly to Savannakhet, a city on the Mekong, halfway down the Laotian panhandle. At an airport where the United States once ran supply flights to troops fighting the Communist Pathet Lao — ancestor of the present government — team members climb off the planes and onto trucks, which trundle them a quarter mile to a helipad. Then, loaded onto Laotian Mi-17s, they fly away from the modern world and into country seen by few Americans in thirty years.

I have flown 12,000 miles and across twelve time zones to join the mission as its unofficial fifty-first member, to witness its work in the jungle and immerse myself in the technological leaps of the past fifteen years that have made it possible. I've come, too, with questions about this massive effort, questions like: Why is the government doing this now? Is it necessary at all? Is it worth $100 million a year? And: Why are the people of Southeast Asia, with hundreds of thousands of their own missing, helping us?

It is my third visit to the region. Like those previous, it began with a seemingly endless flight across the Pacific to the vast weirdness of the

Bangkok airport, a humid stew of peoples and languages, of smells and long lines and impenetrable crowds where, while waiting for a passport stamp, I was mesmerized by a gargantuan video screen that loomed over the terminal; on it, a Thai and his trained parrot whistled the theme from *The Andy Griffith Show*. Jetlagged and muddle-headed, I flew on to Laos, a territory slightly smaller than Oregon and shaped like a long-stalked head of broccoli. China and Burma lie to the north, Cambodia to the south. To the west, beyond the muscular Mekong, is Thailand; no bridge linked the two until 1993, and only one does so today. Vietnam lies to the east, across a border of high mountains.

It is poor even by Third World standards — too poor, really, for its socialist government to control any real wealth or production, or to provide much in the way of services. There's not a foot of railroad track. Vast portions of Laos are unelectrified. Most of the country lacks running water, and in the few cities where it exists it's unfit to drink. Outside of the same handful of cities, health care is virtually nonexistent, education is paltry, the economy is preindustrial, and living conditions border on the medieval. It is a world lit by fire. Much of the population subsists on family rice plots, crossbow hunting, and foraging.

In Vientiane I obtained the papers I'd need to travel into the interior, walked unpaved streets among mildewed concrete buildings, witnessed the capital's uneasy courtship with the West after years of self-imposed exile. My lavish hotel rose from a neighborhood of squalid shacks and patrolling soldiers. Rats swam past my table at a riverfront bar. At one Vientiane nightspot, I saw a Laotian rock band cover Pink Floyd's "The Wall." At a restaurant in the city's center I braved Jeo Mengda, which the menu described as "Chilli sauce with the smell of the water bug served with boiled vegetables." After six days in town, I caught a ride south, into the panhandle, to meet the incoming teams.

Before long the Mi-17 slows, and its pilot sends us corkscrewing downward, fuselage shuddering, blades whacking the air. Some passengers shut their eyes. An army sergeant to my left keeps his open. He stares out the porthole between us, nodding, then glances over to me. I evidently look nervous. He taps my shoulder, jabs a thumb toward the cockpit. "This guy's good," he yells over the rotor.

"Yeah?" I say. "How can you tell?" I look to the cockpit and decide not to do it again: One of its occupants is now trying to catch the drips from the ceiling with a small towel, so that they don't land on the man at the controls.

"He's found a hole," the sergeant says. "He waited until he found a hole, and now he's gonna just circle down through the clouds until we're below them."

Sure enough, our turn tightens until we're heeled over hard, the spinning ground filling the portholes, and we have to steady the luggage to keep it from toppling. We drop as if sucked down a drain, the clouds a white blur as we pass through the overcast. When we level out, we're just below the ceiling and just five hundred feet off the ground. Treetops seem to reach for us. We zigzag over the forest, the portholes pelted by rain, until a narrow strip of asphalt comes into view, its surface pitted with deep holes, shoulders scalloped and broken. We bank into a wide right turn to follow it.

The chopper fishtails eastward, slicing through the misty tentacles dangling from the clouds' bellies, the ground rising gradually beneath us, and so we go for miles, sandwiched in a dwindling wafer of clear air between jungle and blindness. I stare down at the road, which looms closer with every minute. It's cracked and gouged, and in places the pavement disappears completely, is replaced by stretches of cinnamon-colored mud and tiny ponds that reflect the overcast sky.

"Route 9," the sergeant yells. The chief highway across the Laotian panhandle. A major link between Vietnam and Thailand. It doesn't look the part, and I turn a troubling thought: This is a country without money for basic highway repairs. How much can it possibly invest in pilot training? In aircraft maintenance?

The rotors throb. Below, rice paddies shimmer. We cross unbroken miles of forest, then a river stained coffee brown, then a village of thatch-roofed huts on stilts bunched around a bare-dirt clearing, water buffalo loose among the buildings. A second village slides by, no more than 150 feet under the Mi-17's wheels. I can see chickens on the ground and a knot of children peering up at us.

Just beyond the settlement I notice another feature of the landscape: a hole, an almost perfect circle, big enough to swallow one of the village's huts. Another appears. Another. Still another. They're everywhere, some of them fifty feet or more across, most filled with opaque water. They're punched into rice paddies, bunched in threes and fours around villages. They line Route 9. I can see others hidden by the jungle, betrayed by round gaps in the canopy. In places they're so tightly spaced the ground resembles the surface of a golf ball. Bomb craters.

The Mi-17's whining turbines deepen in pitch. The big machine again slows, and ahead, through the veil of a stiffening rain, a patch of bright blue appears. The chopper flares, nose high, and settles slowly onto a concrete pad. The helicopter's crew chief throws open the hatch to a shock of wind and rotor noise; I grab my backpack from the stack in the aisle and follow the sergeant out. A hard rain is falling, and we jog across spongy ground past already-parked Squirrels — and past a concrete pedestal that rises knee-high from the grass, its top adorned with a crumbling Communist star, a relic from the days when this was a North Vietnamese maintenance camp.

These days, the star is at odds with the self-contained Little America that waits beyond. Linking the landing zone with Route 9 is a straight, narrow dirt road, nicknamed Main Street, and around it rises a small town of fifty-three canvas wall tents called the Ban Alang Base Camp.

At the landing zone's fringe the joint task force's commander in Laos, Lt. Col. Kevin Smith, is yelling instructions to scurrying soldiers over the din of what's now a downpour, apparently unfazed by his drenched T-shirt and shorts. Smith pauses a second to point me toward my tent. It's prime Ban Alang real estate, one tent back from Main Street's west side. I duck in and slip off my pack.

My home for the next month is about twelve feet by eight, with screened gables and a drooping roof supported by a center pole. A bare-bulb light fixture is duct-taped to the pole and plugged into a thick extension cord powered by a generator shack at the camp's western edge. The tent is otherwise empty. As I'm assessing it, one of Smith's aides sticks his head in, sees that I don't have a cot, and tells me I'll need to scrounge one up, so for the next half-hour I roam the camp.

Behind the tents platooned on the street's west side, at the end of a long concrete sidewalk, stands a low cinderblock building housing the camp's latrines, which are equipped with otherwise unattainable luxuries in this part of the world: porcelain sit-down toilets. Just north of the latrines stand the showers, floored with concrete, framed with bamboo, walled and roofed with nylon tarp. A bright royal blue, the tarps are ubiquitous at Ban Alang. They're draped over the roofs of all the tents and overhang the narrow corridors between. They shroud piles of gear. They've served, over the years, myriad other functions, so many that they're now considered indispensable; no other gear used by the

U.S. military in Southeast Asia, save for duct tape and a tough nylon rope called "550 cord," is so highly prized. From the air, Ban Alang's blue stands out against the jungle's thousand shades of green as if lit from within.

Just north of the landing zone on Main Street's east side, two tin-roofed, open-sided barns stand side by side. In one, caged in thick chain-link, the teams store their shovels, picks, pumps, and surveying equipment. In the other is one of the camp's social centers: a gym of benches and free weights, along with two hotel ice machines and a couple of big coolers of bottled water. Alongside the barns is a metal-framed canvas mess tent. A chain of portable banquet tables runs down its center, along with a couple dozen folding chairs; along its north wall is another table, on which sit a microwave oven and a pair of two-burner propane stoves. A twenty-five-inch color television and video-tape player occupy a corner. The TV is Ban Alang's readiest connection to the outside world, thanks to a satellite dish outside, and it runs pretty much around the clock.

A dishwashing station stands out back of the mess tent, and beside it, a small, open-air shack with a thatched roof, a Ping-Pong table centered on its concrete floor. A few yards from this modest game room is a tiny building of screened windows and woven-bamboo walls — the hospital. And a few yards more to the north is the most remarkable amenity of the camp's many: Mama's, a dispensary of good, cheap American and Lao meals, cold indigenous beer, cigarettes (a Thai version of Marlboros), soft drinks (mostly aggressively sweet Asian brands), and Oreos.

By the end of my search I've amassed one metal-framed cot with a defective crossbar that causes one end to sag; an army-issue folding field table, wooden, olive drab in color; one folding metal chair, swiped from the mess tent; and an electric fan, which I plug into the open socket.

It's dark and raining harder than ever when I sprint across Main Street to a mandatory camp meeting. The mess tent is already crowded when I step through the door, shirt soaked, and into its sallow light. Half the Americans in camp sit at the banquet tables, which have been rearranged into a long-stemmed T; the rest line the walls. I find a place in a corner as Kevin Smith, sitting at the T's bottom, stands. The room is instantly silent.

Smith is wearing blue jeans and a T-shirt emblazoned "Ohio State Athletics," but even so manages to look like an army officer. His hair, turning to silver, is thick but cropped a shade too closely to be fashionable, and he stares a bit too hard, speaks a little too forcefully, rests his hands on his hips with too much of a "Go ahead, fuck with me" air to be anything but.

"Welcome," he says. "I'm Lieutenant Colonel Smith. I'm the Detachment Three commander of Joint Task Force–Full Accounting. Welcome to Laos. Welcome to the Ban Alang Base Camp." As he speaks, moths flit around the fluorescent strips overhead. The rain's tattoo against the tent roof strengthens. Smith turns up his volume. "Before we go any further, I want you to remember this: For as long as you're here, for the entire time you're in Laos, safety is your number one priority.

"You're in Laos in the rainy season," he says. "In the rainy season, the ground gets saturated. Critters come out of the ground. And there are a *lot* of critters in Laos. Poisonous snakes." He scans the room, as if to ensure that we're paying attention. "Scorpions." Another pause. "Centipedes." Pause. "Leeches." Finally: "Insects."

"Be aware of the critters. When you leave your tent at night, take your flashlight. Take a minute to check the ground outside your tent. Last mission we had a guy leaving his tent at night. Had to use the latrine. He didn't usually take a flashlight with him, but for some reason he decided to this time, and he flicked it on as he was stepping out, and two feet away was a snake." He squints, searching his memory. "What kind was it? Anybody remember?"

"A big-eyed viper," somebody says.

"That's it," Smith nods. "A big-eyed viper. You do *not* want to step on a big-eyed viper. When you go into the latrine at night, stand there for a minute at the door. Take a good look around. Make sure Jake No-Shoulders isn't waiting to say hello to you."

We will have one day off during the four-week joint field activity, the colonel tells us. Every other day, weekends included, we'll fly to our excavation sites. We are to keep in mind that doing business in Laos is expensive and that our carelessness can make it more so: A Squirrel costs the American taxpayer $11 a minute, every minute, and the Mi-17s, $45. "So pay attention," he says. "Don't keep that helicopter waiting. We spent $1.1 million on the last JFA on air transportation alone. That's a bunch of change."

Outside, the rain is producing a loud hiss as it strikes gravel sprinkled atop Main Street. The colonel dispatches someone to fetch our next speaker; at Ban Alang's north end, separated from the American compound by orange plastic fencing, fifteen wall tents house a Laotian military delegation led by a taciturn major. A few minutes later, the officer strides in with a half-dozen assistants. He faces a linguist from Joint Task Force-Full Accounting and commences a gruff monologue, punctuating his speech with little karate chops. "There are many dialects of Lao," the translator relays. "Without official help, you could be misunderstood. The locals could be misunderstood." Therefore, we Americans are never to communicate with the locals without first consulting a Laotian official. One will never be far away, as we may go nowhere alone: We cannot take off in a helicopter without a government escort, nor stray far from camp on foot. We may not stop en route to our excavation sites. We may not take photographs from the air.

The major wraps up his remarks by echoing Kevin Smith on safety. To ensure that we're kept from harm, he adds, the People's Democratic Republic has supplied Ban Alang with eighteen sentries armed with AK-47 assault rifles. "At night, the guards are on constant patrol," he says, "so you don't have to worry about things." He smiles.

Smith stands, thanks the major, then holds up a hand. "This is important," he says. "This is not a sprint, people. This is a marathon. Day three, you're full of vim and vigor, and you can't wait to get out there because it's something new. By day twenty-one, it's starting to get pretty old.

"You don't want to be the guy on day twenty-three who for twenty-two days straight has screened nothing but sterile soil and wishes he were anybody else, any place else — and who isn't paying attention when that piece of bone turns up.

"Remember," Smith says, pointing at us, "that you are here to send home a missing American who fought right where you stand. Whose family has waited for answers all these years. Remember why you're here."

2

POPULAR CULTURE's best-known reference to the search for unaccounted-for Americans is a shoot-'em-up action picture released in the mid-1980s. In *Rambo*, Sylvester Stallone, portraying a Medal of Honor recipient credited with "fifty-nine confirmed kills" during the war, sneaks into the Vietnamese boonies to discover long-abandoned Americans sharing a bamboo cage with spiders and rats. Double-crossed by his own government, and armed only with steely resolve, a compound bow, and his trusty K-Bar knife, the shirtless Rambo shoots, stabs, blows up, beats up, electrocutes, and immolates a legion of Vietnamese and their Russian advisers; commandeers a Russian helicopter in mid-flight; destroys the camp; frees the prisoners; and flies them across Laos to freedom.

The American operation actually under way in Southeast Asia doesn't rely on such heroics. The team I'll join on the search for Jack Barker and his crew is led by a former high school cheerleader, a licensed cosmetologist, and a Marine Corps captain born after the war's end. Most of its thirteen members, seven women and six men, are army sergeants trained as "92-Mikes," the military occupation code given to Mortuary Affairs specialists — soldiers trained at Fort Lee, Virginia, in the basics of physiology and in the science of preparing their dead comrades for shipment home.

We assemble in the barn beside the mess tent just after the meeting, everything beyond the glow of its lights dark and busy with sawing crickets, the air cloying with rain and heat. Water drips from the shed's corrugated metal roof and splashes in puddles at our feet. "OK, y'all," a smoky-voiced black man says, "we got a lotta work to do tomorrow, got a busy day." Sergeant First Class Randy Posey runs his tongue over the bottom of a thin mustache, regards his fellow soldiers with slightly bulging eyes. Posey is the team's senior noncommissioned officer, and rides herd on its ten enlisted members. At forty-four, he is among the oldest Americans at Ban Alang, and after just two years at the lab, he is among its most trusted sergeants — steady, reliable, fair-minded, kind. He peers at a stocky, beetle-browed young man with a "high and tight" haircut, the sides of his head nearly shaved. "Sir, you have anything you need to say?"

Marine captain Patrick Reynolds, twenty-seven years old, is the team's official leader, and Posey's boss. He scans the dimly lit faces around him. Half of his team is older than he is, and most have far more experience than he does: This is Reynolds's first day in Laos, and his first recovery mission. "Let's get an early start in the morning," he says. "We've got a job to do. Let's work together. Let's get it done."

"What time you want everybody here, sir?" Posey asks him.

Reynolds ponders the question for a moment. "We start flying at, what, oh-seven-thirty?"

"Yessir," Posey says. "Usually something like that."

"Very well," the captain says, "let's have everybody meet here at oh-seven-hundred."

Posey nods and turns to an athletic young woman, fine-boned and pretty, her blonde hair tied into a pony tail and threaded through the back of a faded St. Louis Cardinals ball cap. "Ma'am?"

Gwen Haugen is the team's anthropologist, its scientific leader. Reynolds and Posey command people; she commands the work. "We'll take just a few people out to the site tomorrow," she says. "We just need to have a look around, to see how we're going to set things up. I don't expect it to take very long. We won't work a full day out there."

"OK, you heard the doc," Posey says, eyeing the rest of the team. "Some of y'all will go out to the site. Some are gonna stay here to help get things squared away. Either way, be here at seven o'clock."

The members of Recovery Element One, or "RE-1," venture into the night. On my way to my tent, I see other teams huddled in brief pow-wows outside the mess tent and in the middle of Main Street — Recovery Element Two, assigned the task of finding the remains of a navy pilot lost aboard an attack jet shot down in 1968; the thirteen members of

Recovery Element Three, who will seek two aviators killed when their observation plane crashed in a box canyon to our south. The balance of the Americans in camp, huddled around the barbells and benches of the open-air gym, are attached to an Investigative Element, or IE, which will tour the countryside looking for leads on where Joint Task Force–Full Accounting should send REs in the future.

Once in my tent, I plug in my light, pull a chair up to my field table, and open a packet of papers the joint task force has prepared for me, a primer on this last mission of the Vietnam War.

Of the 2,583 servicemen who were unaccounted for when Saigon fell in April 1975, a quarter were next to impossible to find from the start: They were aviators who crashed in deep water, GIs vaporized in artillery blasts. In the years since, investigators have hit dead ends in their search for nearly as many more, which, hoping for new leads, they classify as "deferred." Over the same time, more than one in five of the missing have been found and sent home for burial. Another one in ten have been recovered from the field, but have not yet been identified. That leaves 23 percent of the lost, fewer than six hundred, open and active candidates for recovery missions.

In the Pentagon's shorthand, Jack Barker and his crew are collectively known as "1731," the reference number affixed to their case file. Every unrecovered soldier, sailor, airman, or marine from the Vietnam War has such a file, numbered according to when he was lost. Thus, a man last seen in January 1961 will have a number beginning with three zeros; a soldier missing in mid-1966 will have a number in the 0300s; those lost later in the war, like the four aboard the Huey, will have four-digit numbers beginning with "1" or "2." Some defense analysts have devoted their entire careers to working Southeast Asian MIA cases, and know the histories of each so well that at a mere mention of a "REFNO," they can rattle off the names of the missing, the circumstances surrounding the "incident of loss," and the efforts made to close the case since.

They'd recall, for instance, that the men of 1731 were highly decorated: Between them the four earned five Purple Hearts, three Silver Stars, at least two Bronze Stars, two Distinguished Flying Crosses, and one Distinguished Service Cross, a recognition of valor second only to the Medal of Honor.

They'd recall that the shootdown claimed a commander: Jack Barker was his company's CO, and an up-and-coming major who seemed destined for the army's high ranks.

They'd recall that Bill Dillender was only nineteen years old, and that John Chubb, a few months older, had been in Vietnam for just twenty-eight days when he died.

They'd recall that the Huey's pilots were among their company's least experienced. Barker, a short, stocky Georgian two days shy of his thirty-second birthday, had been flying for less than six months. Capt. John Dugan, the twenty-three-year-old New Jersey redhead beside him in the cockpit, was technically the bird's senior aviator — but was so unschooled himself that he didn't yet command his own chopper.

They'd recall the flight as "basically a suicide mission."

And they'd recall that the four are surrounded by other Americans, for many of the missing have geography in common. Disappearances in Vietnam tended to occur in the country's slender waist, in what are now its central provinces — Quang Nam, Quang Tri, Quang Binh, Thua Thien. Throughout what the Vietnamese call the American War, these were the provinces closest to the demilitarized zone that separated North and South Vietnam, and they were home to some of the fiercest fighting. Most of the 584 men unaccounted for in Laos at war's end were last seen near the border and just west of the DMZ, not far from Ban Alang.

The jumbled landscape hereabouts was a vital component of the North Vietnamese strategy: Faced with the challenge of supplying its guerillas deep in American-occupied South Vietnam, and knowing any troops, food, weapons, or ammo convoyed through that territory would be intercepted, the Hanoi government pulled an end run — it snuck them into Laos, down the Laotian panhandle, then back across the border behind the lines. Westerners nicknamed this back-door route the Ho Chi Minh Trail.

The peaks of the Annamite Cordillera, the craggy highlands forming the thousand-mile border, aren't high by mountaineering standards — the tallest mountain in Laos rises 8,694 feet, a summit that would be lost in the Rockies — but they create their own weather; steep-sided, split by deep river gorges, they attract cloud cover and hold it fast. Cloaked in this soupy air and the jungle's thatch, protected by the border's chaotic topography, North Vietnamese caravans drove, bicycled, and backpacked a steady flow of soldiers, weapons, and rice to their comrades-in-arms.

The American brass recognized the route's importance early in the fighting and ordered its almost continual bombing. One day's strikes might wreck a piece of it; the Vietnamese would reroute the trail around the damaged section. When another strike took out the new stretch, the Vietnamese would move it again. It wasn't long before the trail was a web of a thousand strands weaving through the dense Laotian bush, in places twenty-five miles wide.

The American effort to disrupt the southward march constituted the longest continuous mission of the war. It called on aircrews dispatched on bombing runs, commandos on the ground, electronic warfare specialists — the Pentagon employed all sorts of clever gizmos to combat the supply network, including sensors that detected the footfalls of troops on the move, overheard conversations, even sniffed the odor of human flesh. Nothing worked for long, however, and U.S. losses in stanching the traffic were significant. Case 1731 is among dozens here.

My dossier includes a summary of the case prepared by Bill Forsyth, a joint task force analyst. It is lean on details about the Huey's loss. "On 20 March 1971, the four-man crew of a UH-1H helicopter was attempting to extract an Army of the Republic of Vietnam (ARVN) force from the area of Landing Zone (LZ) Brown," it reads. "The first helicopters that attempted to land were driven off by heavy ground fire. The pilot of the case aircraft attempted to land, but the aircraft was hit. . . . Four other UH-1 aircraft were lost near the LZ on that day and the extraction was suspended."

Forsyth goes on to describe the site where the excavation will take place. It is 5.7 nautical miles southeast of Ban Alang. The wreckage is scattered over an area measuring fifteen meters square. It will require forty to fifty people, working for thirty days, to dig it all up.

He judges RE-1's odds of success as "possible."

Late at night the rain returns. As I lie in my cot, listening to its tattoo on the canvas overhead, the soil around my tent turns to pudding. Sometime around three the wind kicks up, the tent's stakes tear loose, and I jerk awake to a loud, hollow pop — the sound of a light bulb bursting. I sit up and peer into the blackness, can make out the toppled center pole lying on the floor a couple feet away, frosted glass in pieces beside it, the light socket still duct-taped to its middle. A moment later, the tent's sodden roof collapses onto my face.

So I'm not looking or feeling my best when six of us take off for the site shortly after 7 A.M. Gwen Haugen wants to keep the group small; today will offer her only opportunity to examine 1731's wreckage before it's crowded with people, and before those people start changing it. She, Sergeant Posey, and RE-1's linguist, air force senior airman Clint Krueger, crowd into a Squirrel with a pair of Laotian escorts for the first lift. Fifteen minutes later, the chopper is back for Pat Reynolds, me, another couple of officials, and the team's medic, navy chief hospital corpsman Arielitho "Art" Artillaga.

Our pilot is a New Zealander who works for Lao Westcoast Aviation, an Australian outfit under contract to Joint Task Force-Full Accounting to ferry American teams in Laos. The company's six-seat helicopters are small and agile enough to thread their way into tight jungle landing spots, and its pilots veterans of the Laotian bush, New Zealand's Antarctic camps, and logging operations throughout Oceana. The rotors are turning as we climb into the Squirrel's left side, Artillaga and I crowding in the back with our escorts, Reynolds taking the front seat. Snug and spry, its cockpit wrapped in Plexiglas, the Squirrel is a sports car to the Mi-17's school bus. We rise to a low hover, spin 180 degrees, and with our nose tilted downward, skim fast from the camp and out over the trees and five hundred feet into the air.

Little more than an hour after dawn, there's no sign of last night's storm. The sky is clear, the temperature already climbing through the high eighties, and as we fly eastward, we have an unobstructed view of the landscape below. It is a flat-bottomed valley four miles wide, the same broad furrow that Jack Barker's helicopter traveled in its final minutes. In its depths, the Xepon River runs a jagged course of right-angle bends and squarish loops, white flecks advertising the rocks and low cascades in its path. Off to our left, north of the river, I can make out Route 9's straight cut through rosewood, banana, and bamboo, and beyond it, a chain of round-topped highlands that occupy the nexus between mountain and hill.

Close off our right side rises the massive escarpment toward which Barker and company flew. Its upper half is pink stone streaked and stained with grays and browns, a few tenacious shrubs bristling from its clefts. Lower are the escarpment's shoulders, where the valley's bottom climbs steeply to meet the vertical rock, crisscrossed with narrow footpaths, sprinkled with a few lonely huts standing guard over bright green rice fields. And everywhere — along the river's banks, among the wild banana trees sprouting like asterisks at the escarpment's foot, across fields and forest — everywhere are craters.

Four miles from Ban Alang the escarpment, which for most of its length runs east-west, veers sharply to the south. The Squirrel banks around the promontory this bend creates — a mammoth ship's bow pointed to the northeast — and on rolling ground a mile ahead, a patch of bright blue appears.

We set down in a clearing ringed by two dozen crouching villagers, the Squirrel's rotor kicking up a swirling cloud of dust, twigs, and dead leaves. The spectators have little experience with helicopters and don't know to shield their faces against the blast; as we jump from our seats, several are rubbing their eyes and spitting dirt from their mouths. One is a leather-skinned woman about four feet tall, topless and nursing a naked infant. She's also smoking a pipe. Another is a skinny teenager in a black Metallica T-shirt. I pass a knot of smiling little girls in bright gold earrings and long, colorfully woven skirts, and little boys whose heads are shaved save for oval tufts of hair over their brows. One, maybe ten years old, is smoking a cigarette.

Our destination lies forty yards from the landing zone, at the end of a broad path. An advance team has cleared a great circle of vegetation from the excavation site, leaving a scene resembling photographs of the wartime Somme or Verdun, more postapocalyptic than suggesting science is afoot. Dragonflies flit over stumps of bamboo hacked into evil-looking points and termite mounds chest-high and hard as cement built on what, a few days past, was dark forest floor. The ground is muddy and puddled and ugly in its nakedness.

Some of the cleared bamboo has been lashed into the frames of three large, open-sided tents roofed with nylon tarps. In one, at the clearing's southwest edge, thinner poles have been fashioned into a platform for gear storage and two picnic tables, one long and one short. This will be the break area for us Americans. We'll dig for the helicopter with the help of hired villagers, who will rest in another tent of about the same size, fifteen yards away; the third shelter will serve as a rough clinic during visits by the mission's American doctor.

I dump my knapsack on a picnic table and stride among stumps and puddles, boots squishing, to the clearing's middle and the lip of a bomb crater thirty-five feet across and fifteen deep, with sides that dive into an opaque brown pool. Just beyond it, on the site's east side, the ground drops steeply into a still-wooded and shady ravine. I can hear a stream burbling down there, though it's invisible behind piles of bamboo chopped down to create the clearing and dumped onto the gully's bank. A second bomb crater, about half the size of the first, is punched into the slope at the clearing's northeast edge. A third lurks in the brush behind the American break tent.

The escarpment looms over the bush to the west and south, its cliffs glowing warm in the morning sun. I eye its uneven top edge and think: Somewhere up there, beyond view but within a few hundred yards of where I stand, Landing Zone Brown lay. I look around. Haugen and Reynolds, our marine captain, are crouched at the edge of the big crater. Sergeant Posey is walking the clearing's western fringe. Clint Krueger, the linguist, is talking to a small group of villagers with our chief escort, a Laotian army captain named Somphong Sangkhisisavath, who's wearing camouflage sneakers with his jungle fatigues, and another Laotian officer representing the district — something akin to an American county — in which we've set down. He's a tall character wearing a camo ball cap that bears the embroidered legend "US POLO," and a rough facsimile of the Stars and Stripes.

Only one thing is missing: the Huey. There is no wrecked helicopter here, nor any obvious sign of one — no burned hulk, no broken rotors, no mangled engine. I stroll over to Haugen, who is still at the crater's edge picking at something on the ground. When I bend down beside her, I see that it's a candy-striped piece of electrical wire. A couple feet away, a button lies beside a tuft of grass.

Next to it is a thin ribbon of aluminum, maybe three inches long.

A small triangle of broken Plexiglas.

Shards of what seem to be porcelain, a half-inch thick and bright white — as if a bathroom sink has been smashed and scattered over acres of the Laotian bush.

With a start I realize that *this* is the helicopter, that I'm standing in it, that this is all that remains of a machine almost forty-two feet long and fourteen and a half feet tall, a complex marriage of aluminum, steel, and glass that weighed two and a half tons. "I don't get it," I tell Haugen. "Where's the rest?"

She looks up at me. Haugen has spent four years as an anthropologist with the Central Identification Laboratory. This is her eleventh mission. She doesn't seem much fazed by our surroundings, nor the dearth of wreckage. "An awful lot of them are like this, when you have an explosion and fire," she says calmly. She stands and pulls off her gloves. "Then you've got secondary burning from farmers clearing their fields, so a lot of these sites have been burned twice — once in the incident and later by the locals. And these farmers use gasoline. It's a hot fire."

"Yeah, but surely fire didn't do *this*."

She chuckles softly. "Well, no," she says. "Not all of it. But this is pretty typical." She looks around the clearing, then at the splinters at our feet. "There's been a lot of scavenging by thirty years after an incident.

"Have you seen their machetes?" She nods toward a group of local boys perched in deep squats on a nearby termite mound, their knees level with their shoulders, rumps hovering an inch off the dirt. Several hold machetes — in Lao, *bria* — with crude, square-ended blades. "Look at the metal on them," Haugen says. "A lot of times, it'll look suspiciously like aircraft."

Visit other parts of the world, and a half-century after a plane crash, the wreckage will lie relatively intact, untouched by the locals, who regard it as a tomb, a place worthy of respect or inhabited by spirits. Not so in Southeast Asia, where metal is snatched up not only at decades-old wartime crash sites but at the scene of contemporary accidents, sometimes before they've even had time to cool.

True story: On October 19, 2000, a Lao Aviation commuter plane carrying fifteen people smacked into a mountaintop in northeastern Laos, not far from where a recovery team led by lab anthropologist Greg Berg was working a site. The Americans joined the rescue effort. While Berg helped bandage the injured, he noticed that most of the more than one hundred villagers who'd gathered at the crash were clutching pieces of wreckage, and realized that in their zeal to salvage metal, the locals had started to dismantle the plane even as the survivors lay pain-racked and helpless around them.

Haugen's marking the location of each piece of surface debris with little orange flags on wire stalks when Randy Posey approaches from across the site, perspiration beaded in his mustache and dripping from his chin. Posey had never heard of 92-Mikes when he joined the army eleven years ago, after a first career as a schoolteacher. He wasn't even aware the job existed; he meandered into it after holding down another military occupation specialty — field artillery, with a unit stationed in upstate New York. The climate at Fort Drum came as a rude shock after more than thirty years down South, and the work was a lot harder than anything he'd experienced in the classroom — so hard and so unpleasant that after four years he told the bosses he couldn't take it anymore. They asked him: You want a job where you just sit at a desk all day? Posey said, Yeah, I'll take that one. They shipped him to the Mortuary Affairs company at Fort Lee. Three years later, he was at the lab.

Some army assignment officer somewhere has probably been laughing ever since. Posey works harder on the lab's missions than he's ever worked in his life. His T-shirt droops with what must be five pints of sweat. His white tube socks, pulled up over the hems of his fatigue pants to keep out poisonous critters, are soaked through.

He stops a few feet from Haugen and gazes over the debris field. "Not much to it, ma'am," he says quietly.

"No," she replies. "The only wreckage I've seen is over here." She points to the scant evidence at her feet, then to a trail tamped into the muddy grass that angles up the ravine, passes through the debris field, and skirts the big crater. "There's this little path running through here, so once we get this gridded, we're gonna want to keep the villagers from using that."

Posey nods as a steady procession of locals climbs the trail from the ravine's bottom. Haugen watches them come. "I can see it's going to be difficult," she says. I notice that while the sergeant is practically puddling sweat, the anthropologist appears dry, fresh, unaffected by the heat.

Posey wanders off. Haugen returns to our conversation and to picking at the ground with her trowel. "Sometimes you think the heavier items, like the rotor assembly, they wouldn't be able to get out," she says. "You'd be surprised. They just pick it apart over time."

She looks up at me. "We're only a kilometer from a village," she says. "This is pretty much their Home Depot."

Late in the morning, a wiry Laotian with a bushy tangle of graying hair appears at the edge of the clearing, wearing a khaki safari shirt, nylon swimming trunks, and mismatched flip-flops, the left one yellow, the right, blue. In one hand he holds a red, floral-pattern umbrella. Mr. Talin is the chief of a nearby village. More importantly, he's the owner of a war souvenir, the one intact artifact of the helicopter that came to rest where we stand. Haugen turns to Clint Krueger. "Ask him to indicate where he saw the helmet," she says. At the same time, she hands Mr. Talin a wire flag.

Krueger utters a few words in Lao, pausing between phrases to search for the right wording. The chief promptly strides to the crater, sure-footedly descends its side, and splashes through the knee-high muck at the bottom. He plants the flag in the hole's northwest corner, then looks up at us.

"Does he still have the helmet?" Haugen asks. Krueger haltingly relays the question. Mr. Talin nods.

"Would it be possible tomorrow for him to bring the helmet, so we could take a picture of it?" she asks. Krueger hesitates. Captain Somphong jumps in to translate. The man says he could do that.

"Could you ask him whether, when he farmed here, he saw any more pieces of airplane?" the anthropologist asks. She's looking at Krueger, but it's the captain, evidently impatient, who poses the question in Lao. Mr. Talin shakes his head.

Haugen points to the trail through the debris field. "People walk through here," she says. "Did people maybe pick up big pieces and take them to the village?" We haven't been to Ban Satun Gnai or any of the surrounding villages. For all we know, pieces of the helicopter have been incorporated into house construction, a common Laotian practice. The captain translates the question. Mr. Talin stares. Haugen tries a different tack: "Are there any other large pieces, possibly with numbers, that they might have in the village?" Mr. Talin says that could be. Possibly.

"Yes, because it would be very helpful if we could have pieces with numbers," Haugen explains. "Many helicopters were lost here, and it would be very helpful to have a number." Captain Somphong translates. Mr. Talin rattles off a lengthy reply. The captain turns back to Haugen. He has a thick head of longish, wavy black hair, a mustache, and an air of friendly insouciance. "Sold," he says breezily. "So he could live."

Haugen sighs. "OK. I understand." She smiles grimly. We all look at each other for a minute, during which Mr. Talin climbs out of the hole. "He didn't see the helicopter crash?" she asks. The chief nods, pauses for a moment, then says well no, not personally.

Haugen purses her lips, thinking. Captain Somphong and the chief eye her expectantly. Of the many burdens facing an anthropologist in Laos or Vietnam, the language barrier ranks among the toughest. Any successful interview relies on developing a certain rapport with the person questioned, with the establishment of common ground, however small. It's a tall assignment when one's questions are passed through a third party, and the answers received the same way. Haugen's exchange with the chief, like most between recovery teams and their Southeast Asian hosts, has been a stilted, formal affair, and has yielded what one might expect: a polite, superficial conversation uncolored by body language or nuance, a painting of broad strokes in primary colors.

She tells Captain Somphong she's out of questions, asks him to remind the chief that she'll need to see the helmet, and returns to the debris field at the edge of the crater, where she leans onto what resembles a slender post-hole digger, twisting its handles, driving it into the earth. When she pulls it back up, the tool's chrome bit is packed with a narrow cylinder of earth, a cross-section of the ground beneath our feet.

"There's some good news," Haugen murmurs, as she studies the sample. "It doesn't appear that the villagers have been digging around." Below the debris field, and the villagers' trail, lies a layer of disturbed soil about ten inches thick — disturbed by man, by an event like an air crash. "Nice, disturbed soil," she says. "Which tells me we just might find something. It might be good."

3

IN 1774, AN ARMY of Virginians met the Shawnee and their allies in a long and bloody firefight at Point Pleasant, on the Ohio River. When the carnage ended, the victorious whites couldn't say how many of the enemy they'd killed; the Shawnee had carried off their dead as they'd dropped.

During the American Civil War, lulls in the fighting would see teams of litter-bearers take to the battlefield to remove the casualties, and safe passage was accorded this grim duty by both sides. Likewise, in Cuba, the Philippines, and both world wars, GIs saw to it that the bodies of their fellows were carted from the field.

For the bulk of America's experience under arms, and for that of countries with far longer histories, the aim of such efforts was to accord the dead a decent burial. A trooper in the ranks had little expectation that if he were to die, his remains would wend their way back to his family; in the days before electric refrigeration, chemical preservation, and speedy transport, such honor was reserved for only a vaunted few. Romans carried only their leaders home on their shields; low-ranking martyrs to the empire were left behind. Lord Horatio Nelson, fatally wounded in the British victory at Trafalgar, was pickled in a barrel of rum for the voyage back across the English Channel and a demigod's state funeral; his sailors, who died by the score, were simply weighted, wrapped, and thrown overboard.

The terms of the unwritten contract between fighting men and their governments guaranteed only that they would not be left to rot where they fell. So it is that oceans of Confederate graves stud the ground at

Gettysburg, and of Union graves at Petersburg, and that a multitude of Americans lie in the unfamiliar soil of Flanders and Normandy. So it is that Australian thousands lie at Gallipoli, half a world from home, and Englishmen beneath Crimea's valley of death and the grasslands of Natal. And so it is that the crew of a German U-boat, sunk by American ships and planes off the North Carolina coast in World War II, lies to this day in a cemetery in Hampton, Virginia.

On rare occasion, an effort might have been made in centuries past to return at war's end in search of remains, but even then, rank had its privileges. Just after the U.S. Seventh Cavalry charged into disaster at the Little Big Horn, its 266 officers and men were given hasty burials on the battlefield. A year later, in 1877, the army returned to the site to retrieve the slain unit's leader, George Armstrong Custer, and reinterred his bones — or, at least, what were believed to be his bones — at West Point. His horse soldiers were left where they lay.

It wasn't until the mid-twentieth century that the United States opened a preamble to the expeditions now under way in Southeast Asia: For a few years after World War II, teams from the army's Graves Registration Service wandered battlefields and island-hopped the Pacific in search of American bones. They weren't out to account for every soldier who lacked a marked grave. They didn't seek marines who'd been machine-gunned in the surf in the landings at Tinian and Saipan and a host of other far-flung atolls, and who'd washed to sea with the tide, nor the thousands of sailors who'd drowned aboard sinking warships and submarines.

Then came Vietnam, and, after the U.S. pullout, an ambition to achieve "the fullest possible accounting" of the lost. What brought the change? Technology may be part of the answer: For the first time, America had the means to undertake the mission. Political pressure surely played a role: The war was unpopular, seen as needless by a huge chunk of the population, and with that dissatisfaction came the view that an errant Washington owed its boys, at the least, the dignity of a burial on American soil. The Vietnamese style of waging war was a large part of the equation: Hanoi was maddeningly silent on the subject of what had become of men who'd disappeared on its turf.

But perhaps the biggest impetus was the simple truth that the United States did not control the battlefield at war's end. Its unrecovered dead were beyond reach, in territory held by a former enemy.

The most compelling parallel to the anguish this produced can be found not elsewhere in the American experience but in mythology. In Homer's *Iliad*, the Greek warrior Achilles slew the Trojan hero Hector in a fight outside Troy's besieged walls, then desecrated his body by dragging it behind his chariot in view of Hector's horrified comrades. Worse, he refused to turn it over to the defending army.

Everyone in Troy knew Hector was dead; just the same, retrieving his body and giving it a proper funeral was so important to his people that his grieving father, Troy's king, braved a journey into the enemy camp to plead for the return of his son's remains.

When America pulled out of Vietnam, there was little doubt about the fate of all but a tiny percentage of its unaccounted-for soldiers in Southeast Asia.

Yet here we are.

The agency placed in charge of the accounting effort was the Joint Casualty Resolution Center, a branch of the U.S. Pacific Command that was revamped and renamed Joint Task Force–Full Accounting in 1992. For the science and sweat involved in actually digging for the lost, both the JCRC and joint task force have relied on the lab.

The Central Identification Laboratory–Hawaii, usually referred to by its acronym, CILHI — pronounced "Sill-high" — is a young organization, descended from a tiny, ad hoc laboratory in Thailand at the close of the Vietnam War. At the time, it had one anthropologist, largely self-taught, and a staff consisting of a handful of soldiers, most of them 92-Mikes. Like all enlistees, 92-Mikes first endure basic training, then go to school to learn a military trade. At Fort Lee, and on field trips north to the Richmond city morgue, they learn how to recognize the 206 bones of the human body, how to tell human from animal teeth, and the rudiments of recovering and preparing remains.

In 1976, the fighting over, the lab was relocated to Hawaii. For its first several years at Hickam Air Force Base, in Honolulu, CILHI did little work in Southeast Asia, because the Vietnamese, Cambodian, and Laotian governments weren't much in the mood to invite Americans back into their territory. CILHI teams instead ventured to Papua New Guinea, where hundreds of American fighter and bomber aircraft were lost to enemy guns and capricious weather during World War II. The lab's transformation from seat-of-the-pants scholarship to respected scientific program thus occurred as it worked dormant cases two wars and four thousand miles removed from its raison d'être; by the mid-eighties, when recovery operations began anew in Laos and Vietnam, its single anthropologist had been replaced with a cadre of scientists with solid academic credentials.

It was not long after, in the early days of postwar cooperation between U.S. and Laotian officials, that work began on Case 1731.

In the autumn of 1988, America had conducted just four recovery missions in Laos with the help of the People's Democratic Republic, and eager to get back into the bush, the JCRC fastened on the crash that had claimed Jack Barker and his crew as a particularly good candidate for a fifth: The Huey's location was said to be on relatively flat ground and near highways — Route 9 was just a few miles to the north, and a smaller road, Route 92, branched off it to pass within a kilometer of the site. In a region of roadless wastes and seldom-visited mountains, these were rare attributes.

The Laotians concurred. They cleared the way for a visit, and a few weeks later, nearly eighteen years after the Huey's demise, an Mi-17 loaded with Americans and their gear was choppering east along the Xepon. At the spot pinpointed by eyewitnesses to the shootdown they found wreckage, and a lot of it — big, recognizable helicopter pieces, an M-60 door gun, enough stuff that the team leader reported the chopper appeared "relatively undisturbed," despite its setting among cultivated rice fields. The Americans grew even more excited when the senior Laotian on hand, one Major Khampheui, announced that bones had been seen there in the past, lying amid the piled metal.

Two weeks later, a U.S. delegation flew to Vientiane for another summit on future digs. Case 1731 was high on the agenda, the Americans urging that lab and Laotian workers together unearth the wreck as soon as possible. The Laotians again agreed; in the meantime, they said, they'd send technical experts to the site to prepare it for excavation.

In February 1989, Laos invited a lab recovery team to the wreckage of a CH-34 helicopter on the Xepon's north bank, less than an hour's walk from the 1731 site. An American recovery team flew into the valley expecting to dig up Jack Barker's Huey at the same time, because of its "close proximity and potential to yield substantive results." But although they knew the case to be an American priority — or, perhaps, because they knew it to be — the Laotians nixed an excavation at 1731.

Perhaps they refused simply because they could. The Laotians are hagglers, four million souls fond of ad hoc arrangements, their lives minus many of the organizational strictures without which the West would collapse. Book a ticket on Lao Aviation and you'll find that your flight may not take off on the day you expected, let alone at the appointed time. Visit a Laotian market and the price of a pound of rice will vary by the moment and the customer, every transaction subject to negotiation, every negotiation undertaken as if it's the first. Bus schedules, office hours, contracts — any arrangement that requires a particular behavior at a particular time — isn't part of the cultural weave.

So it went with recovery missions in the 1980s. American teams were limited to a handful of people and ten days on the ground. They tackled one case at a time. Beyond those provisos, every detail of every dig was on the table for discussion. Every meeting was a study in reinventing the wheel. "The Lao have never before agreed to establish a year-round program of cooperation," as one U.S. report put it, "having preferred to negotiate every step singly — and often painfully."

Whatever its reasons for keeping the diggers away, the People's Democratic Republic invited the Americans back in late May, and at long last a team headed to the Case 1731 site to bring its four soldiers home.

Little about that mission turned out as expected. Bad weather delayed its start by three days. When anthropologist Pete Miller and his team flew to the site, most of their gear lagged two days behind, on trucks bogged down on Route 9. Even so, Miller — who's now sixty-three, still at the lab, and deployed on this mission as the anthro on RE-3 — quickly found a shallow depression in the earth, marking the spot where the bulk of a Huey struck, and put his people to work scraping away at it. The "impact crater" was littered with shards of helicopter.

Within a few hours, the anthropologist's spadework had transformed the crater into sharp-edged, stairstepped art, the sort of neat hole into which a ziggurat would fit if you were to turn one upside-down. Several hours into the dig, a worker pulled a key piece of evidence from the dirt.

It was a small rectangle of aluminum stamped with information about the helicopter to which it had once been affixed, including its tail number: "69-15505." Unfortunately, it was the wrong tail number — not that of Jack Barker's chopper, but another Huey shot down the same day. Pete Miller halted the dig. The team packed up. Nearly five years passed before anyone came back.

*   *   *

In January 1994, seven American investigators assigned to Joint Task Force–Full Accounting visited Ban Chen, a village beside Route 92, hoping to speak with locals who might give them leads on where next to look. A panel of elders "explained that there are six helicopter crash sites in the area," the team later reported. "Four sites are located in the mountains to the west and the remaining two are located near the base of the mountains, within a kilometer of the village." One of the latter pair, the villagers noted, had already been dug up in 1989.

The unexcavated wreck, a few minutes' walk from Pete Miller's dig, "was associated with a helicopter that crashed during March of an un-recalled year 'during the war,'" the investigators reported. "This was explained to mean 1971, the year during which the most intense fighting in this area occurred." Villagers told the team that they didn't witness the chopper's crash, because they'd fled the area; the combat was fierce hereabouts, and they'd holed up in mountain caves until it eased. They first reached the wreck two months after the fact, finding a partially burned hulk, painted green, its tail section and rotor blades broken off and lying nearby.

"They initially stated that no remains, personal equipment, or other crew-related items were seen at the site," the team reported. Later in the conversation, the elders said they did recall seeing a shirt near the wreck, but figured it was long gone, destroyed when the fields were burned for rice planting. The villagers said they knew nothing of the men aboard the aircraft.

Most importantly, they said they knew of no other American crash sites or graves and were certain that if such things existed in the surrounding countryside, they'd be aware of them: The residents of Ban Chen hunted and raised crops along the escarpment and knew the land well.

The interviews completed, the team followed the village chief through a dense forest of bamboo to the lip of a large bomb crater, where they found "numerous small pieces of aircraft wreckage," several chunks of plastic, and a portion of a zipper. There was no sign of an impact crater, nor human remains, nor personal effects. They found nothing crew-related, in fact, nor any wreckage bearing a serial number — which, as the 1989 dig had demonstrated, is key to telling one crash site from another.

"No witness information or wreckage recovered from the crash site supports a correlation to Case 1731," the team's leader concluded. "However, the possibility exists that the site surveyed *is* Case 1731." Presented this lukewarm assessment, the joint task force opted not to excavate. It placed Case 1731 in a "pending" category, awaiting further evidence.

There it lingered for another seven years, until a new investigative team took up the search for Jack Barker and his crew. In March 2001, army captain David A. Combs led an expedition back to the same wreckage, with orders to further explore the place and to interview the residents of Ban Chen and a neighboring settlement, Ban Satum, about other possible crash sites.

Villagers in Ban Satum told the team that they knew of no sites besides those dug in 1989 and surveyed in 1994. The latter had been burned and planted every three years — at least four or five times since the war — and they'd never seen anything of interest there. About the only artifact of that crash that survived, they said, was a helmet, an American helmet. It was owned by a man who lived a half mile to the east in another village, Ban Satun Gnai.

Combs's team revisited the crash site, picked over the little wreckage they found on the surface, and searched the surrounding woods. A couple hundred yards to the south they stumbled on the sole of a combat boot and a piece of U.S. Army poncho in the vestiges of a foxhole. While interesting, the finds seemed unrelated to the loss of Barker's chopper.

When the team flew to Ban Satun Gnai, however, it hit pay dirt. There the Americans met Mr. Talin, who showed them his helmet. It was unmistakably U.S. Army–issue, the sort of flight gear worn by helicopter crews in Vietnam. Mr. Talin testified that he'd spotted it at the bottom of a crater while he burned a field in 1980. The field was the same piece of ground that the 1994 investigators and Combs's own team had visited, the crater the same one that lay next to the site's meager wreckage. Mr. Talin said he'd left the helmet in place until five years later, when he was working the field on a hot, sunny day and pulled it on to protect himself from sunburn.

More wreckage had once littered the field, he told his questioners. Among the articles he'd seen himself, within feet of the helmet, were pieces of flight suit and melted boots. Combs's report of his team's investigation ended with a recommendation: Excavate.

The joint task force wasted little time in putting together a new dig. To lead it, it chose a veteran of ten CILHI missions, whose intuition and attention to detail had helped close cases, sometimes against long odds, on three continents.

By the time she was assigned the excavation at 1731, thirty-three-year-old Gwen Haugen had overseen the recoveries, or partial recoveries, of nineteen lost men.

A procession of flatbed trucks pulls into camp shortly after we land. It has taken them twenty-six hours to haul our footlockers from Savannakhet, over ninety miles of two-foot potholes and washed-out asphalt, road-hogging water buffalo and blinding dust. The Chinese rigs lack discernable suspensions. Their drivers climb from the cabs with the pained hobbles of men whose spines have been pounded to jelly.

The camp greets the trucks like Christmas. Within seconds their tailgates are down, the tarps lashed across their loads are off, and Americans are passing the cargo to others below. We carry and drag footlockers through a strengthening rain to our tents, and for the next hour, Ban Alang quiets, as everyone unpacks.

My steamer trunk is crammed with eighty-three pounds of self-heating pasta meals, macaroni and cheese, Power Bars, granola, canned tuna, salsa, peanut butter, and clothes — quick-drying nylon shirts and trousers, six pairs of socks, T-shirts, shorts, flip-flops, and underwear of a miracle plastic that I can theoretically wear for days without self-loathing. I have a flashlight, a headlamp, and a dozen candles; shampoo, soap, and razor blades; a minidisk player and two dozen recorded albums; an alarm clock and a mosquito net; three paperback novels; sun block; forty-odd rolls of film; and two pairs of gaiters — waterproof leggings that strap to my boots and calves to keep leeches and worse from slithering up my pants. Once I've dumped and organized this load, I'm struck by how civilized my tent seems, and worry that I've been extravagant.

But on a stroll down Main Street, I realize that I might have the most Spartan quarters in camp. I hear a movie soundtrack as I pass Randy Posey's tent; RE-1's top sergeant has somehow managed to pack in a TV and VCR and a big library of videos. And that's nothing: Some of my fellow campers have computers set up on their field desks, DVD players, PlayStations, complete stereos. They've brought workout gear, lawn chairs, and bed sheets and pillows. Veritable pantries of food. A captain on another team packed an assortment of board games. Haugen's gear fills three footlockers nearly the size of coffins.

"As you can see," she says over beers at Mama's, "this place is technology central." The restaurant around us is crowded with soldiers playing cards, chowing down on fried rice, gripping sweaty bottles of Beerlao, the national brew.

She takes a swig. Haugen's circuitous route to a CILHI career was typical of the lab's scientists, none of whom grew up yearning to exhume the nation's war dead. She was raised by her mother in the St. Louis suburbs, where she played clarinet in her high school's marching band. She earned a spot on the cheerleading squad of a neighboring all-boy's school. When she left home for college, she planned to study marine biology.

After abandoning that major for journalism, and discovering she wasn't cut out for newspaper work either, she switched her focus to physical anthropology, a choice born of much desperation and a bit of affinity — she'd enjoyed the single freshman anthro course she'd taken. Once she got into her new major, she was smitten. Here was a field that bundled hard science, law enforcement, and dime-novel mystery, that was equal parts methodology and intrigue.

Haugen obtained her bachelor's from the University of Missouri and a master's degree from Tennessee, and landed a post with a private lab that supplied anthropological services to big corporate clients. She had a nice office, an easy commute, decent pay — the measures of postgraduate success — but the job was miserable, more demographics than anything; she spent her evenings stuffing questionnaires into envelopes. Before long, she quit to take a part-time post, making less money, with the St. Louis County Medical Examiner.

It was at about that point that she started hearing from former classmates who'd signed on with a little-known military lab in Hawaii and whose assignments seemed more Edgar Rice Burroughs serial than the civil service. "When I was in Thailand, I did this," they'd tell her, and "I was in New Guinea doing that," and the more she heard, the more she grumbled: "I don't do anything."

So it was that Haugen went to work for the U.S. Army. She reported to the lab in June 1997, and three weeks later, was on her way to Vietnam. "Don't you have some things for me to read?" she asked her new boss, the lab's scientific director. "I've never worked with the military before."

"Aren't you an anthropologist?" he replied.

"Well, yeah, I'm an anthropologist," Haugen said.

"Don't you know how to dig a site?"

"Yeah, I know how to dig a site," she said.

"Well, then," her boss told her, "go out there and do it."

Nothing about Haugen betrays those tentative early days as we sit at Mama's. She leans against the back of her chair, beer in hand, showered, hair washed, digging clothes traded for shorts, a T-shirt, and flip-flops, relaxed and self-sure and at peace with the environment. "This is going to be a very strange mission," she tells me.

"Stranger than most?"

"Definitely." She takes a hit off her beer and fixes me with large brown eyes. "We have some very inexperienced people on this team, some very young people. The youngest ever." Haugen herself was only two years old when Jack Barker's Huey went down. Even so, she's a relative old-timer here: One of RE-1's 92-Mikes is just nineteen. Little more than a year ago, she was a high school senior working in her father's Michigan video store.

"I can't imagine coming over here when I was nineteen," Haugen says. "I can't imagine what a trip that would have been."

I admire my beer bottle. Its logo is a ubiquitous feature of the Laotian landscape, and for good reason: Beerlao is a fine brew, despite the shortcomings of the country's tap water. "What about the case itself?" I ask. "How's it compare to the others you've had?"

"Difficult," she answers.

"Because of how picked-over it is?"

"That's part of it, yes," Haugen says, with the slightest hint of a nasal twang. "But more than that, we're at the hard sites now. The easy ones, where we had good information and lots of wreckage and knew right where to dig, they've all been done — and what's left are the hard sites to put together, hard in the respect of: Are we digging in the right place? Are we at the right helicopter?"

"Do you think we are?"

Haugen tips back her beer. "I don't know," she says. "I'm sure Pete Miller thought he was at the right helicopter when he was here in '89."

4

VISIT ANY SUNDAY FLEA MARKET in the American South
and you'll likely meet guys selling Civil War buttons and
buckles they've unearthed from a battlefield's fringe. To hold
one of their wares is powerful mojo: In your palm lies a first-
person, physical link to the past, a connection to epochal events that
you can feel, that has a heft to it, a texture. Roll a 140-year-old minié
ball in your hand and you seem one degree removed from the man who
rammed it down his musket's barrel and fired it in anger — closer to
that man, and that shot, than any book can take you.

So it's not surprising that archaeologists have become favored subjects of film and fiction and that our popular notion of their science
thus centers on artifacts. Hollywood archaeologists spend their days in
dusty holes, whiskbrooms in hand, in hopes of uncovering physical
pieces of the past; the relics they seek are ends in themselves, and a scientist's reputation is formed of the swag he brings home.

What the popular image fails to reflect is that archaeology is as much
an interpretive science as a physical one: The value of an artifact lies
not so much in its age or its beauty as in the information it provides
about the people who produced it and the uses to which it was put. Its
proximity to other relics, to features of terrain — its entire context —
tells a scientist much about the article and its place in the past. Removed
from that context, it's merely a curiosity, a trinket of limited academic
interest.

The lab's digs are not classic archaeology by any stretch. Forensic anthropologists specialize in the human body as evidence; they collect

and examine remains not to glean insight into past cultures, nor to detect minute physical differences between the sexes and races, but to solve smaller, more personal riddles — identifying the dead, establishing cause of death, finding clues to the circumstances surrounding a life's end. They often liken their jobs to those of detectives, their excavations to crime scenes, their lab work to building a criminal case. RE-1 has arrived in Laos knowing that the four men it seeks are dead. Its mission is simply to find and repatriate their pieces.

Even so, the context of the site, the locations at which relics are found, is of great importance. The four died aboard a machine with readily identifiable components. Each of the four occupied a regular station in the Huey — Haugen knows that Barker and Dugan were seated in the cockpit and that Dugan, as the senior pilot aboard, probably sat in the left seat; Dillender and Chubb were a few feet to the cockpit's rear, in the cargo hold. Unearthing a piece of instrument panel or a piece of seat might signal that the team is digging in the debris of the cockpit and that Barker's and Dugan's remains lay nearby. Finding a piece of gear unique to a particular location in the cockpit could tell them which of the aviators they're likely to find. Uncovering a piece of machine gun would, on the other hand, suggest that the team has come across remnants of the Huey's cargo bay.

The distribution of debris can tell Haugen things she doesn't know about the crashed helicopter, as well. She knows it was moving when it hit the ground, but nothing of its forward speed, its trajectory, or its actual point of impact. The debris field may explain all of this — not only where the chopper hit the ground but, by dint of the wreckage's distribution over the site, how hard it hit and in what direction it traveled. If it came in fast and at a fairly flat angle, the helicopter and the people who occupied it might have been flung over a large area, and the tract the team will have to excavate in search of remains will be large. If it ploughed into the earth vertically, the dig will encompass a small piece of ground, but will go deep.

The bottom line is that Gwen Haugen has to be as concerned about the geographical context of anything recovered at the 1731 site as a classical archaeologist would be, but for different reasons. What she'll glean from the location of a particular artifact isn't insight into the lives of the people who died here but clues as to where she should look next to find what's left of them.

Haugen's first task at a new dig site, then, is to define the area to be searched, to establish boundaries for the excavation. To this end, all CILHI anthropologists overlay their sites with a grid of squares, at its center the ground deemed most likely to yield artifacts. From there the grid stretches outward to the farthest point from the center at which debris can be reasonably expected. Depending on the size of the wreck, and the time available, the anthropologist may choose to start the excavation in the middle squares and work out, or start at the edges and work toward the middle.

Like most of her lab colleagues, Haugen divides her sites into four-meter squares. The grid serves multiple functions: It enables an anthropologist to excavate in a deliberative fashion, one square at a time, and to chart where on the site artifacts are found, and thus to map patterns in the debris field — and with this information, to make adjustments to his or her excavation strategy as the dig proceeds.

So when we arrive back at the site, Haugen hammers a stake into the ground a few yards in front of the American break tent. This stake will be the southwest corner of the 1731 grid and the reference point for all of its squares. She positions a surveying transit directly over the stake, and with it establishes the line that will be the site's western boundary. It runs past the Laotian break tent, skirting the lip of the big crater, and along this line she hammers five more stakes, each four carefully measured meters from those to either side. She then uses the transit to map the site's southern boundary, which stretches away from the break tent and over the ravine's lip, and hammers five stakes, four meters apart, down this line.

She now has rows of stakes branching north and east from the site's southwest starting point, and two sides of her first square, the one in the corner. To the first stake north of the corner she attaches a measuring tape and pulls it four meters eastward; she attaches a second measuring tape to the corner stake and pulls it 5.65 meters at a diagonal. Each of the grid's units is two right triangles, so squaring the length of a side, then doubling it, yields the square of the diagonal. Where the two tapes meet is the first unit's northeast corner.

Using her tape measures, Haugen builds other squares adjacent to the first, until, by late morning, the site bristles with stakes. Some jut from the tops of termite mounds; some rise from the sloping sides of the big crater. She then links the stakes with white cotton string. When she's finished, the crater and the ground around it are divided into twenty-eight units — twenty-five of them forming a bigger square, five

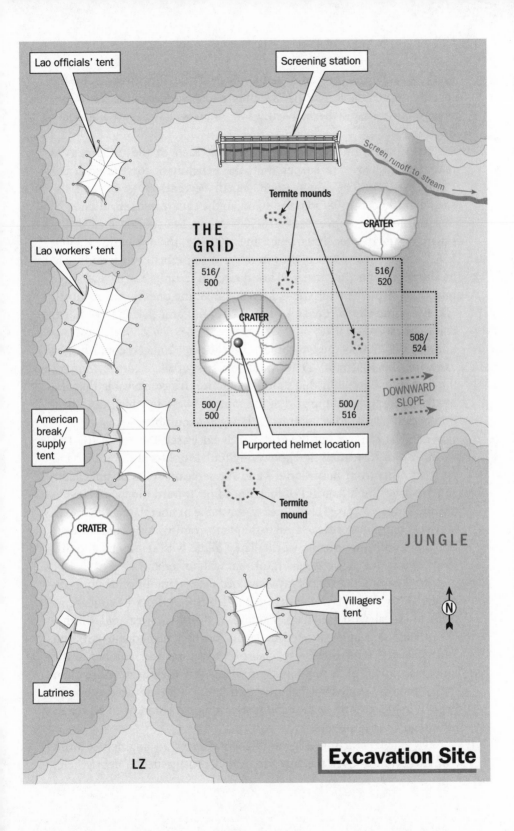

Lao officials' tent

Screening station

Termite mounds

CRATER

THE GRID

516/
500

516/
520

CRATER

508/
524

Lao workers' tent

500/
500

500/
516

DOWNWARD
SLOPE

Purported helmet location

American
break/
supply
tent

CRATER

Termite
mound

JUNGLE

N

Villagers'
tent

Latrines

LZ

Screen runoff to stream

Excavation Site

units to a side, and three attached to the grid's northeast corner, on the ravine's sloping flank. The grid's southern and western edges are twenty meters long; its northern, twenty-four meters. Its eastern boundary doglegs.

Finally, she numbers the stakes so that each of the units can be readily identified. The corner unit, the benchmark for the grid, becomes 500/500. The square to its north becomes 504/500, and the square to *its* north, 508/500, and so on, to the square in the grid's northwest corner, which becomes 516/500. Along the southern edge, the square beside the benchmark becomes 500/504, the one beside it, 500/508. The system gives every unit in the grid a number corresponding to its distance from the corner: The square three units north and three units east of the benchmark stake is 508/508; the one four units north and five units east of the stake is 512/516; the unit five squares north and one east is 516/504.

Using 500/500 as the benchmark is arbitrary; Haugen could just as easily use 100/100, or 40/40. It would be easiest of all, of course, to mark the first square 0/0, but that's an iffy practice: It's conceivable that she might have to expand the grid to the south or west, in which case she'd find herself having to label units with negative numbers.

While Haugen lays out the grid, Randy Posey sets the rest of RE-1 to work. The entire team is here today — it took four lifts in the Squirrel to ferry all of us from Ban Alang — and the sergeant splits us up. Medic Art Artillaga and a handful of locals head off toward the LZ to build a latrine. Three 92-Mikes haul a heavy gray cube of fiberglass to the break tent and open it to reveal a high-frequency radio — our communications link with the outside world. They fiddle with its knobs and antenna and with a gasoline generator that will power it.

Brian Eagmin, the team's explosive ordnance demolition technician, or "EOD," sweeps the site with a metal detector and marks concentrations of metal with pin flags. Eagmin, a thirty-two-year-old Marine Corps staff sergeant stationed in Japan, his hair planed into a blond flattop, is an "augmentee," a specialist on temporary assignment to the joint task force; of a recovery team's thirteen members, more than half — medics, explosives experts, translators, mountaineers — might be such loaner troops, destined to work a single mission, then return to their regular assignments.

Navy Chief Parachute Rigger Victoria Conely, an augmentee from San Diego, pores over the tiny pieces of wreckage in the debris field.

Conely is the team's life support technician; her training should enable her to recognize pieces of the equipment worn by the Huey's crew — to glance at a zipper or a swatch of fabric or a metal snap and say whether it's part of man or machine.

Next to remains, "life support" is an excavation's most valued treasure: If the team unearths anything an aviator wears while in flight, or which is required for his midair exit from his craft — a helmet, for instance, or pieces of flight suit, his oxygen mask, his ejection seat — the man himself can't be far away.

Army staff sergeant David Dingman, the team's photographer and, at forty-five, its oldest member, drags several footlockers of plastic pipe, hoses, and tools to the site's northern edge, where locals have constructed a bamboo frame for the screening station. Besides the grid, the structure is the site's most important element; on it, we'll sift the dirt that's dug from the units. All CILHI digs use the same screens for the task, sheets of metal mesh roughly two feet by three, framed in wood. Dump a bucket of dirt on the screen, push it through, and anything bigger than a quarter-inch across will be left behind.

For all of the technological wizardry the past quarter century has bestowed on America's military — the whiz-bang weaponry, the speed with which it can drop an army anywhere on the planet, the satellites with which it studies its foes — accounting for its lost comes down to a decidedly preindustrial process of digging and dirt and sweat.

If the ground is dry, the soil sandy, a team usually opts to screen the dirt simply by shaking it through the mesh; if it's wet and heavy or rich in clay, it won't fall through on its own, and in such cases the lab typically chooses to "wet-screen," using jets of water to help force the lumpy earth on its way. Wet-screening is clearly necessary here; the site's orange, mottled clay, overlain with a dense gray silt, has been saturated by the rains that have swept this part of Laos for weeks.

Dingman pulls short lengths of PVC pipe from the footlockers, screws T-joints to their threaded ends, and connects another piece of pipe on either side, until he's assembled a joint-studded pipe thirty feet long. He is fit for his age, his fair hair thinning, face lined, a slow-talking Oklahoman who acquired his mechanical expertise before he joined the army. He had plenty of time: Dingman thought about enlisting as early as 1974, when he quit high school, but didn't join the service until nearly seventeen years later, as troops massed in the Middle East for Operation Desert Storm.

Instead, he drove a taxi, pumped gas, fixed cars, and harvested catfish at a hatchery. He washed dishes in the restaurant of a Holiday Inn. He roughnecked on an oil-drilling rig, framed houses, and after hurting his back, left his hometown — Bartlesville, about fifty miles north of Tulsa and twenty miles shy of the Kansas line — for Oklahoma City, where he landed a job with a janitorial company. Before long he moved again, to Dallas, where he painted stripes on highways and parking lots.

He'd been out of school for a decade, with nothing to show for his string of go-nowhere jobs, and the military started to look pretty good. But not good enough: An uncle offered him a job in Los Angeles, an entry-level data-entry post, so Dingman moved west.

He stared at a computer screen for hours on end. He typed. He got soft. He missed being outdoors, and some days he found himself again mulling the military. After a couple of years with his uncle's firm he stopped in to speak with a marine recruiter, just to check out his options, and was shocked to find the Corps wouldn't take him: He was too old to be a jarhead and too old for the air force, as well; his only options, the recruiter said, were the army or navy, where the cut-off age was thirty-five. Disgusted, Dingman left without talking to either.

But back at his computer, his eyes started to fail. He gained a ton of weight. With his thirty-fifth birthday fast approaching, Dingman went back to the army in the spring of 1990. He told the recruiter he wanted a challenge. He didn't want to be a cook or a radar technician or some rear-echelon paper-pusher; he wanted to be a combat soldier, a hardcharger, an Airborne Ranger. He figured that way, even if he stayed for only a single hitch, he'd at least get in shape. At thirty-five years old, he became an 11-Bravo, a U.S. Army infantryman.

It suited him. He'd been dealt some tough hands, and had acquired patience. He'd worked some truly crappy jobs, which had taught him humility. He'd been mellowed by time and hard labor, by unjust foremen and lousy weather. He'd been turned to leather, rendered unflappable; his boiling point was almost beyond reach. He could take whatever the army dished out with a smile, or a shrug, or an unfazed, slow-spoken "Yes, sir."

And he could make himself useful. Dingman knew how to do all sorts of things. When he transferred to the lab, and Randy Posey's team, he was surrounded by much younger soldiers who lacked mechanical skills and the inclination to acquire them. By default he became the team's pump man.

He's sweating as he wraps the threads in Teflon tape before screwing the pieces together; by 9 A.M. it's already well into the nineties. Clouds are building to the north and east, up the Xepon valley, but the sun is outpacing them as it climbs in the sky, and the site bakes in its heat. I'm blotting my forehead with my shirtsleeve, watching Dingman wrestle with one stretch of pipe that seems to be threaded incorrectly, when a shout comes from across the grid. There's a flurry of movement by the break tent, villagers running and pointing at a big termite mound, and I detect another movement at its crown: a thick, black snake, every bit of four feet long. Some of the locals were apparently sitting on the mound, trying to make sense of the activity around them, when they roused the creature. It moves with astounding speed across the stumpy ground and disappears down the ravine. The locals edge back onto the mound and retake their seats.

Haugen takes a break from hammering stakes and wanders over to say she's been nagged by what she suspects is an unreasonable fear. "The coordinates for this site and the one that Pete Miller excavated are almost the same," she says. "They're so close, we've got a couple villagers who are gonna take us to where they say Pete dug. It'll just make me feel better to see it." She scans the half-finished grid, the team members struggling to get the radio working, the crew assembling the pipe. "I'd hate to get into this thing and find out we're digging in the same hole."

I tag along as she, Reynolds, Krueger, Conely, Captain Somphong, and two villagers set out for the wreckage of helicopter 69-15505. We scramble and slide into the ravine, picking our way over a two-foot-thick mat of felled bamboo that clings to the slope, and drop into the creek, then rockhop across the water and claw up the gully's far side. A narrow trail meanders through the bamboo, which is so dense that I can't see beyond a few feet to either side — and can't spend more than a second at a time trying to, lest I catch a swinging branch in the face.

Besides, I'm too busy studying the ground. The bamboo viper didn't get its name by accident; no doubt the brush around us is lousy with the reptiles, whose fangs inject a wildly painful toxin. On her last mission, Haugen led a team into the jungle near here to hunt for the remains of an army helicopter that had blown to bits in midair, and in the space of a few hours the group stumbled on eleven poisonous snakes, including some monster specimens of the infamous "Jake Two-Steps" — so many that Haugen suspended the mission.

At least the lime green viper advertises its presence. Not so the banded krait, another denizen of these woods — a small, insignificant-looking serpent of the genus *Bungarus,* which might as well be Latin for "kiss it goodbye."

The path narrows. Brush closes around us. Vines clutch at our boots. We pass through a grove of hardwood saplings and have to bend over double to slip beneath their lowest branches. Thirty years ago, when U.S. commandos stole through the thickets of eastern Laos, snakes were the least of their worries. We're getting a workout just walking, unencumbered, through these woods; those guys rucked heavy packs and belts laden with ammo and grenades, toted rifles, and — no minor detail — were surrounded by people trying to kill them.

How did they do it? The question presents itself on any trip to the Southeast Asian backcountry, for simple travel remains an enormous challenge. Today we're on relatively easy ground; just east of here, in the borderlands, the piedmont gives way to ridges and knobs that leap a sudden thousand feet without prelude — ridge after jungle-clad ridge, the dank valleys between interrupted by towering mounts shaped like gumdrops, as if children drew them. The earth's crust is thrown into bedlam. Crossing it on foot is hard to imagine. Fighting along the way would be nuts.

Our route, now only faintly discernable in the forest's floor, jogs right, then left, into darkening thicket. "I have a feeling," Haugen says from ahead of me in the line, "that we're gonna have to do a leech check when this is over." Then, with a shout in Lao from the villagers up front, we stop. Off to our left, visible through a picket of bamboo, is a hole about twenty feet across, water at its bottom, its rim furred in ferns and sticker bushes, bamboo and skinny-trunked trees crowded all around.

At first glance, I take it for a bomb crater. Then I notice that its sides are not sloped like the crater back at the site but carved into a neat series of terraces. More than twelve years have passed since Pete Miller supervised the dig here, years of erosion borne on heavy rains and jungle growth and animal activity, and the lab's handiwork is still apparent. "Look at that," Haugen says. "A bull's-eye excavation."

Reynolds fishes in his rucksack for a handheld global-positioning system device, a black, plastic gizmo the size of a cell phone that triangulates our position using satellite signals. The teams use the Universal Transverse Mercator mapping system, which parcels the globe into one-kilometer squares and can pinpoint spots within those squares down to the meter. It's a heck of a lot less unwieldy than traditional latitude and longitude. The marine captain rattles off eight digits, our position off the GPS. "Not far from where we started," he says. "Only about one hundred meters."

"It seemed a little farther than that," Haugen says.

"It sure did," Conely mutters. She's a solidly built woman of forty-four, her red-blond hair carved into a bristly flattop that is wilting and dark with sweat. The sixteen-year navy veteran might have more jungle experience than any American here: After an early childhood in California and New Mexico, she spent several years in Ponape, in the central Pacific's Caroline Islands, where her father taught school and his tomboyish daughter explored the island's coconut palm forests and swimming holes, unbothered by the humid heat. Today her fair skin is flushed pink. We're all soaked — excepting Haugen, who doesn't appear the least bit damp — and now that we've been still for a few seconds, mosquitoes and gnats are gathering. We decide not to linger. I take a long last look at the hole.

One mystery remains unresolved here, and it nags: Why, when Americans first visited this place in 1988, did their Laotian escort mention that locals had found bones on the surface? Was that a lie? Was the major who made that declaration simply confusing this helicopter wreck for another? Could he have meant the site we're digging today?

The Defense Department still stews over these questions. "Maj. Khampheui should be located and interviewed about who told him about the remains being observed, and what exactly this person told him about the crash site," read a Pentagon memo written years later. "Prior to talks between the U.S. and Lao government officials in Vientiane on Jan 2–3, 1989, the Lao pledged to send technical personnel to the suspected crash site associated with REFNO 1731, and other sites in the area. They would prepare the ground for excavations of those sites, which had already been surveyed in December 1988. The Lao PDR government should also be asked to identify and locate these personnel. They should be jointly interviewed about anything they may have found, observed, or were told by the local villagers."

Major Khampheui has never turned up. The advance team has never been interviewed. The "bones" remain a puzzle.

Not long after we get back to the site, the sky abruptly darkens, and a moment later the rain comes down like a fist. The soldiers setting up the radio dash into the break tent, followed by Haugen, Reynolds, and

Eagmin, who've been out on the grid. For sixty seconds raindrops hit the tarp over our heads with such fury that we have to yell to hear one another. Then, as abruptly as it started, the rain stops, and the sun comes out.

"Great," Haugen mutters. "Now it's gonna be *really* freaking hot."

"Hey, listen up, y'all," Sergeant Posey says, as we straggle back out into the sun. "You see that snake this morning? If the locals start moving quickly, move with them." He speaks with a drawl that harkens to his rural Mississippi boyhood, and a gentle firmness he acquired in the classroom. Posey taught part-time for eight years, first in the pine forests and lumber-mill burgs near his hometown, later in Nashville. "They're usually moving pretty slow," he says of our hosts, "so if they start moving fast, it usually means something."

The morning passes. The temperature climbs. Dingman and several other soldiers lash the plastic pipe to the A-frame's ridgeline, connect twelve rubber hoses to its T-joints, then build a trough of blue tarp below. Eagmin finishes sweeping the grid with his metal detector and announces that the site is busy with heavy iron bomb fragments. Artillaga's team, completing a six-foot pit for the latrine, mounts a plywood box over the hole, its top fitted with a toilet seat. The soldiers working on the radio string a long, T-shaped antenna wire in the trees near the break tent, then fire up the generator. The radio squawks impressively, but when they broadcast a radio check, they get nothing but static in reply. Don Guthrie, a tall, mustachioed Australian who's our Squirrel pilot for the day, suggests that the antenna is the problem — it's not high enough and not pointed properly. He tosses a rope over a lofty branch in a tree near the Laotian break tent, then ties the antenna to the rope and hoists the wire high into the air.

While that operation is under way, I notice Krueger standing by himself at the crater's edge and realize I haven't heard the team's linguist utter a word in Lao or English all day. This strikes others as odd, as well. When I join Reynolds and Haugen in the grid, the anthropologist is staring across the site at him. "Krueger is really beginning to bother me with all his talk," she says. "I really am beginning to find it distracting, his constant chatter in Lao. The guy never shuts up."

Reynolds nods. "I'll write him up."

"He's having trouble," she says. "I think the locals are speaking Lao-Theung. I don't think it's regular Lao. Even Captain Somphong told me he doesn't always know what they're saying." Lao-Theung is a label applied to many of the country's mountain tribes, some of whose dialects bear only passing resemblance to the country's official lowland tongue.

"Great," Reynolds sighs. "We've got a linguist who doesn't speak the language."

After fours hours of drenching labor the team quits for lunch. We sit in the break tent's blue shade, talk over the radio's squawks and the generator's growl, drinking bottled water, sweating. A small dog, tan fur stretched tight over its ribs, noses around beneath the table for our crumbs. A gallery of locals stares from the termite mound twenty feet away as Reynolds eats chunky soup cold from a can, and Posey lights a small propane stove to cook noodles. Some of the kids on the mound are naked, some of the women shirtless. One young boy is wearing a black Motorhead T-shirt.

We watch them watch us, and while this mutual examination takes place, two skinny teenagers show up at the clearing's edge, one holding a helmet. Half the team gathers around as the kid hands it to Haugen. Its plastic shell is encrusted with dried mud, stained black, and missing a visor that once lay across its forehead, but it swells at its sides into the bulging ear covers that distinguish Vietnam-era helicopter helmets. On its left bulge is a whorled metal knob from which a boom microphone sprouted. A grommet in the back marks the place the helmet hooked into a chopper's radios and intercom.

There are three other features that aren't standard issue. In the left temple is a bullet's neat, round point of entry. In the right rear quarter is a slightly larger exit hole, its edges beveled outward. And along its lower edge, which once covered an aviator's neck, is a smaller, jagged hole — a leftover of shrapnel, perhaps. It seems a sure bet that whoever wore the helmet when it acquired this damage did not survive the experience.

"It's the old-type army helmet," Conely says, squinting at it. The chief's service as a parachute rigger has afforded her a broader expertise than the title suggests; as a member of an aircraft carrier's air wing and in stints with navy cargo plane and helicopter squadrons, she's been charged with maintaining a range of flight and survival gear. The equipment's changed over the years since Vietnam, but only so much; she knows her helmets. "It's definitely army," she judges. "It's not the type the navy used."

Haugen passes the helmet around. Its interior of foam pads and crisscrossed web straps is intact but blackened, and it smells of smoke. One pad is chipped over the right eye; a tiny fleck of bright white foam shows through. I wonder aloud whether it was a fire that turned it black, or water at the bottom of the crater.

"I don't know," Haugen says. "Both, maybe."

"Even if it wasn't all messed up, it's not exactly what I'd choose to avoid a sunburn," I tell her.

"No," she snorts. "I'd pay good money to see Mr. Talin tending his field in *that*."

Captain Somphong, who's been talking to the boys, strolls over with the news that one of them is Mr. Talin's son and that he reports that when his father found the helmet "in 1973," it "still had blood in it."

"Well, wait a minute," Haugen says. "That's not what Mr. Talin said yesterday. Mr. Talin told us he found the helmet in 1980, left it there, and came back for it five years later."

Somphong, who knows this himself, turns back to the teenager. They talk for a minute. "He says his father found it in 1973 and he didn't take it, and after the slash-and-burn clearing of the fields, he found it again." He delivers the message without expression.

"So he finds it in 1973, leaves it there. He finds it again in 1980 and leaves it there again. And he finds it *again* in 1985, and that time he takes it?"

"Yes," the captain replies. "That's what he says."

"That's a load of crap." She shakes her head. "The crash was in, what, 1971? Two years later and it's filled with blood? *Right*."

Somphong gazes at her, a blank.

"We're going to take some pictures," she announces. She spreads an empty sandbag on the ground, places the helmet in its center, and starts snapping photos with a digital camera, turning the helmet this way and that to capture it from several angles. I squat next to her to watch. "When this becomes important is if we find pieces of a skull, and we can match up those holes," she tells me, clicking off a shot. "I'm going to measure it, and we may be able to recreate it in the lab."

"Why not just take the helmet? Wouldn't that be easier?"

Haugen sighs. "Mr. Talin doesn't want to give it up."

Somphong and the kid are just a few feet away, eyeing us impassively. "He can keep it?" I whisper.

She keeps shooting pictures. "He found it."

"Well, that doesn't seem right." It looks as if someone died wearing this helmet, I'm thinking. Surely the Laotians understand that it doesn't belong in a village hut, in the hands of a guy who purportedly uses it for shade.

"Usually, if we tell the Lao officials that we need a piece of evidence, they'll get it for us. But the IE asked Mr. Talin for it, and he didn't want to turn it over, and the officials didn't do anything. I asked for it yesterday, and the same thing happened."

A few minutes later, she hands the helmet back to Somphong, reminding him that the team needs it, asking him to explain to the kid that it's important to the families of the dead. Somphong looks unenthusiastic about pressing the point, but talks to the chief's son. He comes back, shaking his head. "He says no."

"We could really use it," Haugen says again.

The captain nods, but does nothing. The kid walks off, helmet in hand.

"OK, let's go," Sergeant Posey says. "Let's go to work."

By late afternoon the grid is staked and strung, the radio works, and Dingman, directing a handful of local helpers in an Okie drawl that even his American colleagues struggle to interpret, is close to finishing the screening station. He's dragged a gasoline-powered pump to a narrow earthen shelf halfway down the ravine. He's connected its intake to a thick rubber hose that descends to the creek, and its outflow to another hose running uphill to the A-frame. Theoretically, the machine will force creek water into the PVC pipe dangling from the A-frame's top bar and down rubber hoses positioned over each of the station's twelve screens.

We gather in the break tent. The skinny dog reappears and feasts to a rain of crackers, cookies, and pieces of Power Bar as Posey calls the team to order, then turns the floor over to Haugen. "We had a really good day today," the anthro says. "We got a lot done. We gridded in twenty-eight four-by-four-meter units." She looks around. To the team's augmentees, the number doesn't mean much, but its veteran 92-Mikes know that twenty-eight units is a big piece of real estate; the surface of each square measures roughly 170 square feet, or the size of a single-car garage.

"The thing is, I don't foresee us going very deep," she says, "probably fifty, sixty centimeters at the very most." This is little comfort: If the units are dug sixty centimeters down, each square will produce close to

340 cubic feet of dirt to sift, perhaps a thousand bucketfuls. "You'll probably want to avoid walking in the gridded area," she adds. "Walk around it, because the Lao people will see you walking through it, and we don't want them to do that."

Posey salutes the team's hard work. "It was hot out there today," he says. "Y'all did good." He invites comments from the rest of his team. Reynolds reports that the radio seems to be working and reminds everyone to drink plenty of water. Eagmin, the EOD, reports the ground is laced with bomb fragments, or "frag." Dingman describes the work remaining on the screening station.

"Art?" Posey asks, turning to Artillaga.

"The shitter's up and running," the medic says.

"Let's try to keep the seat sanitized in the latrine area," Posey says, sounding more like a parent than a sergeant. Back when he taught, his big-city students were mostly kids from the projects, a lot of them raised by their mothers. It was good training: When he entered the Army Reserve to earn a second paycheck, he was a ready-made NCO, a father figure to the youngsters under him. "Be considerate of our female . . . of our female . . . um . . ." He searches for the right word before finally blurting "soldiers," and quickly adding: "And sailors. And marines."

"For a second there," Haugen says, laughing, "I thought you were gonna say, 'female *flowers.*'"

"I couldn't get that shit out right," Posey replies. "Krueger?" The linguist shakes his head, wordless. Posey moves on to Conely. "Chief?"

"This is my first mission," the gear expert says, "so I don't want to predict what we'll find. But I'm very optimistic about what I've seen today." She nods her crew cut toward the grid. "There's a lot of stuff out there."

5

HECTOR HAD BEEN DEAD for twelve days when Priam, the king, ventured from the walls of Troy to seek his son's body from the enemy. He found the corpse uncorrupted, its wounds closed, its skin fresh: Hector had faithfully paid tribute to the gods in life, and they repaid him in death by sparing his father the sight of his decomposition.

Alas, most of us don't enjoy such deals. When we die, our remains invite agents of decay in multitude, and these bacteria, insects, and larger scavengers arrive for the banquet with astounding speed and voracious appetite. Within minutes of death the body's temperature begins to drop, from the outside in; the extremities and outermost tissues grow cold first, followed by the body's core. Lactic acid accumulates in the muscles, and in concert with the body's chemistry creates a gel in its tissues that produces a stiffening rigor mortis. Microbes that reside in our intestines reproduce exponentially, devouring the body's blood and digestive tract, and producing gasses that cause the corpse to swell until its soft vitals rupture, opening the way to the surrounding organs.

Flies arrive, laying their eggs or depositing their young in wounds or body cavities. Within a day, in a hot, humid climate such as Southeast Asia's, a newly hatched corps of maggots has started devouring the remains. As the body's internal structures collapse and the collected gasses escape, a succession of new insects comes calling, each species bringing a specialized diet to the corpse. Ants, scarab and carrion beetles. Dermestid beetles, equipped with mandibles capable of cleaning muscle and tendon from bone. Mites and cheese skippers. Bees and wasps attracted by the body's fluids. Tineid moths, the familiar versions of which chew through wool sweaters in Western closets, but which in the wild feast on fur and hair. Assuming that no larger scavengers happen by, the remains are soon desiccated and stripped. Before long, all that remains is bone. By thirty years after death, that bone may be gone, too.

So as RE-1 begins its first day of actual excavation, its prospects for success are difficult to gauge. The remains of the Huey's crew will have had to withstand not only the typical agents of decay but a host of others specific to the site — the corrosive quality of its soil composition, the effects of erosion and past floods, the presence of man-made chemicals around the remains, any number of variables. To complicate things further, nature doesn't always follow its own program; the reliable order of events that govern a body's disintegration can be confounded.

An example: After Gwen Haugen graduated from the University of Missouri in 1991, she spent a summer waiting tables at an Olive Garden, then headed for Knoxville, and the University of Tennessee. Its anthropology program was headed by William Bass, renowned for an outdoor laboratory at which he and his students tracked decomposition rates. The "Body Farm" — a nickname popularized by novelist Patricia Cornwell, and, to the chagrin of some UT scientists, one that's stuck — is a wooded tract ringed in razor wire and sprinkled with cadavers in varying states of decay. On a typical day, one corpse might be stuffed in the trunk of an abandoned car, a few others in coffins buried at different depths, and others might be lying in the sun or shrouded by tarps or buried under leaves and twigs. Some are clothed, others wrapped in plastic or sheets or nothing at all.

Before Bass started planting the farm's crop, little useful research had been conducted on the many factors affecting what happens to the human body after death. Scientists knew that decomposition occurred in predictable stages, but were poorly equipped to determine the date or time of a person's exit from the ranks of the living based solely on his or her physical decay.

Bass, now retired, learned this the hard way in 1977, when he was asked to view a body that turned up near Franklin, Tennessee. The owners of an antebellum estate had been leading a tour of the place when they'd made a grisly discovery: Someone had dug up a grave on the property and broken into the iron coffin it contained. A headless body dressed in a pressed tuxedo was jutting from the coffin's broken lid.

The grave was that of the estate's original owner, Confederate lieutenant colonel William Shy, who'd been killed in the Battle of Nashville in December 1864. This corpse was fresh-looking, however, its bones covered with tissue, some of it still pinkish. The cops figured that they had a modern homicide on their hands, that the killer had attempted to hide his victim in Shy's old grave, and that he'd been interrupted before he could finish the job. Bass studied the remains and decided the deceased was a white male aged twenty-four to twenty-eight, and that he'd been dead for six to twelve months.

He nailed the body's sex, age, and race but was off on the time of death by 112 years. Further research revealed that the tuxedo was ancient, and portions of skull were recovered that suggested the man had died of a large-caliber wound to his forehead — the sort of wound caused by a Civil War–era rifle ball. It was Lieutenant Colonel Shy himself, wonderfully preserved thanks to his sealed coffin and liberal embalming with arsenic.

The Shy case demonstrated that remains entombed in an anaerobic environment — denied oxygen and the organisms that require it to break down tissue — can remain remarkably intact for far longer than one might expect. Bass's subsequent experiments at the Body Farm catapulted the UT anthropology program into the scientific spotlight.

Haugen witnessed the effects of anaerobic preservation herself not long after leaving Tennessee in 1993. That summer the Midwest was inundated by disastrous floods, and among the many towns swept away by the swollen Mississippi was Grafton, Illinois, an old steamboat stop on the river's edge backed by high limestone bluffs. The Federal Emergency Management Agency financed Grafton's relocation to the high ground on the cliff top, where construction crews unearthed a forgotten cemetery. Haugen became a part-timer on a team hired to excavate and catalog the contents of 280-odd graves.

In some, all that remained were the crowns of teeth. But one contained an iron-skinned, torpedo-shaped coffin, a type of hermetically sealed vault popular among the nineteenth century's wealthy. Haugen and her fellow anthropologists didn't know what they'd find inside, so they trucked the coffin to Washington University in St. Louis to videotape its disassembly. When they cracked it open, they found the body of a young boy within, wonderfully preserved: Flesh still covered his face, and dried rose petals encircled his head. He wore knickers, a ruffled shirt, kneesocks. His hands were folded on his chest.

Within minutes, as the casket filled with fresh air, the boy began to vanish before Haugen's eyes. Nature's course had been held at bay for 130 years by the coffin's airtight seal; it caught up all at once. Decay consumed the child's remains so quickly that it seemed she was watching the process on time-lapse film.

CILHI's scientists have encountered the phenomenon in the search for America's war dead, as well, though their discoveries are rarely so dramatic. In 2001, a team unearthed remains that still had meat on their bones — and a portion of a human ear — from the wreckage of a World War II bomber in Papua New Guinea's Owen Stanley Range.

In May 1998, during Haugen's first year with the lab, she was dispatched to France to recover the nine-man crew of a B-24J Liberator, a big, four-engine bomber that had failed to return from a bombing raid in December 1944. The plane had dropped from the sky almost vertically; its nose had burrowed twelve feet deep into heavy clay, most of the fuselage compressing like an accordion into the hole behind it, encasing the crew in a fuel-soaked chamber of metal and dense, nearly impermeable earth. Excavating the wreck was cold work, on ground still dimpled with foxholes. Haugen used a backhoe to scoop the clay and dump it onto a tarp, where her team went through it by hand, squeezing the wet, clumping earth flat. If a member felt something hard in a clump, it went into a bucket for further examination.

The results were spectacular. Haugen found soft tissue, and skin with hair attached. She found pieces of maps, and dog tags, and military identification cards, two class rings (one carved with initials), two wristwatch backs, three pocket knives, flight suit pieces, socks, boots — all preserved, like Lieutenant Colonel Shy and the Grafton boy, because they'd been denied contact with the elements.

Most impressively, her team found bone: on Haugen's first day at the site, 50 fragments; on the second day, 145; on the third, 38; on the fourth, 75. By the time she closed the dig, she and another anthropologist had recovered more than 1,800 bone fragments, enough to enable the lab to individually identify eight of the Liberator's crew.

Another CILHI anthropologist, Bill Belcher, had a similar experience while excavating a B-17 Flying Fortress felled by friendly fire on the English coast in March 1945. All but two members of the bomber's crew, its pilot and copilot, had safely bailed out before the plane nosed into a tidal flat. Belcher, arriving on the scene more than fifty-five years later, dug through the compressed wreckage, starting at the tail, and recovered eight of the plane's thirteen machine guns as he worked downward through muck and mangled aluminum toward the nose. Some of the weapons were almost complete. One, cleaned up, might have worked. He also found, laced among debris from the bomb bay, the remains of two people, both holding or wearing their parachutes, neither chute deployed before the crash. Aboard a flying B-17, the bomb bay was the primary point of exit from the cockpit; the two airmen had been scrambling to get out of the plane, and had simply run out of sky.

When I visited Belcher's tiny lab office, he reached into a desk drawer for a Ziploc containing a folded square of silk. So well-preserved were the deeply buried portions of the English wreck that he'd found this intact survival map of northwestern Europe among the crew's belongings. Its ink was still sharp, its colors bright; the only clue that it had been buried for more than half a century were round, brown footprints left by rusted .50-caliber rounds.

Early in the morning, RE-1's thirteen souls lug picks, hoes, shovels, and several dozen black, plastic buckets from the break tent to 516/520, the unit in the grid's far northeast corner. It is at the top of the ravine, next to the smaller crater, and slopes downward at about thirty degrees.

Haugen has team members rake the unit and place the dead leaves, vines, roots, and rocks they collect into buckets, then calls everyone together to formally introduce the team to the villagers. Fifty locals have gathered for the day's work. Krueger assumes the role of emcee.

The military has always employed foreign-language specialists, mostly in intelligence posts. Until the early nineties, more than half of them studied Russian, German, or Czech, but the Eastern Bloc's collapse, coupled with the outbreak of the Persian Gulf War, prompted a change in priorities: Knowledge of Arabic and Farsi became urgent needs, and nobody much cared about Czech anymore. Weirdness in North Korea, the emergence of Southeast Asia, and China's ever more extroverted stance prompted a call for experts in other Asian languages, as well.

Krueger looks more like a wrestler than such a specialist. He's a muscular, broad-shouldered twenty-five, with a deep tan and a neck as wide as his head. Tattoos crowd both of his upper arms. One depicts a squat, cartoonish devil with goat's feet and a mischievous grin, the number "666" emblazoned around its head.

He was born in Milwaukee and lived there until his family moved to a dairy farm when he was fourteen. It was a decidedly rural place to spend his teens: Krueger knew everyone in his class, at a high school that shared space with all the other grades. A lot of the electives were farming related. He joined the air force both to immerse himself in language and to get out of southwest Wisconsin.

He settled on Lao because he'd be able to train on the East Coast, at the Foreign Service Institute in Rosslyn, Virginia — a bit more easygoing in matters of dress and decorum than the Defense Language Institute in Monterey, California — and because he'd been exposed to Lao while a kid: Milwaukee was home to a large Laotian refugee community. He and three other students sat in a classroom six hours a day, five days a week, for a year, speaking nothing but Lao, until his graduation in December 1998.

Our hosts study him closely as he greets them, smiling, then — after a brief preamble in which I assume he's describing the mission and what we hope to find — points to each American, announces his or her name, and describes our various jobs: Eagmin, a marine for fourteen years and an explosives ordnance disposal specialist for ten; Artillaga, our thirty-eight-year-old navy corpsman, who completed three years of medical school in the Philippines before joining the service fifteen years ago; and Conely, a sixteen-year navy veteran with a degree in community studies and a past career as a nurse's assistant.

Posey wastes no time once the formalities are concluded. "OK," he barks. "Let's do it, y'all." One of the team's 92-Mikes volunteers to shovel the unit. Haugen and Krueger line up locals an arm's length apart between the square's edge and the screening station and explain that they're to pass full buckets from the hole to the screens and empty buckets from the screens back to the hole. Villagers come running to take their place in the line, negotiating the ravine in rubber flip-flops with a surefootedness we Americans couldn't manage in hiking boots.

The bucket line in place, Haugen and Krueger select a dozen Laotians to step onto a platform that protrudes from the screening station's legs, two feet off the ground. The rest of us walk to the A-frame's backside and step onto a matching platform. We Americans each now face a Laotian, a screen at waist level between us. The twelve screens are built like short stretchers, with handles protruding from each end. These handles rest on bamboo struts that run the length of the A-frame; when in place, the screens form the crossbar of the "A."

Dingman starts the pump. Water gushes onto the screens. A whoop goes up.

With that, the diggers start shoveling at the lower, eastern edge of 516/520, dumping dark soil into buckets. The line passes them hand-to-hand up the ravine's edge and across the site. They're dumped onto the screens, where the clay is sprayed with water and pressed through the mesh, falls into the tarp trough beneath, and is carried in a muddy stream back downhill to the creek.

The soil is laced with pebbles and slivers of bamboo and tiny chunks of aluminum melted into monkey's fists and formless blobs, and the team members carefully pick the metal from the mess, drop it into artifact buckets that hang from the A-frame.

Within a minute, the 92-Mike yells from the hole: "Gwen!"

"What?" Haugen shouts back.

"Do you want this in the bucket?" The soldier holds a small, black rectangle overhead. An M-16 magazine, still loaded, the copper jackets of the bullets within tarnished lichen green, their brass cartridges fuzzed with corrosion.

An excited murmur goes up on the screens.

It is a good omen.

The morning is overcast, shadowless and muggy. Dragonflies dart over the grid, but the rain they promise does not come, and as the hours pass and the site settles into a steady rhythm of buckets marching heavy and slow uphill, of splashing water and busy eyes and hands, the temperature climbs.

Just after lunch I'm in the hole, swinging a pickax at a bamboo stump. The heat is baking moisture from the ground, and it rises steamy and suffocating around me. My clothes are soaked through. Sweat cascades, stinging, into my eyes. The pick's handle is slick, its head caked with mud that doubles its weight. A dozen swings and I'm lightheaded and breathing hard, and discouraged — few of my blows have landed where I aimed them, and those few have only nicked the bamboo's tough, shiny hide.

Two villagers shovel dirt beside me, while another couple offer a running commentary in Lao, presumably on my digging style. I straighten up for a moment, winded, and the teenager shoveling beside me taps me on the shoulder, says something I can't even begin to understand, and points at his feet. At the bottom of the hole left by his last bladeful of dirt is a bright, smooth patch of green.

At first I mistake it for sugared glass, like you'd find on a beach. When I crouch down and push some of the dirt away, I see it's opaque. "Valerie."

Staff Sgt. Valerie McIntosh, a 92-Mike, is on the far side of the hole, squaring its edge with a shovel. "Yeah?"

"There's something here."

She crosses the unit and squats beside me. She runs a finger over the object, brushes away a little more dirt, exposes one edge. "We better call," she says, and pulls a walkie-talkie from her belt. "We got something metal down here. Could somebody come have a look?"

Haugen materializes above us. She glances at all the workers gathered around. "I think it's *phak pon*," she says, using the Lao term for "break." She makes a show of looking at her watch. "Yep. *Phak pon!*" She waves the workers back. A few wander off, but most simply retreat a few steps as she and McIntosh kneel beside the hole and gently scoop dirt from around the mystery object. They expose a round corner. "We should probably get EOD down here," Haugen murmurs, but she keeps sweeping dirt away with her fingers. Another round corner appears. Whatever the thing is, it's fairly small: Judging from the one straight edge and two corners we can see, it's about the length of a paperback book. Then a letter, embossed on the object's surface, appears through the soil: "E."

"It says something," McIntosh observes. Haugen brushes back more dirt. A second letter: "N." More brushing. Another: "I."

And a moment later: "M."

"It looks," Haugen says in a near-whisper, "like it says, 'Mine.'"

As in *land mine.*

Haugen is on her feet. "Everybody back!" Some villagers take off running. Some don't move at all. "C'mon!" she shouts, taking a couple by the shoulders, turning them around, pushing them away. "Back! Get back! Get out of the grid!"

From the break tent we watch Brian Eagmin walk alone to the hole. He marches steadily, silently, brow furrowed. He was in boot camp three days out of high school; he'd sought out the marines because he sensed he needed the discipline, needed his ass kicked. It worked. Eagmin learned discipline.

The Grid as of August 13, 2001, 8:15 A.M.

He kneels calmly beside the green thing; we can see just the top of his blond crew cut beyond the ravine's lip as he trowels it loose. EODs rely on their knowledge of worldwide ordnance, which among long-term practitioners is encyclopedic. They study the arcana of fuses, switches, and chemical ingredients. They understand risks, and which they can afford to take. But more than anything, an EOD who aims to reach retirement age learns to concentrate and to hold his focus — to achieve an unflagging, obsessive oneness with the task at hand.

No one in the break tent says much. This is a scene all too common on CILHI digs in Southeast Asia. Teams have uncovered vast caches of Howitzer rounds, their explosive innards destabilized by years of jungle heat. They've dug up live grenades and fuses and blasting cord and mines designed to kill tanks. Mortar rounds. Air-to-ground rockets. Rocket-propelled grenades. And those aren't the greatest perils — that distinction belongs to supposed duds that fell from the sky. Most of America's unaccounted-for servicemen were lost aboard aircraft, often in the company of bombs, some of which may have failed to explode thirty years ago but could blow a fifty-foot crater into the here and now with no more than a sneeze.

And, in Laos, small antipersonnel bomblets that were sown over the Ho Chi Minh Trail pose a particular danger. The BLU-26, for instance, a baseball-sized *"bombie"* filled with ball bearings: Planes dropped hundreds of them at a time from canisters slung under their wings. Tiny fins in the balls caused them to spin, and when they spun they armed themselves, and if they didn't explode on hitting the ground, they've lain there since, waiting for someone to happen along. People do, all the time. Unexploded ordnance, or "UXO," is one of the biggest threats to life facing rural Laotians along the country's border with Vietnam.

UXO is trouble elsewhere, too — some Pacific islands are littered with the ruins of World War II bombers downed with full loads in their bays — but Laos poses dangers on an entirely different scale: From 1964 to 1973, the United States conducted just shy of 581,000 bombing sorties over the trail and nearby enemy strongholds. A single ambitious day saw 1,500 such runs. Those planes dropped more bombs here — more than *two million tons* of them — than have been dropped anywhere, by anyone, at any time before or since. One province was hammered with better than two tons per resident.

Those two million tons took the form of six million conventional bombs and more than a hundred million *bombies*. It would take a steady rain of them, scores upon scores falling every hour of every day for nine years, to achieve the pile of explosives dumped on Laos. God knows how many villages they flattened, how many of their craters still puncture the landscape, and how many so-called duds lie unexploded today.

But think: If one in a hundred didn't work as advertised, there'd have been 60,000 big bombs and a million *bombies* lurking unexploded at war's end, waiting for an unlucky step or plow blade. And the bulk of them would have been in the neighborhood of where we stand.

American parents fret about their kids riding their bikes without helmets or dropping by a friend's house after school without first calling home. Imagine having to worry over your kids stumbling across a little ball in the backyard that looks and feels like a toy until it blooms fire and jagged steel. More than a hundred Laotians are killed or maimed by

UXO each year, nearly half of them children. And it's the innocent-looking *bombie*, not the big stuff, that most often gets them.

Eagmin is alone in the hole for ten minutes, then saunters across the grid to the break tent. "Claymore!" he yells as he nears us. He shows off a curving rectangle of plastic, flips it over. Chunks of some beige substance, brittle and powdery, cling to the back. It reminds me of the insides of a malted-milk ball. Thirty years ago, it was C4, a decidedly unsweet plastic explosive. A claymore mine was packed with a pound and a half of it, in which were embedded 700 steel ball bearings. Set in the ground on little spikes fixed to its bottom and touched off with an electrical detonator or tripwire, the mine fired the bearings in a sixty-degree fan and could kill people caught in this spray up to fifty meters away. I take it from Eagmin, rub my thumb over the raised letters on the plastic:

BACK
M18A1 APERS MINE

Below is stamped, in faded black, "LOT LOP 10-44 4-70."

"Four-seventy," I mumble. "April 1970. The date fits. Would this have been carried on a helicopter?"

Eagmin shrugs. "Could have been." His voice is surprisingly high-pitched, given his size — he tops six feet — and soft around the edges, a bit like Ernie's on *Sesame Street*.

"They could have had all sorts of stuff on there," he says. "But who knows? It could have belonged to the guys they were picking up." In other words, a find of little significance, despite its potential danger.

Randy Posey waves everyone back onto the grid. "Time to get back to work."

"Time to make the doughnuts," Eagmin agrees.

I head back to the hole, and again hoist the pickax. I hardly notice the heat as I take my first swing at the bamboo; my entire consciousness is focused on the possibility that my consciousness, along with the rest of me, will cease to exist when the pick strikes the ground. What if there are other claymores down there? Or a grenade? Or a *bombie*? Eagmin had already swept this unit with his metal detector when McIntosh found that rifle magazine this morning, and hell, *that* was made of metal, and loaded with bullets that were, too. So who's to say what lies a few inches below our feet?

The pickax slams into the soil beyond the stump. Nothing happens. I swing again. Nothing. Again. The bamboo starts to splinter. Once more. The stump splits in two. On the next swing, the pick's head wedges deep in the wood, and I'm able to pry the bamboo from the ground.

It's hard to relax, however. One of the locals on the bucket line is wearing a T-shirt emblazoned with a cartoon strip. The first panel shows a young man sitting in the woods, smoking a cigarette and examining an object he's found. A thought balloon floating over his head indicates that he thinks it's a stove or lantern. The second panel shows him consumed by a forceful explosion. The third panel has him sitting at a table, left eye missing and face disfigured, right arm a stump just below the elbow.

An hour passes. I'm attacking more bamboo, ripping it loose from its roots, when a Laotian kid on the bucket line jumps forward and reaches for something trapped in the tangle. I glance that way, see black metal, and slap his hand back, hollering, "No!" McIntosh grabs the object, holds it up for all to see: another M-16 magazine, this one empty.

For the rest of the afternoon, we find only little, inconsequential pieces of helicopter — a few shards of glass, chips of plastic, a bolt or two. But the red clay is loaded with bullets, most of them slender M-16 rounds, a few of them bigger, .30-caliber rounds from a Huey's M-60 machine guns. Some are buried points-up. Bright green with exposure, they resemble tulip shoots.

The only sounds reaching the hole are cicadas calling from the trees, the swoosh of water on the screens, clinking buckets, quiet conversation, occasional laughter. The bullets are a reminder that where I stand a battle raged, busy with terror and noise and gore. That tragedy happened, and men died.

Here. On this spot.

PART TWO

The Missing

■

1

WHAT HAPPENED had a name. It was Lam Son 719, and it was a grand-scale invasion of Laos involving thousands of troops and more than six hundred U.S. Army helicopters. It was the largest airborne assault ever attempted, eclipsing all others in what was largely an airborne war. Thanks to the courage of the crews aboard the choppers, it may well rank as the finest hour in the history of U.S. Army aviation.

It was undoubtedly also the darkest: When the operation ended, eight weeks after it started, nearly one in three of its helicopters had been lost outright or damaged beyond repair. Dozens of others were so shot up they could only be fixed at the factory. Entire gunship companies were knocked out of the sky. The lessons learned in Lam Son 719 would prompt the army to rewrite its tactical playbook and birth new chopper designs that, twenty years later, would help win the Persian Gulf War.

The invasion's target was the Ho Chi Minh Trail and the network of logistics and supply depots along its route. In late 1970, allied leaders developed a plan to drive into eastern Savannakhet Province, block the trail's north-south flow of men and materiel, and capture Xepon, a major North Vietnamese ammo, food, and fuel dump twenty-six miles from the border. The brass figured the strike would starve Viet Cong guerrilla forces operating in South Vietnam and head off any major Communist offensives that might be in the works.

They chose Khe Sanh as the operation's launching pad. It was a Vietnamese burg just south of the DMZ and eight miles east of the Laotian border, along Route 9, and infamous: Three years before, a Marine Corps firebase there had survived a seventy-seven-day siege by a vast North Vietnamese force and what seemed impossible odds. American forces had abandoned the base not long after their attackers quit the fight.

The Lam Son plan called for South Vietnamese tanks and infantry to roll west along Route 9 into Laos. At the same time, U.S. helicopters would airlift infantry and ranger units to the high ground on the highway's flanks — the hills north of the Xepon River and the escarpment along its south bank. They'd set up a chain of firebases to cover the lowland invasion, which would culminate with the capture and destruction of enemy targets in and around Xepon the town.

The invading army would be entirely South Vietnamese. American personnel would stay in the air, aboard helicopters ferrying the troops, gunships providing them cover, reconnaissance planes, and air force jets that would "soften" North Vietnamese resistance with bombs.

The first phase of the operation went well. South Vietnamese soldiers were trucked from Dong Ha, where Route 9 dead-ends at the South China Sea, to Khe Sanh, where hundreds of helicopters met them with food and equipment. They filled the sky like swarms of bees, more choppers than anyone had ever seen flying at a time, so many that even the most jaded air crews found the scene fantastic. Khe Sanh was a moonscape of fine, red dust, littered with souvenirs of the past siege — boots, spent shells, little bits of aircraft. Army engineers transformed it in days to a gargantuan helipad.

The attack began at 8 A.M. on February 8, 1971. The rotorwash of the lifting Hueys kicked up such billowing clouds of dust that aircrews could see Khe Sanh as a red smudge in the sky from thirty miles away. South Vietnamese tanks and armored vehicles rolled across the border, meeting no resistance, and with great speed reached the intersection of Routes 9 and 92, where they set up a fire support base they dubbed "A Loui." Huey crews airlifted soldiers to the high ground north of the Xepon, where without much trouble they created Fire Support Bases 30 and 31.

But once the armored column left A Loui, it bogged down, not at all far from today's Ban Alang Base Camp; back then, Route 9 was minus thirteen bridges that had been bombed in past American air strikes. Worse, by mid-February the North Vietnamese were moving elements of five divisions into Savannakhet Province. Within a couple of weeks they had half again as many soldiers as the allies had expected, along with a sophisticated web of antiaircraft artillery that could punch holes in the sky all the way from the border to Xepon.

The firebases became fixed targets for North Vietnamese guns, and as enemy units encircled them, they morphed from redoubts to traps. On February 24, tanks and infantry burst through the perimeter at Fire Support Base 30. The South Vietnamese who survived the experience fled to Fire Support Base 31, which came under siege three days later. Down on the road, Russian-made tanks, backed by infantry, turned up to do battle with the invading column.

The drive for Xepon continued south of the river. In early March Huey crews airlifted men to the escarpment, where they created firebases named for Hollywood leading ladies — Liz, Sophia, and Lolo, for Gina Lolabrigida — and pushed downhill into the town. They reached Xepon on March 6. The town was a ruin, empty of anything but symbolic value.

North Vietnamese resistance was so fierce by this point that allied commanders shifted their focus to getting the South Vietnamese out of Laos before the entire army was chopped to bits. As invasion evolved into evacuation, the landing zones along the escarpment were surrounded by North Vietnamese troops, strafed by machine gun fire, terrorized by the nearly continuous detonations of mortar rounds. Some friendlies were so paralyzed by fear they threw down their weapons and waited to die.

The North Vietnamese were patient, however, because so long as they didn't immediately overrun the LZs, bigger game would come along: American helicopters would show up, and they'd have a chance to shoot them down, then kill the South Vietnamese at their leisure. So they hunkered down close to the perimeters around the LZs, too close for warplanes to attack them without killing the allies they were trying to save. They moved in heavy weapons — 27mm guns, which U.S. crews nicknamed "golden ropes" for the streams of deadly lead they spat, and fearsome 37mm antiaircraft cannon that could knock Hueys out of the sky at 5,000 feet, and .51-caliber machine guns that could tear through armor plating. They dug in, and they waited.

Their patience paid off. The helicopters came. In one of them were Barker, Dugan, Dillender, and Chubb.

*   *   *

Jack Lamar Barker was the last of seven children born to blue-collar, Baptist parents in a blue-collar, Baptist town in southeastern Georgia, on the Okefenokee's swampy fringe. People in Waycross pulled shifts at a King Edward Cigars plant, at a shoe factory, or at the big repair yards of the Atlantic Coast Line, a railroad that today is part of the CSX system. Jack's mother, Nettie O'Berry Barker, was a Waycross girl. His father, Clarence Winfield Barker, had grown up in Alma, a dot on the map a few miles to the north, and had come to Waycross looking for work. He found it at the railyard; C.W., as he was usually known, spent his adult life with the Atlantic Coast Line as a crane operator, mechanic, and clerk.

The Barkers met and married young: Their first child, Eloise, was born when Nettie was six months shy of her eighteenth birthday. By the time Jack came along, on March 22, 1939, Eloise was a high school senior, and Jack's oldest brother, Carl Edward — nicknamed "Honeybee" because he kept hives — was fourteen. Jack had three other brothers and another sister, besides. The Barkers were a close family. Crowded as they were in their small house, they didn't have much choice.

Jack was a quiet kid, inquisitive and brainy and eager to please. He wasn't much given to sports — like all the Barkers, he was small — but he spent a lot of time outside, fishing and exploring. And he could sing: Jack had a voice that all his neighbors noticed. He joined the choir at First Baptist as a youngster.

Waycross was a postcard of mid-century rural America: Its Main Street was flanked by diagonal parking spaces, wide sidewalks, and mercantile fixtures of the period — a McCrory's department store, a locally owned hardware store, an S.S. Kresge five-and-dime with a soda fountain. When Jack was young, the Barkers moved to the town's edge, into the old O'Berry home place, the brick bungalow in which Nettie had grown up, five miles from the business district. It had land, and soon C.W. Sr. augmented his railroad pay by farming part-time, raising a few beef cattle out back of the house along with chickens — three thousand broilers at a time, which he housed in a long, low outbuilding. He knew nothing about poultry farming when he started and was still guessing his way through it when ten-year-old Jack joined the local 4-H Club in 1949.

Like chapters throughout the country, the Ware County 4-H was run by the state's farm extension service, and aimed to introduce future farmers to the science of growing crops and raising stock. Club members devoted themselves to improving the techniques, and thus the yields, of a farming specialty, and they entered their projects in county, district, state, and national competitions. Jack Barker took on chicken farming. He struck Ware County's extension agent, Tom Boland, as "a little old boy, dimple-faced" and "smart enough to take discipline and to pay attention to adults," and under Boland's tutelage he proved a gifted farmer, whose affinity for his birds helped him win the district poultry competition, then the state title and a trip to the national convention in Chicago.

By his early teens, Barker had acquired traits he would carry into adulthood, traits that won't be reflected in anything that Gwen Haugen might pull from the ground. Boland's young charge was "a good, clean, moral boy," a quiet kid who didn't smoke, didn't drink, didn't run around, and who didn't, as he got older, hang around the county's juke joints. At 4-H summer camp he befriended Christopher Boyd, another fledgling farmer, who was impressed that Barker "was always a Southern gentleman," that he "never heard him say even a slang word," and that he was deeply religious: The world, in Barker's eyes, was a sharply defined place, with little detectable gray separating sinful thought or deed and the bright light of righteousness. Treating a classmate disrespectfully was sinful. Indulging in drink was sinful. Sex before marriage was sinful — so unwavering was Barker on this last point that he considered masturbation a sin and even announced to the campers sharing his cabin that he'd never done it and never would. Some of the boys laughed at him. The self-sure Barker wasn't much troubled by them.

Childhood came to an industrious end at Wacona High School, where he was one of eight honor students, only two of them boys, in the sixty-three-member Class of 1957. In his senior year he was president of the Beta Club, open only to the school's most academically gifted, and of the young people's temperance union at First Baptist. He held state office in 4-H and was vice president of the boys' district chapter. He led a local choir. He was business manager of his class. He worked in town at Sietzer's Food Store, helped raise the family's chickens, and did his homework. Jack Barker's classmates didn't have to use a lot of imagination to vote him the boy most likely to succeed.

Barker left Waycross the following autumn for Stetson University in Deland, Florida. He planned on a career in veterinary medicine, though preaching was a possibility; some of his classmates, family, and fellow churchgoers were sure he was destined to be a minister of the Gospel. If flying or the army interested him, he kept it to himself.

An hour before dawn I claw free of the mosquito net shrouding my cot, pull on shorts and sneakers, and step into the dark outdoors to join Haugen, Pete Miller, and the several other Americans who meet most early mornings to jog or power-walk along Route 9. I'm looking forward to a few minutes outside Ban Alang's well-guarded perimeter, which in a mere three days has tightened around us, and to seeing the surrounding countryside without it racing by in a blur. I crunch noisily down Main Street as the camp sleeps around me, pass through the Lao compound, and climb a gentle hill to the highway.

The junction is where everyone supposedly meets, but I find it empty. I peer east down Route 9, but can make out nothing in the dark. A breeze kicks up, and on an easterly gust comes a snatch of conversation, or what seems one. I strain to hear more. Surely the others can't be far off. With a glance back at camp, I head east.

I walk quickly, loose gravel skittering and scratching underfoot, stumbling as unseen potholes catch me by surprise. The sky is moonless, and the highway a ghostly charcoal against the utter black of the scrub and jungle beyond its edge. I can see nothing ahead. I can see nothing behind. I hear no voices now, nothing but the rustle of invisible trees.

I look back again, wondering whether anyone could have seen me leave. It's against the rules to walk the road alone: Our hosts allow Ban Alang's Americans on Route 9 only if they travel in groups and venture no farther than two kilometers from camp. The Laotians say this is out of concern for our safety, and indeed, armed bandits roam a few of the rural provinces, mostly up north, and some of the Hmong tribesmen in the mountains along the Vietnamese border are in a constant state of near-rebellion.

And Laotian officialdom has reason to be more safety conscious than usual these days. Late in 2000, a series of bombings rocked the main market, bus station, post office, and several restaurants in Vientiane, within blocks of the American embassy, causing untold casualties. "This has affected peace and security to some degree," the Laotian embassy in Washington allowed.

So granted, there might be some risk to being out here. But it seems small, very small, when balanced against the hazards we face every day at the site. The heat can bring on headache, unconsciousness, even death. The ground underfoot is uneven and slick and studded with sharp stumps that can transform a simple misstep into a punctured lung or a deep gouge. Infection and disease are ever-present threats. Animal perils abound: The land writhes, as Kevin Smith warned on our arrival, with "critters" — not just the much-feared scorpions and centipedes, but hornets of outrageous dimensions and all manner of wasp and ant and steel-jawed beetle.

Layered atop these natural perils are myriad man-made worries, of which UXO is but one. A team excavating a site in Vietnam unearthed U.S. remains booby-trapped with grenades during the war — whether by Americans or Vietnamese was unclear. A recovery team in Cambodia had to flee its site in the face of a mortar barrage, which may or may not have been accidental.

My odds of getting hurt are far better on the job. Besides, Vientiane's paranoia about an American presence in the hinterlands has been in full bloom since the first joint recovery missions, sixteen and a half years ago, long before banditry and bomb blasts. What's really at work is that we're guests of an authoritarian regime that has no money, few sources of new income, no international standing, and little influence beyond a few of its own cities, let alone beyond its borders. It has a small, widely scattered population. It poses no threat, militarily or otherwise. It controls little, so what little it can control, it controls with a vengeance. And one of the few things it can control is us.

So it is that we use ancient Russian-made helicopters that cost far more to operate and are far riskier to ride than the American military's own models. And that we're capped at fifty people per joint field activity — until early in 2001, the number was forty — when all involved recognize that such a cap limits a JFA's efficiency and unnecessarily retards the rate at which recoveries might take place.

Americans are not allowed to take pictures from the air, no matter how innocuous the subject. Away from camp, American team members are tethered to their dig sites — Gwen Haugen's asked to visit the villages around 1731, and has been turned down. Wartime landing zones such as Brown are usually off-limits to us and our pilots.

It's not as if there are a lot of secrets out there. The best maps of the place, the only ones that depict the terrain in any detail, far surpassing anything that Vientiane has drawn on its own, were produced by the United States, during the war.

The sky lightens to a deep, velveteen purple, and as it does, a bobbing patch of white appears on the road ahead. It becomes a T-shirt, then Haugen, power-walking in toy-soldier strides, headed back to camp. "Not much further to the turn-around," she says, and disappears into the gloom behind me. Pete Miller chugs past a minute later, bathed in sweat, breath rasping, and behind him a chain of other walkers and joggers.

A few minutes later I reach a wide spot in the highway, where I can see muddy footprints looping back westward in a wide arc. The sun is not yet risen, but in anticipation the sky has turned a dull gray, and before me the highway is empty. Off both sides are leggy and thin-limbed trees of too few leaves, and bristly, waist-high shrubs, beyond which nothing is visible.

I stop. A rooster crows off to my left, suggesting that somewhere past the bushes there a house lies hidden, perhaps even a village. Route 9's chewed and pitted asphalt limps on toward the border.

Two hours later. As the team carries its tools to the hole shortly after touching down, I stand with Bounmy Vanmany, my escort from the Press Department of the Ministry of Foreign Affairs. Bounmy — the Lao go by their first rather than their family names — is supposedly my guide and interpreter, though I've seen him only occasionally since our arrival at Ban Alang; he spends most of his time in the base camp's Laotian compound and in a tent that Captain Somphong and other government officials have erected for themselves in the woods near the screening station so that they needn't socialize with the local hoi polloi.

Government functionaries constitute an elite in the People's Democratic Republic, which was created twenty-six years ago to rid the nation of elites but which, in fact, simply substituted a new group of the anointed for the old. The swap wasn't a good one: When the socialist regime seized power in 1975, more than 400,000 people, including most of Laos's teachers, business leaders, seasoned civil servants, degree-holders — in short, its brains — promptly fled the country. Those left to lead the gloriously liberated new republic weren't drawn from the head of the class; the American war-era maps are still useful because despite the self-sufficiency, strength, and toil of the population at large, not a heck of a lot has been accomplished here since.

I met Bounmy in Vientiane, where, like all American journalists, I was driven to the ministry's offices to obtain my credentials and to pay an array of "service" and "registration" fees that totaled $500. Another bill waited on top of that: all of Bounmy's food and lodging expenses, an amount that had to be negotiated and paid up front. We settled on $15 a day for thirty-two days — all told, a big chunk of the average Laotian's annual earnings. I left the ministry nearly a thousand bucks poorer than I'd gone in.

That Bounmy has proven a not particularly great value for the dollar hasn't bothered me; I certainly don't need the Ministry of Foreign Affairs dogging my every step. But now he has sought me out at the edge of the big crater, and we stare at the sludge obscuring its bottom. You could empty a large backyard swimming pool into the breach, and have room left over.

"There were many bombs," Bounmy says quietly. He purses his lips. He's a handsome, well-groomed man, with thick black hair and friendly eyes and, during most of our exchanges, the hint of a smile lurking beneath a stony veneer. He's also far better nourished than his rural countrymen — taller, bigger-boned, bordering on pudgy.

I squint at him. I can't imagine how big a bang would have accompanied this one hole's creation. "Terrible," I say.

"Yes." His hands are in his pockets; he points with his entire body toward the crater. "Why do they not dig up here? Why do they start digging way down there?" I follow the tilt of his head to Haugen and Posey, who are over on the ravine's lip, opening another unit and setting up a second bucket line.

"I think Gwen does that for a reason," I tell him.

"To me, it seems to waste so much time," Bounmy replies. "I would start there." He nods again into the crater, then looks at me. "That is where something from the helicopter was found, I think."

"Yeah. A helmet."

"Yes. So there are probably other things there, too. So why not dig there?"

"I think there's a methodology to this," I offer. "A certain plan to it." As a rule, Haugen chooses to start digging at a site's lowest point and works uphill; freshly turned earth is far more vulnerable to erosion, and if we were to start excavating the higher ground first, what with all the rain the area gets, we'd risk seeing its contents washed downhill into the creek.

"But why, when they know that something has been found *there?*"

I shrug. "Science."

Bounmy is silent for a moment. "Maybe that's true," he mumbles. "But I would start *there.*"

We watch as the bucket lines begin passing dirt to the screens. Everything that comes out of the second unit — 512/520, next to the first unit on the grid's doglegging eastern boundary — is in buckets tied with blue tape. The tape also marks half the screens, which will be dedicated to sifting only the soil from the blue buckets. One of the team members has set a small boom box on a termite mound near the screening station. The Eagles' "Hotel California" drifts over the site, distorted by too much volume from too-small speakers.

I recall my predawn trip down the highway. "You know, Bounmy," I say, turning back to him, "I'd like to walk to the site one day."

"Walk here?" he says. "From the base camp?" He looks confused. "But you can ride a helicopter."

"Yes, but I would like to see Route 9. This whole area was the scene of a huge battle, and that road was at its center. I haven't seen much of it, and I doubt I'll get to on the Squirrels."

Bounmy stares into space for half a minute. I notice that he has tucked the cuffs of his trousers into his black dress socks, as a defense against leeches. "I will ask," he says.

The first unit closes. The square just to its west, 516/516, is opened. Haugen, examining the walls of the finished unit — which are smooth and vertical and sharply angled — notes that here, in the grid's northeast corner, disturbed soil gives way to "culturally sterile" earth at fifteen centimeters, about six inches, below the ground's surface. A precept of archaeology holds that we are unlikely to find anything below that line, for every human activity leaves a footprint. Dig a hole in your backyard, and a century from now an archaeologist will be able to find it; even if you refill the hole with the same soil you extract, it will settle differently and never match its surroundings. A wooden fence will be detectable long after the wood has rotted to nothing, thanks to its post holes; the palisade around Virginia's Jamestown settlement, built nearly four hundred years ago, left marks that have enabled diggers there to establish exactly where it stood. Likewise, a falling aircraft will leave clues to its presence: Its pieces invariably will penetrate the soil, displacing it. You can pick every last sliver of debris from a helicopter's point of impact, but you can't return the earth to its state before the crash.

On occasion, the ground's stratography can play tricks on an archaeologist. If a plane flying horizontally strikes a steep hillside and punches its way deep, one can dig into the soil directly over the debris and encounter sterile earth before hitting any disturbance, provided the excavation is uphill of the point of impact; such situations produce a layer of disturbed soil sandwiched by sterile. But in most cases, hitting sterile soil means you can stop digging; there will be nothing below it but more of the same. Haugen decides that unless the debris field goes deeper we'll excavate to twenty centimeters, or about eight inches down.

I work a screen, sifting buckets of dirt from the new "plain hole," as opposed to that marked with the blue tape. My Laotian partner is a skinny man whom I guess to be in his mid-thirties, wearing a T-shirt so torn and holey that it serves little function. He speaks no English and I know no Lao Theung, forcing us to communicate with points and pantomime, but not much exchange is necessary: Time and again he picks out a piece of wire or plastic from the dirt dumped on our screen, often before we've even had time to wet it down, and as the morning passes, his eyesight only seems to sharpen. We turn up swatches of thin metal foil wadded into tight balls, a circuit board of translucent fiberglass, a long shard of rusted steel. I lose all peripheral vision: After a couple of hours, all I see is the screen, and the clay on top of it, and the rocks in the clay, and the pebbles among the rocks, and pieces of stone and wood the color of bone.

It took Jack Barker five years to get a degree in biology. Halfway through his freshman year, he left his classes for six months in Switzerland with the 4-H Club's International Foreign Youth Exchange, and took more time off to help his parents rebuild after their house burned down.

Stetson, Florida's first private university, was small, academically solid, rural, and conservative, traits that no doubt appealed. But it wasn't cheap, and Barker struggled to raise money — he was a lab technician with the Georgia Department of Health one summer, helping to conduct research in virology, and further defrayed his expenses by accepting a scholarship from the army's Reserve Officer Training Corps.

When he graduated, he was obligated to serve as an officer in the Army Reserve for six years. There's little evidence that Barker planned to make a career of the service at that point; he simply set out to do his time. He attended ROTC summer camp at Fort Benning, Georgia, in the summer of 1962, and that August took the oath of office as a second lieutenant. While he waited for a post in uniform, he taught a semester of science back at Wacona High. He finally went on active duty on February 4, 1963.

Barker knew that an army paycheck swelled with each new skill one acquired. That might explain why, on his first day on the job, he applied for airborne training, which in a few tough months turned foot soldiers into paratroopers. He entered Jump School at Fort Benning in April 1963. Later that year, wearing a winged parachute on his uniform, Barker reported to the U.S. Army Training Center at Fort Jackson, South Carolina, where he worked as an instructor on the firing range and his by-the-book, no-excuses approach to life and work earned raves from his superiors. "Lieutenant Barker presents an immaculate appearance at all times and carries himself according to the highest standards of military bearing," one officer wrote in the young lieutenant's first fitness report, adding that Barker's leadership style "both educates and motivates."

He stayed busy. Shortly after arriving at Fort Jackson, he became choir director at a Baptist church in nearby Columbia, which required his Wednesday nights for practice and his Sunday mornings for worship. After church one Sunday, Barker looked in on a Columbia "huddle house," a venue for coffee and talk that drew lots of local college students. Among them was nineteen-year-old Esther "Dee" Bryan.

Bryan, deeply religious herself, was an undergraduate at Columbia College, an all-girls Methodist school that warned its students they'd best avoid the wild men of Fort Jackson. Wearing his uniform, Barker sat down beside her and asked where she was from, what she did. He never asked her name, but a few days later he turned up in the lobby of her dorm; he'd sought out a Columbia yearbook, found her picture, and tracked her down.

The two sat in the building's parlor. Barker spoke of his college years, his time in Switzerland, his six siblings. Bryan had never met anyone

so young who'd done so much, nor anyone with such command of conversation: Barker was good with words, quick-witted, curious, and he
seemed genuinely interested in what she told him about herself. He was,
she decided, a real grown-up, perhaps the most mature, confident
young man she'd ever met.

Barker came calling in the lobby a few more times before she decided
to chance a date with him. Even then, the college's admonitions about
military men had her worried. She packed scissors and a nail file into
her purse — "an arsenal of things" — with which to defend herself, and
borrowed money from friends for emergency cab fare. Barker signed
her out of her dorm — standard operating procedure at Columbia —
and took her to see Alfred Hitchcock's *Psycho* at a downtown movie
house. During the shower scene, Dee spilled popcorn and Coke all over
him. She wasn't sure he'd invite her on a second date, but before long,
they were steadies.

Late the following spring, Barker left for an assignment at Fort Bragg,
North Carolina. Not for long; still trying to earn extra money, he applied to flight school, and a couple of months later, in July 1964, began
the Officer Fixed-Wing Aviation Course at Fort Rucker, Alabama. He
wasn't a natural in the cockpit: His instructors held him back "due to
slow progress" when his twenty-six-member class graduated in April
1965, and he had to persevere through an extra week of instruction before earning his wings.

By now promoted to first lieutenant, Barker transferred to Bragg for
six weeks, then to Fort McPherson, Georgia. Dee had graduated from
Columbia and landed a teaching job in nearby Atlanta, and the couple
reunited — but only for a few months, until Barker received new orders.
"Indiv will arr Vietnam wearing khaki trousers and short sleeve shirt
and will have in poss basic rqr khaki unif, fatigues and cbt boots," they
read. "Dress unif not rqr. Summer civ clo desirable for off-duty wear."

Late in the afternoon, Conely dumps the artifact buckets onto a screen,
and we circle her as she picks through the day's bounty. There's no
bone, but a lot of helicopter: big chunks of the same white porcelain I
noticed on our first visit to the site, actually the armor that protected
the cockpit's seats; pieces of instrument panel, including one fragment
that reads BRIGHT in white on black, another, MASTER CAUTION; slivers of glass, some green, some clear, some flat, a few curved; lots of M-
60 bullets without cartridges; and several soaked, frayed pieces of fab-

ric. Perhaps most remarkable is a wire attached to two screws, evidently a safety feature to keep the fasteners in place. It did its job admirably: The screws and wire held, even as the aircraft around them did not.

"That's interesting," the chief muses, with the sage air common among navy chiefs and senior army sergeants accustomed to riding herd on teenagers — and that has come, in Conely's case, with being ten years older than her equals in rank and experience.

Like Dingman, she enlisted to put an end to aimlessness: After her family's adventure in Ponape, she lettered in track at a California high school and earned a degree in community studies at the University of California at Santa Cruz. She married at twenty-one, a day out of college — one of her classmates in "T-grouping," a decidedly 1970s undertaking in which a dozen or so students sat in a circle sharing their deepest thoughts and feelings.

But life failed to live up to its promise. Her marriage failed, and work didn't satisfy; she sold vitamins door-to-door and pulled shifts as a certified nurse's assistant, caring for elderly patients in their homes and at a retirement center. She went back to school to study physical therapy, couldn't hack the science courses, returned to nursing care. And despaired: She couldn't imagine emptying bedpans and taking temperatures for the rest of her days. In a late-night phone call, her cousin Bobby, who'd joined the navy years before and risen quickly through the enlisted ranks, asked her whether she'd ever given any thought to the service. She joined in July 1985, at the age of twenty-eight.

"We have some pieces of visor, big pieces," the chief says as Haugen approaches. She shows off a few large fragments of clear Plexiglas. "And some pieces of flight suit." A swatch of torn green, a few inches square. She hands it to Haugen. "That's flight suit?" the anthropologist asks.

"That's definitely flight suit." That voice of authority. At home in San Diego, Conely's with a navy H-60 helicopter squadron. One thing the seagoing service has in common with the army is the material used in flight suits: Nomex, a tightly woven, flame-retardant fabric.

We stow the tools in the break tent, shut down the pump, turn off the generator, lock the radio in its case, and sit in the shade for a few minutes, drinking water, in clothes soaked and clinging. The dog again shows up and again stuffs itself on handouts as the Squirrel spools up beyond the trees, ready to take the first lift back to base camp.

"We found some good stuff today," Haugen tells the team. Her dossier on 1731 warned that several helicopters were shot down in this area, she says, every one but Jack Barker's an "operational loss" in which no one was killed. Without breaking out shovels, it can be difficult to distinguish such wrecks — of jets from which pilots safely ejected, crunched helicopters from which passengers and crew walked away — from others in which men died, and might still be found.

"I came into this thinking that we had about a 25 percent chance of being in the right place," Haugen says, eyeing the evidence on Conely's screen. "But what we've found means this probably wasn't one of those operational losses."

2

ONCE IN VIETNAM, Jack Barker reported to the Third Radio Research Unit in Saigon. The outfit was a cover for the Army Security Agency, a secret organization that sought to disrupt the Viet Cong's operations in South Vietnam by severing its communications, using direction-finding gear to pinpoint enemy radio transmitters. It had started as a ground operation, but in December 1961 the unit had learned that using short-range radio gear to seek the hidden and highly prized transmitters risked American lives; the first U.S. Army soldier killed in the war was a direction-finder for the Third RRU, ambushed that month on a road outside the capital. The army's solution was to mount direction-finding equipment in aircraft, and it was as a pilot in these unarmed DeHavilland Beavers and Beechcraft Seminoles that Barker joined the unit, nicknamed "TWA" for "Teeny Weeny Airlines."

The Beaver lacked any inertial navigation system or global positioning gear, both standards today; its pilot had to rely on ground landmarks to figure his position and the locations of the transmitters he detected. His effectiveness was only as good as his flying and sense of direction. The twin-engine Seminoles were more advanced, but in any plane the work was dangerous: Missions invariably called on the unit's pilots to fly low and slow over hostile terrain and to loiter there while his passengers homed in on the Viet Cong.

Barker, as usual, gave the assignment his all and proved a standout. He was awarded the Air Medal twenty-four times, along with the Bronze Star. His fitness reports were almost tedious in their praise.

"This officer's performance of duties while serving in the Republic of Vietnam has been truly outstanding," one commander wrote. "In a mission characterized by the need for technical knowledge, the association with highly classified material and of vital importance in the counterinsurgency effort, [he] was without peers in his accomplishments."

Just how good Barker proved to be is suggested by a letter he received from his boss's boss's boss after an April 4, 1966, flight. "The quality of your performance," Col. Clayton Swears wrote, "is clearly demonstrated by the fact that the exact, measured, unquestioned results of your mission on that date exceeded the results by any aircrew on any of the hundreds of similar missions previously flown by members of this command." His company's executive officer offered perhaps the highest accolade: "I would gladly serve again in combat with this officer."

Barker was promoted to captain in May 1966 and a month later transferred to the 146th Aviation Company as a platoon commander. Just before Thanksgiving, he rang up Dee, who was still in Atlanta. Telephone calls from Vietnam to the States used military phone lines and radio patches; connections were spotty and monitored by an operator, and callers had to use radio lingo.

"Will you marry me, over?" Jack Barker asked his girlfriend of three years.

"Yes," Dee replied, "I will. Over."

For an hour after RE-1 lands back at Ban Alang, the LZ throbs with incoming choppers; Squirrels touch down, disgorge their passengers, and spring skyward again at such a pace that when the last sortie's done, and the last turbine shuts down, the camp seems suddenly blanketed in an eerie quiet.

I head to Mama's with Pat Reynolds, who marches across Main Street with such carefully measured steps and arm swings that at first I take it for a put-on. As we near the restaurant I realize the explanation is simply that the man's a jarhead. Until Reynolds, army captains always led recovery teams, but these days interservice cooperation is a priority among military leaders struggling to trim budgets and manage expensive new technologies and match America's fighting prowess to the world's changing threats. The lab has not escaped this cultural shift; while "U.S. Army" remains part of its title, it's going "joint." Reynolds is symbolic of the lab's future.

Not that he planned it that way. Reynolds joined the Corps hoping to someday lead a rifle company, but instead wound up in logistics — not an altogether swashbuckling line of work but one that gave him the skills to deploy people and equipment in the middle of nowhere. They were the same skills developed by the army's Quartermaster Corps, of which Mortuary Affairs and the lab are a part. The call went out for CILHI's first marines when he was up for a new assignment, and not only did he seem a good fit but the nature of the lab's work intrigued him. It sounded like good duty, important duty. A peacetime job that mattered.

We get a table, order beers, pore over the menu. The big Beerlaos arrive. That Reynolds joined the marines at all was an unexpected development. His parents were Irish immigrants in the Bronx, and barkeeps; all of his living paternal forebears, in fact, owned or worked in taverns — which, considering his father was one of thirteen kids, meant the Reynoldses were well represented in the New York hospitality industry. An only child, he spent his days in Catholic schools, where he was "reprimanded highly," and many an evening in his parents' establishments.

It was the navy that fascinated him as a boy. His folks would take him to Fleet Week each year to see an armada of warships pull into New York Harbor, and he'd thrill to the carriers, cruisers, and destroyers that lined the wharves or anchored just offshore, pennants flying, sailors lining the decks in their whites. His enthusiasm faded as he got older; by the time he settled into his classes at Manhattan College, he had no intention of pursuing a military life. He instead majored in finance and information systems, planning on a corporate career. He rowed crew. He fell for one of his female teammates, started thinking about marriage and family.

But in his junior year he came across an advertisement for the marines, and for reasons he can't explain it entranced him. Maybe it rekindled something in his genes: His dad had been a medic in the U.S. Army, even as an Irish citizen. Perhaps it was just the Corps's bravado: *Think you're hot shit? Think you're good enough to be one of us? OK,* the marines said, *let's see you prove it.*

The recruiters wouldn't even talk to him at first. Despite all his rowing, Reynolds had ballooned to a stout 235 pounds when he wandered in to see them six years ago. "Come back when you've lost twenty pounds," they told him. He went home and lost the weight, and they told him to lose another ten. When he did that, they let him in.

We're joined by Ray Walsh, the camp's doctor, a veteran of the Peace Corps in East Africa who signed on with the air force to help pay for his medical schooling. Every joint field activity in Laos includes an MD, whose primary duty is to provide care to locals living near the digs and any who might come calling at base camp. Before long, Haugen and Pete Miller pull up chairs, as well. Miller, among the seniormost CILHI scientists, the overseer of the 1989 dig for 1731, sits to my right. He's wearing a T-shirt from some past dig emblazoned "Low Priority." His hair, longish and gray, is lank with sweat. We all take long pulls from our Beerlaos.

RE-3's team leader sits down with a brand-new Trivial Pursuit game. We split into pairs — Haugen and the newcomer, Reynolds and Doc Walsh, Pete Miller and me. My partner is a good one, with a fantastic memory of the arcane, and we rapidly earn two wedges while the others skip luckless around the board. Between turns I scan the other tables at Mama's. Eagmin and three female soldiers from RE-1 are playing cards at one. Members of the IE are seated at another. The camp's linguists, minus Krueger, are at a third.

The scene poses a stark contrast to the amenities on most of the lab's missions. On a July 2000 trip, I camped in Vietnam with a team excavating a helicopter that had broken up in mid-flight. The group's ridgetop landing zone was ringed by high peaks and swathed in clouds that marooned the diggers for days at a time, and its members slept and ate in a camp they built in the gloaming of a teak and mahogany forest. It looked like something out of *Swiss Family Robinson:* They lashed bamboo into tent platforms and porches, into showers, tables, even into a sectional sofa they arranged around their campfire. They didn't play any board games, though, and at night they heard tigers growling in the trees.

The accommodations get a lot more primitive than that. In March 2001 I visited a team working on a giant limestone massif in Laos's Khammouan Province, about an hour's flight from Ban Alang. Just approaching the place, I had to shut my eyes: My helicopter performed an aerial ballet to reach the only practical landing spot, a boulder peaking from the jungle canopy, barely large enough for the chopper's skids. The closest thing to a campsite on the mountain was a sloping shelf of leech-infested, rocky dirt, so uneven and thick with trees that wall tents wouldn't fit. The team and its Laotian escorts lived for weeks in tiny backpacking tents, every one of which was tipped uphill or down, each too small for all but the most essential gear. Water was flown in when the weather allowed — which is to say, just often enough.

Randy Posey found himself at one remote excavation in central Vietnam where it rained so hard and for so long that over the course of a month his team spent four days actually digging. The weather kept resupply and rescue choppers away, too, leaving him no choice but to hunker down, soaked and thirsty and bored witless in the jungle gloom, praying no one got hurt or snakebit.

CILHI files are busy with that brand of low-grade misery, and worse. Another team was excavating a World War II crash site on a mountaintop in Papua New Guinea when a storm moved in, grounding its helicopter at the mountain's foot. Its members stayed put for a couple of days; then, low on water, out of food, and with the weather showing no improvement, they decided they had to hike out. Guided by native tribesmen, they stumbled a thousand feet down the mountain, hit a dead end, and climbed back up, at which time the natives abandoned them to a cold, rainy, tentless night on the mountainside. Had a sergeant on the team not packed extra clothes in her duffel, they'd have been in deep trouble.

Even on missions on which the teams commute to work by road or air, the lodgings are rarely up to Ban Alang's standards. Many a digger has shared his or her rural Vietnamese "guest house" room with lice, leeches, rats, and cockroaches big enough to brand. Hot showers are unattainable luxuries. The toilets, at their best, are porcelain holes in the floor, over which one has to balance to complete one's task; at worst they're the same without the porcelain, and sweltering and unlit and swarming with bugs, to boot. One whiff of the air percolating from their grim depths and you'll opt for the woods, snakes be damned.

So this little outpost of comfort in the Laotian jungle is an anomaly, at the cusp of weird and familiar, East and West, danger and safety. Lucky is the soldier who camps here, particularly if he or she is new to CILHI and without experience in the Third World.

Our game crawls into its second hour. Exhausted, we alter the rules so that any correct answer earns a wedge. Grow up in a family of bar owners and you absorb sports; within a couple of turns, Reynolds and Doc Walsh have left us behind. Somehow Haugen and her partner, who in the early going looked hopeless, storm past us, too.

"So, Pete," I say to Miller, as we wait for our turn, "we went out and saw your 1989 excavation at Gwen's site."

Miller has overseen more excavations than any of his peers at CILHI — he reached the fifty-case mark two years ago and has ventured regularly into the field since. He nods, a wistful smile forming. "Oh, yes," he sighs. "That's one I remember well."

"It was pretty amazing to see how well-preserved it was, after thirteen years," I say. "You could still see where you'd built steps going down the sides of the hole."

"Oh, it was a beautiful little excavation," he says. He swallows a mouthful of beer. Hours after sundown, our resting arms leave sweaty spots on the table. "And this TV crew shows up. And we found a radio with a data plate, and OK, there we are, on national TV, the cameras rolling, when we find it, and everybody's excited, and we look at the numbers and realize it's the wrong helicopter." He shakes his head. "On national TV."

Luckily, it was *Laotian* national TV; the indignity Miller suffered was only so big. That first 1731 dig came four years after Miller's first in Laos, in 1985, but three years before Joint Task Force-Full Accounting arrived on the scene. The restrictions in place back then were far more stringent than those of today; for one thing, the People's Democratic Republic permitted teams into its territory for only ten days at a time.

"That's all you needed," Miller says. "Ten days was plenty of time, because back in the eighties, we had nothing but good cases, easy cases. All the sites were intact, and we knew exactly where they were. Every time out, you recovered remains." He shakes his head. "Those were the days."

"Not like now?"

"Nothing like now," he says. "Now we're into the hard cases. We're into the isolated burials, and sites where there's just nothing left."

That's just as true of Vietnam; the pickings are getting slim. Haugen has a .500 record — she's found remains on five of her ten digs — and it's that good only because she's worked in Europe, where crash sites are protected from looters. The last JFA in Laos saw three teams digging and not a bone recovered. The mission before that, one team in three found remains.

The experience of Dingman, sitting at a table across the room, is typical of many rank-and-file members of the lab staff. His first dig, in the summer of 2000, took him to two sites in Vietnam's Central Highlands, just across the border from where Jack Barker's chopper went down. The first was a blind hunt for a GI who'd fallen from a Huey during an extraction. The odds were long, so it didn't surprise anyone when the team found nothing.

The second site was a burial, and at first, it looked to be a bust, as well. They were about to give up when a witness told them they'd passed right over the grave, that they simply hadn't gone deep enough. Sure enough, they found remains in the center of their grid. He was one for two.

He returned to the field later that year for a dig along northern Vietnam's rugged coast. The team found lots of aircraft parts but no remains. One for three. Six months before coming to Laos, he went to Vietnam a third time, to the "Money Pit," a particularly complicated aircraft crash site that had seen American digs before, and would see others after. His team found nothing. One for four.

In April 2001 came his oddest trip yet, to Korea. He and Posey were part of a small team that ventured into the DMZ to excavate a spot where a roving South Korean patrol had stumbled on surface bones. Propaganda blared from gargantuan loudspeakers on both heavily armed frontiers, and they dug with the knowledge that the North Koreans were watching them through gunsights. They found remains, however. Two for five.

"Nothing like now," Miller says again. When we wrap up this JFA, he's scheduled to spend eight days home in Hawaii before he leaves again for Vietnam, to do advance work at the point where a jet is said to have "lawn-darted" vertically into the ground. The rear of the plane, the portion closest to the surface, was supposedly scavenged by locals years ago, but its forward portion, including the cockpit, was left deep in the soil.

"Ten meters down, eight meters, whatever," Miller says. "But what's bad about it is that a salt-processing plant was built years ago on top of the site, so we have to tear up this plant to get to it." He swallows a mouthful of beer. "*Buildings* have to be moved."

Jack Barker shipped home in December 1966. He sang "How Great Thou Art" at his father's funeral within days of his arrival, and sang "The Lord's Prayer" at his own wedding a few days later, on January 14, 1967. The latter ceremony, at the Methodist church in Dee's South

Carolina hometown, was also a sendoff: In March, the newlyweds moved to Hanau, Germany.

Just north of Frankfurt, Hanau was home to Fliegerhorst Kaserne, a former World War II Luftwaffe airfield, where Barker occupied an odd niche as a fixed-wing pilot in the leadership ranks of a helicopter battalion. As always, the sharp, squared-away young officer attracted the attention of his superiors. "Extremely dependable and completes his assignments with zeal and forcefulness," one wrote. "One of the finest officers of his contemporary group," judged another, adding: "His dependability and skill in overcoming obstacles are unmatched." His commanders underlined their pleasure by nominating him for the Army Commendation Medal.

Between kudos, Barker toured Europe with Dee, took square-dancing lessons, and — more good fortune — started a family. The couple's first son, Bryan Lamar, was born in Frankfurt, and when they left Germany in June 1969, Dee was pregnant with their second, Michael Winfield. He was a doting father to the boys: He woke for their 2 A.M. feedings, bathed them, read them stories, took them to the doctor.

He and Dee had talked about his leaving the service. They missed their families, and friends who never stayed long before the army snatched them away to Vietnam or some other far-flung duty station. They longed to establish roots, a real home. But as the end of Barker's tour approached, the army issued him orders to the Infantry Officer Advanced Course at Fort Benning — a plum for an officer who'd entered the service through ROTC and who'd remained in the active-duty reserve, rather than the regular ranks. It tagged Barker as a real up-and-comer.

So he stayed in. He and Dee bought a house in Columbus, Georgia, and he entered the school in September 1969. He made major the following month, far ahead of the standard advancement curve, and when he was graduated from Benning in June 1970, his instructors rated him suited to someday command a battalion.

He was immediately accepted into the Rotary Wing Qualification Course, or "Q Course," at Rucker, an assembly line that churned out helicopter pilot officers in eleven down-and-dirty weeks. The four Barkers kept their house in Columbus, renting a trailer in Alabama and driving home on weekends. When Barker was graduated, he was qualified to fly the Bell OH-13 Sioux — a bubble-enclosed, two-seat trainer

— and the Bell UH-1 Iroquois, the army's ubiquitous "Huey," a workhorse used as troop transport, gunship, freight hauler, and ambulance.

Then new orders arrived. The major was to report to the 101st Aviation Battalion of the 101st Airborne Division, as second-in-command of an assault helicopter company. The unit was based at Camp Eagle, a sprawling airfield complex south of Hue, in northern South Vietnam.

Dee had befriended the wife of another Rucker student while Barker was in class. The woman's husband was headed for Vietnam at the same time, and she invited Dee and the boys to stay with her in Phoenix. Dee took her up on her offer, moving the family to Arizona when Barker left for Southeast Asia.

He arrived at Camp Eagle on October 20, 1970. His new unit, Bravo Company, also known as the Kingsmen, was a rowdy bunch accustomed to combat. Their quiet, religious new executive officer had been out of helicopter school for less than a month.

Bomb craters pock the rice paddies along the DMZ a few miles east of the Case 1731 site in Vietnam. As visible as such scars in the landscape remain, more than a quarter-century after the war's end, they're nothing compared to the craters found in Laos. (*Vicki Cronis*)

The cloud-shrouded escarpment looms over the 1731 site. Thirty years before, those heights concealed Landing Zone Brown. (*David Dingman / U.S. Army Central Identification Laboratory*)

Photographs not credited are by Earl Swift.

Gwen Haugen, Recovery Element One's anthropologist. The veteran of ten overseas missions had found the remains or partial remains of nineteen lost American servicemen when she embarked on the search for Jack Barker and his crew.

Army sergeant first class Randy Posey, RE-1's top enlisted member and a father figure to a young and inexperienced recovery team.

Marine captain Patrick Reynolds. RE-1's senior military member, he was the first marine to lead a recovery team and was on his first mission with the Central Identification Laboratory.

Air force senior airman Clint Krueger, the team's reticent linguist.

Gwen Haugen and Pat Reynolds examine a bullet-damaged U.S. Army helmet. Entry and exit holes in the artifact were the key piece of evidence suggesting Americans died at or near the site during the war.

The chief of Ban Satun-Gnai, a village east of the dig, points to the spot where he says he found the helmet on the floor of a big crater.

Army PFC Tracy Gummo and marine staff sergeant Brian Eagmin haul equipment across the Case 1731 excavation site.

Navy chief parachute rigger Victoria Conely, RE-1's expert on gear worn by Vietnam-era flight crews.

A Laotian villager swings his *bria* at a piece of timber intended for the screening station, taking shape at left.

Clint Krueger, center, converses in Lao with the Laotian army's enigmatic Captain Somphong.

Supervised by Tracy Gummo, villagers dig at the ravine's lip above a pair of already excavated, carefully stairstepped units.

Villagers at the Case 1731 site wait to go to work. The dig's indigenous muscle ranged from the juvenile to the elderly.

Victoria Conely picks through the meager wreckage recovered one day halfway through the dig.

What a crash, a fire, and thirty years in the jungle can do to a flying machine. These bits of a Huey instrument panel were snared by a screen's quarter-inch mesh.

The most telling piece of wreckage unearthed in Gwen Haugen's excavation: the Bell helicopter data plate found in 504/508.

3

BAN ALANG MORNINGS begin much as American soldiers started their days thirty years ago. I escape the mosquito netting draped over my cot, unzip my tent, lurch groggily to the latrines, filling a bucket with water on my way in — the toilets flush, but only if you dump water in the bowls after you've used them — then venture back through the wet, predawn chill to the shaving station, a thatched, open-sided shelter between the latrines and my quarters.

And on the way, I look south to the escarpment, just as Kingsmen crews gazed on a hill near Camp Evans every morning. Ground Control Approach Mountain, they called it. If they could see it, they could fly, and likewise, if these days the escarpment is visible, the choppers can leave our camp. It might not be scientific, but it's reliable.

This dawn, like most, finds the ridge completely obscured by a bank of low clouds that slowly burns away as a crowd of us brush our teeth at the shaving station, all puffy-eyed and torpid and spitting opaque streams of bottled water into the grass. RE-1's junior members shovel ice into sandbags for our cooler at the site. The Squirrel pilots stumble onto the LZ for a "bushman's breakfast" — a yawn, a stretch, a piss, and a look around.

I pull on a long-sleeved shirt and long pants, a first line of defense against microscopic nasties; like all the Americans at Ban Alang, I've been vaccinated against Japanese encephalitis, cholera, yellow fever, typhoid, tetanus, hepatitis A and B, even rabies, and each day I swallow a little doxycyclene pill that theoretically protects me from some strains of malaria. But the best safeguard against disease is to avoid it in the first place, and there's no vaccination against some of the stuff lurking out there. Some Laotian mosquitoes, for instance, are known to carry dengue, also known as "breakbone fever," a brutal ailment that at its worst can turn you into an oozing bag of blood. The mosquitoes that pack it, unlike their malarial cousins, bite only when the sun is up.

By the time RE-1 meets at the equipment shed, at 7 A.M., the clouds have usually dissipated enough to expose two-thirds of the escarpment, and one of the pilots will leave with the team's first lift; from 500 feet up, he can better judge whether the weather will permit RE-2 and RE-3, whose sites are farther away, to head to work. By the third lift, the escarpment's ragged top typically is showing, the valley is bathed in sunshine, and the temperature is rising fast.

The site has settled into an even more predictable routine. I spend the morning on the screens, working opposite a cheerful young villager in an ancient black T-shirt decorated with a fierce-looking eagle, its head encircled by "The United States of America" in florid script. I wonder where he got it — from a soldier on one of the two IEs that were here before us, perhaps? He takes charge of the rubber hose feeding water onto the screen, while I press the thick clay through the mesh. Nothing but "ACS" — "aircraft shit," or "aircraft stuff" — turns up, metal shavings, slivers of glass, wire, washers, a few rivets.

More interesting debris appears on other screens, however: more pieces of what Conely identifies as helmet visor, some olive-drab fabric she believes to be part of a flak jacket. It's largely guesswork: Conely's experience has been with intact components, not shards caked with mud and rust after thirty years underground. There's much, besides, that challenges even approximate identification, pieces of clear and green glass that could be from cockpit windscreen, or instrument panel, or God knows where else — assuming it comes from a helicopter at all.

The chief talks aloud to herself as she pores over the artifacts. A lot of parachute riggers seek out the rating because they're interested in skydiving or aviation. What drew Conely was the knowledge that others would rely on her: Back in San Diego, aircrews know she's packed their chutes and trust that if they have to use them, those chutes will open as they should. They know she holds their lives in her hands.

And now the members of RE-1 rely on her to tell them what they've found. The stakes aren't quite as high, but if she's wrong — if she were to misinterpret a piece of unimportant wreckage for life support — she might prompt Haugen to focus the team's efforts on the wrong spot. To waste days. To miss bone.

She dumps another bucket onto her screen. It yields a pile of Plexiglas, a bracket fitting from a helmet, a D-ring, M-60 and M-16 rounds, wire connections, more chunks of porcelain seat armor. Shards of bomb frag, rusted and curved and heavy. Most impressive is a rubber earcup from inside a flight helmet. "Standard issue on American aircraft," Reynolds says. "That's a good sign."

Haugen is excited by the discovery. "I really feel like we're at the right aircraft," she tells the team. "I have a really good feeling. Keep a really good eye on those screens."

The air turns gummy. At first break Artillaga staggers to the break tent, his shirt sopping. The medic is accustomed to tropical heat — he was born in the Philippines and lived there into his mid-twenties — but now he collapses onto a bench. "I have never sweated so much the whole time I've been in the navy," he gasps. He smiles deliriously.

Conely's stout frame is drenched, her face pink. The rest of the team is too drained for conversation. I sit on a footlocker, eyes closed, conscious of little but my soaked underwear. Some soldiers listlessly feed the little dog, who actually seems to have filled out a little.

"Y'all drink water," Posey says, studying his charges. "Gotta keep that water in you. Gotta stay healthy. We gotta push some dirt today." He runs a hand over his soaked head. "God *damn*, it's hot."

I head back to my screen by way of the big crater, a detour that takes me past Don Guthrie, who is standing at its edge. Haugen is closing 512/520 and opening the unit to its west, 512/516, which covers the ground on the ravine's lip just a square away from the highest concentration of surface debris. The pilot and I watch her shovel dirt into a bucket. "Bloody hard work," Guthrie says. "I wonder how many people realize what it's like, doing this. How bloody hard it is. I reckon 50 percent of the people in the States think this is worthwhile, and 50 percent don't give a fuck, or think they're spending too much money."

"Might be right," I say. "Of the people who even know it's going on." I was surprised by the reactions I got back home when I mentioned I was coming here, and why: My younger friends were wildly jealous of my upcoming adventure and expressed admiration for the rightness of the mission; a sizeable minority — older and male, mostly, and veterans —

shook their heads at the expense of it all, told me they didn't understand why, all these years later, the government felt it necessary to disturb the bodies of American boys who were dead and would stay dead no matter how much cash was dumped into recovery operations. The most adamant I encountered were men who'd fought in World War II and Korea, and who presumably had wartime friends who'd vanished. Leave them, they said. Let them rest. It does nobody any good to dig them up now.

The screens are back up and running. I can see my partner in the United States of America shirt, working alone. "But listen," Guthrie says, stretching, "at the end of the day, it's mighty nice to be able to go to the families and say, 'Your son died on that helicopter. We know that, because the bones we found at the site, the teeth we found, wouldn't have been there if he were a prisoner at some bloody prison in Hanoi.'"

True enough. All we have to do is find those bones.

John Francis Dugan had been with the Kingsmen for four weeks when Jack Barker arrived. Like his new boss, he was a short man, five foot six and a chunky 172 pounds, and like Barker he was on his second tour in Vietnam: Dugan had spent his first as a forward observer with an artillery unit, a post that required him to get close to the North Vietnamese positions he pinpointed for shelling.

On one occasion, Dugan's artillery unit misplaced him — an administrative screw-up — and he was declared missing in action. The army telegrammed his parents, who waited for word of his fate for days, until a letter turned up that he wrote after he'd been reported missing. So it was that when John Dugan arrived in Vietnam on his second tour, his family had already lost him once.

His father, Joseph, was an accountant who'd worked the books for several companies before joining a small accounting firm in Roselle, New Jersey. There he met Mary Edna McDevitt, whose family enjoyed such local prominence that the street on which she lived bore her name. John was born on November 10, 1947.

Roselle was a bedroom community, forty-five minutes from Newark, and Joe Sr. did only so well. John and two brothers shared one of two bedrooms in a cramped apartment tucked above a stationery store, a Chinese laundry, and a barbershop. One summer, when John was about ten, the family returned from vacation to find that the landlord had repossessed one of the apartment's bedrooms — had emptied it of its furniture, put up a new wall, and rented the vacant space to a dance studio. For several years after that, Dugan's parents slept on a pull-out couch in a space off the living room.

At Roselle Catholic High School, Dugan earned good grades without exerting himself. He worked at a local restaurant after class; built a large, carefully alphabetized collection of rock-and-roll 45s and LPs; and slavishly followed the Yankees: He and his younger brother, Mike, often took bus and subway to summertime day games, where they'd worm their way from the bleachers to seats in the field boxes.

He developed a passion for cars, as well, despite an inauspicious early acquaintance. His older brother, Joe Jr., was teaching him how to drive in the parking lot of the local A&P when John lost control of the family's 1959 Volvo; the vehicle leaped over a concrete parking barrier and smashed through a fence. A further indignity came with his first driving test: He took it in a car with touchy brakes and came close to catapulting a license examiner through the roof. He eventually passed the test, bought a 1952 DeSoto, and just out of high school traded up for a white-on-blue 1959 T-bird convertible, which he drove to classes at nearby Union College and an after-school job at a chemistry lab. He'd spend a couple of years at Union, he figured, then move on to a bigger school for his chemistry degree.

But an unexpected drama rearranged his plans. One day Dugan failed to turn up for classes at Union, and failed to come home from his after-school job. The Dugan boys often had visited a buddy's house for marathon Monopoly games, and Mike had noticed sparks between John and their friend's fifteen-year-old sister, Barbara, who sometimes joined them. Still, Mike wasn't expecting to hear, when Dugan finally called nearly a week after his disappearance, that he and Barbara had eloped and were living in a Maryland motel. John had found a laboratory job in the D.C. area, but he hadn't been paid yet, and they could sure use some cash. Could he borrow some?

Mike drove south with a family friend. They found Dugan alone and heartbroken; Barbara's parents had swooped in on the newlyweds and snatched her away, and were already working on an annulment. The romantic flight, brief though it was, bore other, and rather more dire, consequences: Dugan had dropped out of Union to head south, and no longer had a deferment.

He met with an air force recruiter, but signed up with the army when the service offered him a shot at officer candidate school. He completed basic training at Fort Dix, then OCS at Fort Sill, Oklahoma. He left for Vietnam in April 1968, put in his year as a forward observer, and earned a Purple Heart, the Vietnam Service Medal, and the Bronze Star. He never mentioned the decorations to his parents or brothers, who had no idea he'd earned them until long after he was home.

What he did talk about were the pilots he'd met and worked with — the spotters in small planes with whom he'd speak by radio to arrange artillery barrages, and the steady-nerved commanders of medevac choppers, or "dustoffs," who'd put down anytime, anywhere, to pluck the wounded from the field. Those guys, especially the chopper pilots, actually helped people, Dugan told his family. There they were, in the middle of a war, in the midst of all that killing and destruction and brutality, serving their fellow man.

He started flight school at Fort Wolters, Texas, shortly after his stateside return. One of his classmates was Pete Federovich, a young officer with a wife and a baby and a house in Mineral Wells, a few miles from the base. Federovich liked Dugan as soon as he met him; the Jersey man had a sly sense of humor that kept him laughing, and the two became close friends. Dugan drove to the family's triplex almost every weekend for backyard cookouts.

While at Wolters he traded the T-bird in on a new Mercury Cougar XR7, and couldn't be pried from its bucket seats; he insisted on doing most of the driving when he and Federovich bounced among airfields or went into town. He was a fast, and not terribly good, driver, with a fondness for eye contact during conversation and for conversation while he drove. When he broke his right leg playing softball and was set back in his training, he had to gas and brake the Cougar with his left foot. It did little to improve his skills.

In the spring of 1970, now rated to fly the UH-1H Iroquois, Federovich got orders to Vietnam. Dugan did not: Having served one tour, he could have remained stateside for quite some time, perhaps until the fighting was over. But Dugan was eager to return, and his friend wasn't gone long when he volunteered for combat duty.

His mother tried desperately to talk him out of it. Dugan told her he had to go, that the people in Vietnam needed him. Everybody in the family told him he was crazy, or stupid, or both. It did no good. Before he left home, Dugan treated his mother to a Yankees game, then to an outing to Shea to see her favorite team, the Mets. In September 1970, he was gone.

The excavation inches westward. A sergeant lays claim to my screen partner in the United States of America shirt, who's acquired the nickname "Uncle Sam," or "Sammy." My new partner is a villager in his twenties who stands about five foot six and can't weigh more than a hundred pounds, and who parrots everything I say. I point to clay clinging to the bottom of a bucket and pantomime rinsing it with the hose and tell him: "Wash the bucket," and he cries, "Wash the bucket!" I point to a particularly dense lump on the screen and tell him, "More water," and he says, "More water!" When we stop work for lunch, I announce, "*Phak pon.* Break." He hollers, "Break!"

As we pluck a slew of M-60 rounds from the screen, more pieces of flight suit, chunks of Plexiglas melted and charred black along their edges, he teaches me to count in Lao from one to ten, and I reciprocate in English. He teaches me the Lao-Theung word for water (*nam*), and rock (*heen*), and wood (*mai*). "Hello," I learn, is *sabaa-di,* and "thank you," *khoop chi.* But beyond this meager glossary, we achieve little connection, and the same goes for the men and women on the screens beside me. Even veterans of multiple missions retain only a few phrases they learn in the course of a mission, for they might be in Vietnam one month, in Papua New Guinea a few weeks later, in Laos or Cambodia or North Korea or Russia after that. Keeping the currencies straight is a job, let alone so many languages.

Besides that, the Americans tackle an enormous amount of work on each outing, and exertion, exhaustion, and deadline pressure conspire to chill small talk. The phrases a visiting team member is most likely to employ with regularity are work-related: Do this. Go there. Come here. A GI who fought here thirty years ago would most likely recognize the few Lao words on which the team relies. They're the same ones he learned.

The diggers move slowly across the two open units. Posey supervises one square, stairstepping its sloping surface to keep it a consistent depth. Locals use picks to break the reddish-yellow soil loose; the sarge shovels it into buckets and hoes the hole flat behind them.

He speaks softly to the villagers as they work. They don't understand a word of it, but he keeps it up, a stream of gentle encouragement from a man who, to look at him, seems in his element, completely at ease in the hole. It is remarkable to behold, in that before Posey settled into teaching, he pursued another line of work completely at odds with this place and all the sweat and shoveling and months away from home that the lab requires: The sergeant cut hair. Growing up, he discovered he had a flair for barbering — "I was blessed with it from God," he says — and by the time he left his teens he was shaping the heads of much of Centerville, Mississippi, south of Jackson near the Louisiana line. An older brother convinced him to go to barber college. Today he's the only licensed cosmetologist among CILHI's senior sergeants.

The years that followed toughened him — if not his time in the class-room or his years at Fort Drum, then certainly his early days in Mortu-ary Affairs. Most 92-Mikes don't work for CILHI; the specialty is geared to handling fresh casualties. Shortly after he got to Fort Lee, Posey was sent twice to Bosnia to prepare and ship home the bodies of Americans killed in the peacekeeping efforts there. He was just back from one such trip when Commerce Secretary Ron Brown's plane, a Boeing 737 loaded with people, piled into a Croatian mountainside. Posey was flown back to the Balkans to help. He saw bodies burned to cinders, pieces of others scattered hither and yon, clothes and papers and skin in the high branches of trees. He helped remove and bag the secretary's Rolex.

The ground he oversees coughs up some bigger stuff — the mud-caked workings of a radio or some such electronic device, its broken chassis filled with tiny cogs and wires and studded with knobs. A drizzle starts to fall, then erupts into a downpour that stops before we're a step away from the screens. The sun emerges. The temperature climbs until it almost hurts to breathe. Then, abruptly, clouds move in again, bring-ing more rain. As it intensifies, the locals working the screens grow im-patient to leave. Haugen finally turns them loose when it starts to pour, and we retreat to the break tent.

Conely picks through the day's artifacts on a clean screen. Besides the electronic component, it's mostly knots of melted metal, little bits of plexi. Captain Somphong looks over her shoulder. "Many glasses."

"Yes," she says. "Lots of glass." She sighs. Deciphering glass is a chal-lenge for a modern-day navy parachute rigger; the chief's spent her time in modern H-60F Seahawks, not Vietnam-era Hueys, and minus such experience she's hard-pressed to distinguish pieces of a cockpit's chin bubble from those of a Huey's massive windscreen, and both from slivers of busted helmet visor. Of the three, the visor is the only debris of real interest to RE-1; the trick is knowing it when she sees it. A lot of Huey veterans probably wouldn't be able to do it. And manuals don't help — Conely might be able to use them to identify the helicopter's fractured mechanical innards, but they're of little use in making sense of window smashed into small pieces. She looks up at Haugen. "Not much here, Gwen."

Haugen moves over to the screen and runs her fingers over the piled ACS. "Did you see this?" She picks up a jagged piece of green Plexiglas. On it is etched a handwritten notation:

205-030-

CHG I   B.H.C.   11-70

Conely looks startled. She says nothing as we crowd in for a look at the site's first potential piece of traceable evidence. It is not complete: Whatever followed the number's first six digits must be on another piece of busted Plexiglas.

"B.H.C.," Reynolds reads aloud. "That must be 'Bell Helicopter Company.'" Bell, among the world's biggest helicopter producers, designed and built the Huey. It sold Jack Barker's bird to the army in March 1967.

Our Squirrel pilot says "205" is the company's model number for the aircraft. The "Chg," Haugen theorizes, stands for "change."

"November 1970," Conely murmurs. "When did our guys crash?"

"March '71," Eagmin answers.

"So that fits," Conely says.

"It was probably a piece of the greenhouse," Eagmin suggests, referring to the windows that enfolded the Huey's cockpit. "Got changed out." The EOD has read more about the helicopter war in Vietnam than RE-1's other augmentees and most, if not all, of its regular members, and has a pretty solid understanding of the UH-1H.

"Would Bell have written that on there?"

"No," the pilot says. "The guys in the field would have put that on there, when they installed it."

"Maybe there's a maintenance record somewhere of when they replaced the windows," Conely says. "We could find out whether they replaced one on this particular helicopter in November of 1970."

"Maybe," Haugen says. "We can always ask."

Making a request for information, or RFI, is a simple procedure for a CILHI anthropologist or joint task force investigator working in an office in Hawaii; he or she needs only to fire an e-mail to the appropriate agency — the National Archives in Washington, or Bell Helicopter in Texas, or the Armed Forces Record Center in St. Louis — and wait for a reply. Putting out an RFI from Ban Alang isn't quite so easy: It requires typing the request onto a computer disc at the camp's communications shack, from which it's transmitted as a stream of digital signals to the joint task force's Detachment Three headquarters in Vientiane.

Assuming it's not garbled beyond understanding, a worker at the detachment — housed in a suite of large offices in the gated and heavily guarded U.S. embassy — retypes the RFI into regular e-mail or includes it in the message traffic regularly dispatched from the embassy with the aid of overhead satellites. Most often it's routed to the joint task force's main headquarters in a windowless concrete building at Camp H. M. Smith, a marine post on a hillside overlooking Pearl Harbor. There, the analyst overseeing the case in question forwards the RFI to the appropriate agency and gets an answer back to the team in the field in the same manner.

All of which can take some time. Haugen puts in a request when we land, and our wait begins.

4

WILLIAM EDWARD DILLENDER showed up in the Kingsmen compound seven weeks after Dugan and three weeks after Jack Barker came aboard as XO. He had just turned nineteen, but was already a veteran of the war: The six-foot-two, straight-backed soldier had been a radio-telephone operator in an airborne unit before he was given a chance to switch to helicopters. He came to Bravo Company figuring he was in for some excitement.

He was born on October 6, 1951, to William Thomas Dillender and Mattie Ann Quarles, both Southern people; his birth in Waltham, Massachusetts, was a geographical accident, the product of his father's nomadic career as a firefighter and crash-rescue crewman for the air force, and his first years were spent on the move. When he was still an infant, his father was reassigned to a base in England, and four years later to Davis-Monthan Air Force Base outside of Tucson, and a year after that to Tampa. Billy started school while the family lived for a year in Wiesbaden, Germany. From there, they moved back to Florida and Eglin Air Force Base.

It was an exciting, if not entirely happy, childhood. Bill the elder could be a kind, sentimental man, but he was also in the thrall of what's now labeled post-traumatic stress disorder. One night in Herzogenaurach, Germany, at the close of World War II, he'd been alarmed by the sound of footsteps tailing him as he walked in a thick fog. Mindful that other GIs had been targeted by bandits in the past, sure he was about to be robbed, Dillender unloaded his service revolver into the mist. His trackers turned out to be five unarmed teenagers, mere boys. He killed them all.

The episode preyed on him. Years later, a tormented Bill Dillender would bark at Billy and his two brothers to stand up straight, to pull their shoulders back, to keep their mouths shut at the dinner table. If they transgressed in some minor way, he'd have them stand at attention with their noses in a corner; if they slouched the slightest bit, they'd get more time. He wasn't bashful about using his hands.

Which is not to say that Billy didn't need the discipline. From the start he was an impulsive, mischievous kid; when he was little more than a toddler, his mother told him his father would be home late, and Billy loosened all the carpet stays on the staircase so that he'd know when his dad had arrived. It worked. Bill Dillender fell down the stairs.

Billy didn't calm down when, in 1960, his father retired from the service and the Dillenders settled in Cookeville, Tennessee, Ann's home place. Every time Bill drove through the town center, it seemed, the deputies would flag him down: Billy had borrowed a neighbor's pet dog and sold it at a local flea market, they told him, or stolen a farmer's pumpkins, or, in one memorable episode, ridden around Cookeville with some Tennessee Tech fraternity brothers, his ketchup-soaked arm dangling from the trunk of their car.

It was Billy who, playing with his friends, invariably swam the roughest water, jumped from the highest cliffs, braved the greatest dangers. He stayed wild through a year living with his brother Jim, in Detroit, hopping a rolling boxcar to steal rotgut whisky, staying out all night with girlfriends.

By October 1968 his parents were working at a church-owned hotel in Naples, Florida, and for months, while seeking a bigger place, Bill and Ann and Billy and his younger brother, Dan, lived in one of its rooms. Billy entered Naples Senior High School.

With his father's encouragement, he enrolled in the army's Junior ROTC program there, and after class worked at a gas station and later at a lawn equipment place. But by the fall of 1969 he was sick of school and eager for change, and he'd discovered in JROTC that he enjoyed drilling and inspections and the chain of command. Ever impulsive, he and a buddy decided to enlist in the army.

His father backed the idea. The service was a little less enthusiastic. A recruiter wrote to the high school, asking whether he might be convinced to graduate before enlisting, to which one of his JROTC instructors replied that Dillender had been "a very cooperative and enthusiastic cadet," that he'd be "an asset to the Army," and that "in view of the particular circumstances of this student, I feel that it would be of benefit to him to enter the service now if possible."

Dillender reported to Fort Jackson in November 1969. He qualified as an expert — the army's highest rating of marksmanship — with the M-16, the .45-caliber pistol, and the 106mm recoilless rifle. He made private the following March, and at Bill's urging, sought Airborne training. Bill and Ann drove to Fort Benning to witness his first paratroop jump.

A few weeks later he got orders to Vietnam.

A swampy heat envelopes the screening station. We push dirt throughout the morning, sweating, quiet. Little is turning up on the screens; the units that in past days have coughed up so much ACS seem to have suddenly run dry. Finding artifacts in the clay is energizing — it suggests that the next blob of dirt, the next screen, might yield a piece of bone, might answer decades-old questions. When the screens don't produce, however, rubbing the clay through the mesh for hours is numbing.

The buckets marching uphill from the hole contain soil from the western ends of the two open units, the portions of the squares closest to where the greatest concentration of surface debris lies. We should be pulling more stuff off the screens, not less. The dirt should be thick with it.

No one says much at lunch. Reynolds eats a can of cold chunky soup, then falls asleep on the equipment platform. One 92-Mike dozes on a bench, head resting on her knapsack, her ball cap shielding her face. Others listen to portable stereos or read or feed the dog, which several team members have taken to calling "Chubby," or simply stare across the grid. I watch a kid over in the Laotian tent, no more than five years old, smoke a cigarette. Eagmin wanders over and plops heavily onto the bench beside me.

Our EOD was born in Chicago, spent a few childhood years in Minnesota, settled with his parents and younger brother in Tucson, Arizona. He passed a pretty typical boyhood there, playing baseball (second base) and football (offensive guard), getting good grades, minding his elders.

All that changed halfway through high school. It's a bit difficult to

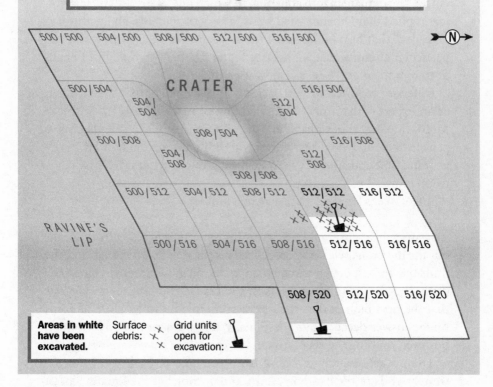

The Grid as of August 19, 2001, Noon

500/500 504/500 508/500 512/500 516/500

500/504 516/504

CRATER

504/504 512/504

508/504

500/508 516/508

504/508 512/508

508/508

500/512 504/512 508/512 512/512 516/512

RAVINE'S
LIP

500/516 504/516 508/516 512/516 516/516

508/520 512/520 516/520

Areas in white have been excavated. Surface debris: Grid units open for excavation:

picture now, as quiet and studious as he's become, but in his mid-teens Eagmin morphed into a wild child, motivated to excel at partying and not much else. His grades tanked. His relationship with his father went to hell. Even as he was doing it, he knew he was screwing up, and knew that he had to do something to correct the course he'd set. He also knew it wouldn't happen while he was living at home. He was almost sold on the army when he spoke with a marine recruiter, and the more he heard, the more he liked. The recruiter promised Eagmin would get heaping helpings of jarhead discipline. He promised Eagmin hardship. He guaranteed pain. Eagmin lapped it up. Three days after he graduated from high school — barely — he reported for boot camp.

He spent four years as an administration specialist in Okinawa and Quantico before he grew so sick of being stuck indoors, minding paperwork, that he applied for a transfer. Explosive ordnance demolition was a lateral move, but to Eagmin it represented a giant leap in job satisfaction. This was front-line work: Wherever marines went ashore — and they were often the first American troops to go ashore — EOD guys were among them.

He pulled a shift in the Persian Gulf, and in 1992 deployed to Somalia for six months. Mogadishu was lousy with ordnance; Eagmin and his colleagues destroyed captured arms caches and cleaned up after raids on ammo dumps. On one memorable job, they blew up 100,000 pounds of explosives and ammo. It made one hell of a bang.

After a few years at Camp Pendleton he was shipped back to Japan. He spent a year at Camp Fuji, on the side of its namesake mountain, where he met and married a young Japanese woman. Back at Pendleton, the couple had two sons, who are now three and five. They stayed in California until a year ago, when Eagmin was shipped a third time to Japan.

Which is where he was when word came around that the joint task force was looking for explosives experts. He first heard about the missions years ago: Marines in the Pacific are offered a small number of augmentee slots each year, as are the other services — the marines and air force usually draw EOD assignments, and the navy life-support tech and medic posts. Eagmin had become a student of the Vietnam War, fascinated by it, devoured everything about it that he could get his hands on. He saw recovery operations as a necessary denouement, the fulfillment of a compact between those who take up arms in the American cause and their leaders: You may be hurt in the nation's service, may even be killed, but you won't be left behind. You will come home. Until now, he was never in the right place, professionally or geographically, to land a mission. "It really is a grand-slam assignment," he says, "a career highlight, to bring home heroes."

Most augmentees feel the same way. All are volunteers who competed for this assignment. Conely caught wind about the missions while at sea aboard the carrier *John C. Stennis*, and thought: "We're still looking for people?" She was fascinated by what she heard of recovery missions, but at the time her ship was too shorthanded to spare her. Five months ago word again came down that the joint task force needed life-support techs. She brought the subject up with her husband. He'd served on a carrier during the war, had watched strikes launched on targets in Vietnam and Laos, but just the same, he was surprised by his wife's enthusiasm. "You don't really want to do that, do you?" he asked her.

Yes, she replied, she did. He told her in that case she should go. She went back to work and put in her name.

For Krueger, the assignment was a rare opportunity to put his skills to use. The government keeps its linguists busy — there's much to read and translate, radio and television broadcasts to summarize for the brass, the occasional foreign national to interview. Still, one doesn't get many opportunities to converse in Lao at Fort Meade, Maryland. A trip with the joint task force is a terrific plum. Assuming, of course, that the locals actually speak the language you've been taught.

I tell Eagmin I can't imagine having his job. "The other day, with that mine," I say. "That had to be scary as hell."

He shakes his head. "Nah. As soon as I walked up I knew exactly what it was that I was looking at." There's no boast to the statement; it's delivered as simple fact. "I knew what the risks were, and I knew how to take care of it. I was real confident that I wasn't in danger, in that particular case.

"What gets you killed is complacency. And, of course, Murphy's Law." He smiles grimly. "Things go wrong. I've had some friends killed that way."

"How do you defend yourself against Murphy's Law?" I ask.

He chuckles softly. "You don't."

Faith Hill, on the boom box, is drowned out by a hard rain on the tarp overhead, but it ends after a minute, and the sun reemerges. "Let's go, y'all," Posey says gently.

"Time to make the doughnuts," Eagmin sighs.

We trudge back to work, a sorry-looking bunch: The rain has turned the ground to a slippery ooze, and yellow-brown mud has caked on our boots, up our legs, and — thanks to the splashing water on the screens — across our bellies. In the early afternoon we close the two units and open two new ones — 512/512, the square under the surface wreckage, and 516/512, just to the north. The temperature soars, topping 100 degrees. My brain bakes inside my sodden hat.

I work a screen with Sammy, picking through dirt from 516/512. We find a few M-60 rounds, a metal snap, more burned Plexiglas, gnarled aluminum. Haugen pulls two large pieces of curving Plexiglas from her screen, which Conely identifies as helmet visor. The team's mood brightens. Conversations resume.

When we quit, Conely and Eagmin, examining the day's accumulated wreckage, identify a blasting cap, unexploded but crimped flat and empty; several more pieces of what Conely believes to be visor; a green plastic button from an army-issue shirt; several components of a boom microphone, once attached to a flight helmet; a broken corner of a claymore cover, probably the one we found earlier; and a pile of snaps, washers, rivets, and transistors.

Posey solicits comments as we wait for our chopper rides back to camp. "We found some more life-support items," Haugen offers, "some pieces of helmet. We opened two new units and closed two. I think things will move a little more quickly now that we're in a groove on the screens."

"Doc?"

"Keep drinking water," Artillaga says. "Stay hydrated."

"Krueger?"

The linguist shakes his head. Posey insists. "Say something, Krueger."

"Come on, Krueger," Captain Reynolds says. "I *order* you to say something."

"I have nothing to say," Krueger mumbles.

Most Kingsmen pilots, like those of helicopter companies throughout the army, were warrant officers, men who were appointed, rather than commissioned, and had entered the flying community from the enlisted ranks or civilian life. When they weren't in their machines they were often at the Castle, an A-frame social club a short walk from the flight line at Camp Eagle. They tended to measure each other by their capacities in both venues.

Only a handful of the company's men were "real live officers," or RLOs, and they were viewed as a breed apart by the Kingsmen warrants. RLOs, in their eyes, were far more likely to be careerists. RLOs were far more likely to worry over army regulations and military decorum and the chain of command. Most especially, RLOs were far less likely to be good pilots, because their management duties cut into their flying time.

The upshot: Any RLO faced a challenge in gaining the respect of the pilots in his command, and Jack Barker faced a bigger one than most. He was a newbie, and he was a stickler for army procedure, and not only did he waste few words but when he did say something, it was softly, in more a poet's voice than a commander's. And within weeks of his arrival, he replaced Maj. Retsae Miller, beloved by many warrants and enlisted crewmen, as Bravo Company's CO.

The new boss rubbed some Kingsmen the wrong way from the start.

They thought him far too intense, far too committed to satisfying the brass, far too spit-shined and buttoned-down for the muddy heat of Vietnam. They resented his lack of experience in helicopters. They disliked being upbraided for failing to salute, or for not wearing their hats. His five-foot-five-inch height spawned inevitable allusions to Napoleon.

Barker knew himself that he had a tough act to follow. "Rex Miller, the company commander of B Company, had to go to the States on emergency leave," he wrote Dee. "The battalion C.O. informed me of the decision to make me C.O. about 9 P.M. the same day Rex left. Needless to say, I was surprised and worried. Rex was an outstanding officer. The men in the unit just worshipped him."

The challenges of keeping the Kingsmen on a by-the-book course soon seemed overwhelming. "For example," he wrote Dee in late November, "about 10 or 12 of my troops use pot, three or four use harder drugs, yesterday I sent a (staff sergeant) packing with instructions never to return to this area, this A.M. I gave three Article 15s [the army's term for nonjudicial punishment] and advised one man unless he straightened up he would go to jail. These were my first Art 15s since I have been here. I don't have a supply sgt., I don't have a motor sgt., my maintenance detachment is about 50 percent strength, enlisted men of which I am short are getting [early transfers home], I am not getting replacements, but my mission remains the same. And honey, every day it's this way, over and over. Every day my 30kw generator breaks down and we repair it, etc., etc."

By New Year's the company's problems prompted him to write that he was "ready to give up my future Army career. . . . We are now so short of personnel that it is difficult to accomplish anything. And then there is always the drug problems, the racial problems, the mission accomplishment and the normal day to day problems we have here such as food and water. What a life! In four days I will have been the B Co. company commander for two months. Seems like forever."

Through these trials, some of his warrants came to appreciate him. One, Thomas J. Hill, found him "very fair, very likeable." Pilot Gene A. Haag thought him more mature than most of the officers, a guy who "knew his business," who told the truth and didn't pussyfoot around. A guy worth following.

*   *   *

The day after it opens, 516/512 closes, and the members of RE-1 are happy to see it go: The square of earth at the grid's northern edge, one unit away from the center of the debris field, has produced little of interest. Haugen, wearing a blue-gray ball cap that reads "RELAX," studies her drawings of the grid, and decides to next open 508/520, the last of the three units forming the doglegged eastern boundary. She had initially planned to leave it until later but now wants to double-check her hypothesis that most of the helicopter's wreckage lies to the west, in the ground between the ravine's lip and the crater. If the team unearths a great amount of debris from the new unit, the bulk of the wreckage may not lie that way at all, but under the ravine's steep bank.

Conely dumps the last of the closing unit's gains on a screen in the break tent. She finds some shredded material she believes may be seat upholstery — it is woven, with a shiny vinyl finish — along with a few pieces of bomb frag and the shattered remains of a porcelain rice bowl of unknown vintage.

Late in the morning, a piece of black plastic, its surface etched in crosshatches, turns up on a 512/512 screen. It is obviously a handle of some sort; Conely theorizes that it may be part of the Huey's cyclic, the stick with which the helicopter's pilot controlled the pitch of its rotor, and thus the craft's direction. At lunch I walk over to the LZ and examine the cyclic on the Squirrel. It looks a lot like the artifact.

But despite a painstaking excavation that has left two-thirds of the unit a smooth-floored, square-edged hole ten inches deep, 512/512 otherwise produces nothing but inconsequential ACS. The unit that seemed the center point of the helicopter's fall to earth is pretty much empty.

Nobody is more surprised than Haugen. "I thought that unit would yield," she mutters as we work the screens. "I thought for sure we'd find something good there."

Midway through the afternoon, the water spraying from the screening station's rubber hoses suddenly turns milky, then dark brown, then sputters to a stop. We can hear the pump whining, halfway down the ravine; the trouble, it seems, does not lie with the machine. Dingman leaves the screens and runs downhill, and as he tries to sort out the problem, Haugen's Laotian partner steps away from the screen they share and strolls off.

"Now where's he going?" Haugen says. Before the words are out of her mouth, there's an exodus of labor from the A-frame: A fellow in a leopard-print shirt that the team has nicknamed "Travolta" walks away, along with Sammy and "Ringo," who sports an early Beatles haircut, and a handful of others.

Were I among the French who lorded over Southeast Asia for the first half of the twentieth century, I might explain it away with a casual "*Su-su*," a label that bundles lazy, apathetic, listless, disengaged, simple, backward — and which, in colonial days, became an almost self-fulfilling put-down for Laos's natives.

In truth, there's nothing lazy about the locals, and certainly nothing thick. Simple survival in the Laotian backcountry requires brains and energy. How many Frenchmen can build a house from nothing but a thicket of bamboo and a *bria*? How many would survive more than a few days in the Annamite Range, left to their own wits?

Stay alive till adulthood here and you're worthy of respect. That said, the people of the high country along the Vietnamese border do have operating styles that at times conflict with those of their Western partners on recovery missions, and it's such a conflict that we're witnessing now. The locals know we can't push dirt without water, can see that we don't have that, and evidently have decided that there's little point to waiting at their posts for its return when they could do so in far greater comfort elsewhere.

"Hey!" Haugen yells. "Hey, come back here!" The deserters glance over their shoulders, but keep moving toward the Laotian tent. The rest of us look on helplessly. What do you say to quell a mutiny when the only Lao words you know are the integers from one to ten? "This is out of control," Haugen mutters. She spots Polo, the district representative, across the site. "There's an official," she hollers. "Tell him to tell them to stop!"

Krueger yells to Polo in Lao, and he walks without great urgency to the officials' tent, where Captain Somphong has been napping, shirtless, since lunch. The captain stumbles out of the tent and orders the workers back to the screens, just as Dingman succeeds in restarting the flow of water. The workers climb back onto the A-frame, seemingly untroubled by Haugen's glare. "We're not done," she tells them. "Work is not over!"

It might as well be. The water runs dry again a short time later, and when Dingman gets it going it pours muddy from the hoses. And the new unit isn't producing much more than the old: When Haugen asks Posey whether he is pulling much off his screen, he grimaces. "Couple pieces of glass."

Haugen strides, frustrated, to the break tent. Time on any dig is always short. Every day is precious, and this one feels wasted. Early on a mission, pulling up pieces of the past is thrilling, the science of it fascinating, but as days pass with no sign of bone and only a smattering of life support, the operation's human stakes loom. Four men are lost. It's up to her to find them. It's not happening.

Bringing peace to the relatives of the missing is part of what drives the lab's anthropologists into the jungle several times a year, but over time, the people who come to matter most are the missing guys themselves. They want to be found. Crazy as it sounds, that's how a mission comes to feel — like the missing men are watching, waiting, hoping. If Haugen goes home empty-handed, it's the undiscovered dead, not the disappointed or bitter living, who haunt her.

The afternoon meeting feels like a pep rally for a losing high school football squad. "We're not recovering a whole lot, like we were earlier," Haugen tells the team. "We're advancing toward the crater, though, and we'll hope it's the area of greatest possibility. We'll just keep plugging along. We've only been here a week. I know it feels longer than that, but let's stay with it."

Conely sounds the same theme. "Just keep thinking positive," she says, leaning on a screen scattered with the day's meager discoveries. "I know it's difficult. Negative thoughts creep in, but I try to keep trucking, and I encourage you all to do the same. We can still find these guys."

"Amen," Posey says. "Gotta take 'em home."

5

JOHN DUGAN HAD HOPED to land in Pete Federovich's unit. He came close: His friend was assigned to the battalion's Alpha Company, the Commancheros, quartered a short distance away. Of the 101st's four companies, the Kingsmen were the rowdiest. Dugan seemed to feel more comfortable with Alpha. He visited often.

Like Barker, Dugan was an RLO, and like Barker, he had responsibility thrust upon him quickly: He was named commander of the company's second platoon soon after his arrival. But unlike the major, Dugan was an easygoing boss who got action from his warrants via requests, not orders — "I need somebody to do this," he'd tell a pilot. "Could you do it?" — and made it a point to stay friendly with his enlisted crewmen, as well. One afternoon, crew chief Joe Kline was flying with Dugan when all aboard noticed a vibration in the rotor. After most missions, the pilot and copilot would walk off, leaving the chief and door gunner to service the bird for the next day's flight. On this day, Kline knew he had a long night ahead of him. He went to the Kingsmen's hangar, got a replacement part for the rotor assembly, and started the repair. A light rain began to fall. The sun set.

Kline was on top of the Huey, tired and hungry and feeling sorry for himself, when he spied a figure with a flashlight across the flight line, coming toward him. As it drew closer, he made out that it was John Dugan, toting a couple of cans of Coke. The captain climbed onto the Huey, handed Kline one of the sodas, and trained his flashlight on the rotor assembly while the chief fixed his bird. He sat there in the dark, in the rain, until the job was done.

Typical Dugan. Everyone in the company, from the lowliest private to the most experienced warrants, liked the guy. On the ground, anyway: In the air, the Kingsmen weren't so keen on him. A Huey had two men at the controls. The more senior, the aircraft commander, rode in the cockpit's left-hand seat; an incoming aviator flew on the right as a "peter pilot" — a copilot, or apprentice — until he got the hang of things. He'd take turns riding with each of his platoon's aircraft commanders into situations he could expect to encounter in the air, and would witness how the senior man dealt with them, so that over time he'd be able to deal with them himself. Apprenticeship was stressful, beyond simply controlling a craft that required the simultaneous use of all four limbs. A pilot's headset was filled with chatter: He listened to four radios, his door gunner and crew chief were talking to him on the intercom, the other pilot was talking, and he'd be trying to talk back to the people in his bird and in others, trying to juggle eight conversations at once, and over all this was layered the din of the guns. The aircraft commanders paid particular attention to how their newbies behaved under fire. Concentration had a habit of flying out the hatch when the M-60s opened up.

Over a few weeks' time, the aircraft commanders developed a pretty good sense of a new guy's abilities, and would meet to discuss whether he was ready to join their ranks. It was a decision reached by their consensus; the regular chain of command usually had little say in the matter. After the usual three-month apprenticeship with the Kingsmen, Dugan didn't get the nod. Nor after four months. Nor after five. Some of his peers viewed him as sloppy, others as hesitant. One pilot with whom he flew often, Gerry Morgan, sensed that Dugan simply wasn't built for the job.

Barker, too, failed to win status as an aircraft commander; as the company's CO, he didn't spend enough time in the air to hone his skills. "I have only flown 3:50 this month," he complained to Dee in a January 1971 letter. "I need ten more minutes just to qualify for flight pay."

Word comes back from Hawaii: The numbers on the Plexiglas are untraceable. They cannot be correlated to Jack Barker's Huey. Haugen delivers the news to Reynolds and me shortly after we return to camp from another unrewarding day at the site; while we dug, finding little, an e-mail arrived for her at Ban Alang's commo shack.

She's not surprised, she tells us — it was a long shot that a changed-out window would prove the key to identifying the wreck. Still, it is disappointing, for a necessary first step to finding Barker and his crew is establishing once and for all that we're digging in the right place. Even if it doesn't produce remains, RE-1's excavation will be a partial success if it accomplishes that. In fact, the dig can be logged in the "Win" column even if the team finds a data plate that proves it is *not* the target bird, because so much of this work is a simple process of elimination: If RE-1 finds a serial number that proves we're in the wrong place, as Pete Miller did in 1989, the joint task force can at least cross the site off its list of open excavations and concentrate its efforts elsewhere.

What Haugen has to hope doesn't happen is that her team spends an entire month digging the site, and turns up not only no remains but no hard-and-fast evidence of the helicopter's identity. She's not suffered that experience often, but it's happened. On her first mission to Laos, and her third overall, she pursued the case of a navy OP-2E Neptune shot down in February 1968, an hour's helicopter flight north of Ban Alang. The Neptune belonged to a secret navy squadron of sub-hunting planes modified to drop sensors on the Ho Chi Minh Trail, a duty that made the big, slow, low-flying craft a fat target for ground fire. Sure enough, an antiaircraft shell had exploded against this plane's chin, killing a crewman; its pilot, Commander Paul Milius, had stayed at the controls so that the seven others aboard could bail out, and was himself last seen jumping from the burning Neptune's hatch. CILHI teams found the dead crewman's remains in an isolated grave in late 1996, at about the time the navy was commemorating the pilot's courage by putting his name on a new guided-missile destroyer. Before Haugen's arrival, however, no sign of Milius had been found in three CILHI missions.

The crash site was on a remote sixty-degree slope thick with jungle — so steep and overgrown that local workers had nowhere to camp and had to hike two hours to work each morning. Trees had grown around and through some of the wreckage. Even so, most of it had been carted off by scavengers. By the time she closed the site, CILHI had excavated 2,291 square meters of soil — an area nearly equal in size to half a football field — and there was no dirt left on the hillside to move. Haugen, like her predecessors, found no remains, nor anything that positively identified the wreckage; she could say with certainty that she'd dug up the right model of plane, of which only three were lost in the war, but could not establish with certainty that it was Milius's Neptune.

RE-1 has established that the wreckage here is that of a Huey, but a lot of Hueys went down along the escarpment. Haugen needs a data plate. She needs that proof.

We split up. En route to my tent, I run into my press escort. "So when can we walk to the site?" I ask him. "Have you asked your bosses?"

Bounmy looks at his feet, then toward the LZ, then toward the mess tent, obviously looking for an escape from conversation. "I have asked," he finally says. "I do not think anyone will go with you."

"I can go alone?"

"No," he says. "You must have someone with you. But I do not think anyone will go. It is too far." He smiles weakly. I've estimated the walk at about sixteen kilometers — ten miles, maybe a little less. Not a particularly taxing distance. "Too far?" I say. "It's a three-hour walk, and on roads the whole way. How is that too far?"

"Lao officials, they do not want to walk that far," he says.

"How about you?"

"No," he says, chuckling. "No, I cannot walk that far."

"Of course you can."

"No," he says again. "But I will keep asking."

I have the shower to myself. Its water is gravity-fed from a tank across Main Street and pours into a fifty-five-gallon drum that's positioned over a propane burner cobbled from an old stove. On most days, the system produces only a tepid spray, but this evening the water's hot. Refreshed, I head for the mess tent to cook up some macaroni and cheese. Eagmin is cooking noodles the next stove over. Captain Reynolds, looking spent, is sitting at the long table, silently reading a month-old edition of *Stars and Stripes*. No one feels much like talking. The TV is tuned to an old Tom Hanks movie, *Joe Versus the Volcano*. We watch it as we eat.

Sergeant Posey walks in while Hanks floats shipwrecked on a raft. "Is this *Cast Away*?" he asks as he waits for a stove. No, somebody replies, it's *Joe Versus the Volcano*.

As Posey boils water, Haugen enters the tent with a dish of leftovers. She glances at the TV while she opens the microwave. "This *Cast Away*?" No, several people answer, it's *Joe Versus the Volcano*. She nods, starts the microwave, and the electrical circuit feeding the tent blows. The TV goes black. A groan goes up in the dark. Somebody runs outside to flip the breaker, and a minute later we have lights; the TV picture returns, without sound.

Posey takes a seat beside me, defiantly upbeat. "I'm just waiting for that moment," he says. "It's going to happen, too. Dr. Gwen is optimistic right now, and I am, too. It's going to happen." The sound returns to the TV. Haugen resumes cooking her dinner. Within a minute, the circuit blows again, to the accompaniment of loud swearing.

Later, as thunder rumbles over Ban Alang, I nod off while sitting at my field desk, reading by candlelight. I wake with a start when rain begins to strike the roof of my tent, decide I don't feel much like socializing at Mama's, and crawl into my cot, pulling my mosquito netting closed around me. Perhaps Posey is right, I think. Tomorrow we might find something big.

Through the late fall of 1970 and into the next year, the Kingsmen flew combat missions — picking up platoons of ground-pounders in the bush, dropping them elsewhere in hopes of flushing out the North Vietnamese — mixed with "ash and trash," or logistical support runs. On the latter they'd deliver hot meals to troops in the field or sling-load water buffalo or transport three-hundred-pound pigs that stunk up the cargo holds. "Yesterday I flew a VIP mission," Barker wrote Dee on January 22. "I flew a bird colonel up to a radio site just south of the DMZ. For the first time I got a chance to see North Vietnam. Funny thing — it looks just like South Vietnam."

The little piece of South Vietnam within the Kingsmen compound didn't look like much. The company's birds were parked in revetments dug into a tiered hillside. A minute's walk away, the warrants slept two to a small, tin-roofed hooch walled and floored in plywood. Heavy netting hung overhead, a translucent ceiling between roof and living quarters. Besides that, the only furnishings were metal cots and wall lockers. Barker, Dugan, and the other officers lived in a second set of hooches linked by a network of lumber sidewalks, necessities during the monsoon season, when Camp Eagle's dust turned to paste. Sandbags were stacked around the hooches to guard against shrapnel, and the men were never more than a few yards from a slit trench, in which they could dive for cover if the compound came under rocket or mortar attack. Barker spent most of his waking hours hunched over a desk in a shack that housed his office and the company's flight operations center, an American flag on a pole behind him.

The company's workdays started before dawn with "crank and commo," checks of the birds' engines and radios, and ended late, often long after dark. In what little time they had away from their machines, the Kingsmen took meals at the battalion mess hall, washed their clothes in metal tubs using the "Camp Eagle Stomp," wrote letters, drank. Dillender was too young to get served at the Castle; he and the company's other youngsters relied on older colleagues to sneak them beer.

The uncomfortable routine came to a halt on January 29, 1971. Dillender, by now a crew chief with two months of flying behind him, had returned from a short day in the air when he and the company's other crews were told to stay with their aircraft. Darkness fell, and rain with it, and then an order came down: The Kingsmen were to move to Camp Evans, up near the DMZ.

They flew low out of Camp Eagle and over Route 1, Vietnam's main north-south highway, which was packed with vehicles moving north in the dark. Something was up, and the crews traded theories about what it might be. The most popular was that at long last, America was going to invade North Vietnam.

In truth, Laos waited. "We got up at 0315 this morning and started to prepare for a big troop movement," Barker wrote to Dee the next day. "Right after daylight we insert [sic] troops out as far west as Khe Sanh. By now I am sure you have heard about it and seen it on TV."

In a letter he wrote the following day, the major assured his wife that the company had returned to Camp Eagle and was not part of what promised to unfold across the border. "As I told you in an earlier letter my unit is no longer involved with the big move by Khe Sanh," he reiterated on February 21. "I only mention this again because you indicate how worried you have been." He repeated the claim on March 1 and again on March 5: "As for the war in Laos, I know most of the wheeler-dealers that are directing the aviation aspects," he wrote in slanted, looping cursive. "From my point of view, the effort is correct, but we sure do waste a lot of lifes, helicopters and other equipment in the process. But don't get upset. My unit is still flying ash and trash missions in the rear area. We are flying people and supplies for the 1st Brigade and resupplies up to Khe Sanh. Forward of Khe Sanh is where all the action is. I'll tell you if we get involved in that area."

He was lying. Two days before, on March 3, Barker had been part of a troop insertion at Fire Support Base Lolo, a high point on the escarpment two miles from Ban Alang and on that day the worst place to be in Southeast Asia, if not on the planet. He was awarded the Distinguished Flying Cross for his performance; the citation reads that "as pilot of an UH-1H helicopter involved in the emergency relief of a South Vietnamese unit in prolonged heavy contact and in imminent danger of being overrun" at Lolo, he "came under sporadic automatic weapon fire" and with "superior skill and determination" was able to "avoid the enemy fire and previously downed aircraft in the LZ to effect insertion of the troops on board his aircraft."

The Kingsmen may have returned to Camp Eagle after that first trip into Khe Sanh, as Barker told Dee. But they went back, and they flew into Laos, too.

On the screens, Dingman announces that he's sick of drinking water. "An ice-cold Beerlao sure would be nice with lunch," he says, then studies the muddy water flowing down the A-frame's trough. "That looks like butterscotch."

"Mmmm," replies Conely, who's working next to him. "Butterscotch."

"Imagine yourself back in the States right now," Dingman drawls, his words slow and stretched and twangy as a wire fence. He wipes sweat from his creased face. He wanted to be here from the moment he heard of the lab, two years into his army career, when he was assigned to an infantry division at Hawaii's Schofield Barracks; two guys transferring from his unit told him about their new assignments with this outfit that traveled the world in a quest for remains.

It wasn't just the adventure that appealed. In his teens, Dingman had been sure he'd be drafted and read everything he could about Southeast Asia and the war's botched management and, when the fighting ended without him, about the 591 prisoners released by the North Vietnamese, far fewer than anyone expected. Washington, he decided, had been so eager to quit the place that it wrote off hundreds of its unaccounted-for sons.

Here, finally, was the government doing right by its soldiers and their families — decades late, perhaps, but making the effort to stick to the contract, just the same. He envied the guys leaving for the lab but had no expectation he'd ever be able to pursue the mission himself.

"Imagine," he says, "you're at one of those drugstores that serves milkshakes, and having an ice-cold butterscotch milkshake." In Oklahoma, apparently, such places still exist. "Or an ice-cream soda," he adds. He closes his eyes and whimpers.

It took him years to get here from the infantry. Toward the end of his first hitch, Dingman figured that maybe he ought to acquire a specialty that would play well in the civilian job market, in case he decided to leave the service. The job that caught his attention sounded "almost like some sort of show business job," he recalls: He became an army videographer and shipped off to the National Training Center at Fort Irwin, California. He spent more than three years there, chasing soldiers and tanks around the battlefield, shooting thousands of hours of tape with the hope that a minute or two might capture an image that drove home a war-fighting fundamental.

A guy who ran his team's supply shop transferred to CILHI, and Dingman was again intrigued. He figured the soldier won the post because of his supply expertise, but never asked. In truth, the man was a 25-Victor, an army photographer. Just as civilian police departments photograph crime scenes, so too the lab photographs its dig sites before, during, and after its excavations. Every recovery team has a 25-Victor on its roster, who labors most days in the hole or on the screens alongside the 92-Mikes, but who has his cameras close at hand. Whenever a key piece of evidence is unearthed, the photographer preserves the moment, and the discovery's context, on film.

Oblivious, Dingman transferred to Fort Riley, Kansas, so he could live near his mother. She died while he was there, and a year later he was sent to South Korea, where he shot video for a training unit and again crossed paths with the lab: His boss, a master sergeant, had just finished a stint at CILHI.

He was stunned to learn she'd shot pictures. Dingman was up for reenlistment again when he left Korea, at the same time the lab had an opening for a staff sergeant. The army promised that if he re-upped, they'd give him the job. It was too good a deal.

Haugen closes 512/512, the team having unearthed no further artifacts there. As she's standing in the hole, contemplating where to dig next, she notices that the soil exposed in the unit's west wall, closest to the big crater, is oddly layered: Along its top is disturbed earth, from which the team has pulled what little ACS the unit offered; below it is a stratum of mottled orange clay — sterile ground. And below that is something that has not been present in the other units: a second layer of disturbed soil.

She recognizes this lower disturbance as a byproduct of the blast that created the bomb crater. In addition to blowing a hole in the ground, a large bomb sends shockwaves horizontally, often producing fingers of roiled earth radiating outward from the explosion's center. Haugen crouches at the wall and picks at the bomb-disturbed layer of ground with her trowel. The dirt appears clean, free of debris. She interprets this to mean that the crater probably existed before the crash. If true, this is good news. The U.S. Army routinely ordered its downed choppers bombed to prevent the North Vietnamese from salvaging anything useful from the wrecks. While the joint task force has supplied her with no evidence that Barker's chopper was so destroyed, the crater's proximity to the surface debris certainly has suggested the possibility. She reckons, however, that had the chopper been sitting here when the bomb dropped, the blast would have carried some of its pieces through the lower level of jumbled soil. A helicopter falling next to an already-existing crater would produce just the stratography she's discovered.

She opts to open the next unit to the west, 512/508, the southwest corner of which dips into the crater. Several locals and I start digging in the unit's east end. Bees and flies orbit us. Yellow wasps, drawn by our sweat-soaked clothes, hover close by. The soil has absorbed so much sun that it's hot to the touch, even through my gloves. What slows our progress most, however, is a man-made irritation: The locals at the screening station are hoarding buckets, waiting until they have a pile of empties before sending them back down the line to the hole. While this might make efficient sense to those in the line, our digging consequently proceeds in fits and starts; we get twenty empty buckets all at once, quickly fill them, then stand around for ten minutes, waiting for a new supply.

"We need more buckets!" I yell up the line, during one imposed break.

My Laotian helpers second me. "Buck-cats!" one yells. "Need buck-cats!"

It does no good. The men and women in the bucket line just stare at us. I eventually mention the problem to Captain Reynolds, who's working in the other unit. He calls over Krueger, who walks to the men at the head of the bucket line. He is gentle with them, even-toned; the Laotians regard displays of anger or frustration as shameful. Whatever he says does the trick: The buckets start coming in a steady flow, and by lunch we've excavated a neat square in the unit's southeast corner.

We file into the break tent, flop out on its benches and footlockers. It's too hot to eat much; instead, I drink a half-gallon of water into which I dump a Southeast Asian electrolyte powder. Its package advertises that it's "for those who loss of energy such as hard workers, sportman, athletes, heavy sweating people as well as dehydration and in hot climate."

"So," Conely says, as Dingman walks in from the latrine, "how was that Beerlao?"

"Good," he sighs. "Real good." He says it with such conviction that someone new to the conversation might think he'd really stashed a beer away.

"And how about that shake?"

Dingman fishes around in the cooler for a cold bottle of water. "I'm saving that for the next break," he says.

Time drags on the screens. Brian Eagmin encounters a two-inch leech on his, but that aside, there's little excitement. Haugen, working down on the ravine's edge, and Krueger, overseeing diggers in the northeast quadrant of 512/508, pull up a smattering of ACS, but nothing that indicates we're any nearer to the bulk of the wreckage.

"Not a lot today," Conely says, during an afternoon break. She raises her eyebrows and invites us to look in the bucket containing all of the day's finds. There is so little there that we can see its plastic bottom.

"It gets boring when you're not finding anything," Captain Reynolds says.

"It won't stay this way," Sergeant Posey promises. "It'll pick up."

Haugen looks up from a paperback. "Just be glad we're not looking for an isolated burial." A crashed airplane, no matter how scavenged or consumed by jungle, at least gives a team a reference point from which to begin its search for remains. A grave, on the other hand, might be miles from a missing GI's last firefight. It might be miles from the nearest village. It might lie in ground that was occupied by foreign troops when it was dug, and about which the locals know nothing. Even when the lab is lucky enough to find someone who claims to have been part of a burial, he or she often thinks of the grave's location in terms of ground features — streams, trees, and such — that may have moved or disappeared altogether in the years since.

Haugen got lucky in searching for one buried soldier, an army air corps technical sergeant lost in an August 1944 plane crash in Albania. Wayne O. Shaffner and his nine fellow crewmen had been returning to their Italian base when a shell tore through their B-24, blasting a gunner overboard and the rudder off the tail. Four men successfully bailed out of the bomber as it limped south, into the Dolemite Mountains. The navigator and Shaffner, who served as the plane's engineer, waited longer. They jumped as it cleared a 650-foot ridge — too low an altitude to parachute and too high to survive a freefall. No Americans witnessed their fates.

So an anthropologist was sent to Goraj to excavate a gravesite that turned out to be the navigator's, and Haugen pulled into town to look for Shaffner. There she met the son of a farmer who, six years before, had told his children that he'd witnessed a bomber crashing in the village — and the son's story proved to be that rare case of reliable hearsay. He told Haugen that his father described seeing two men jump from the plane as it passed over the ridge, which now was terraced and planted with olive trees. The men had landed on their knees and fallen forward. Both had died instantly. What's more, the witness said, his father had taken him and his sister to one of the gravesites. He led Haugen to the spot.

The excavation was wrapped up in a day. Haugen's team found the remains right where the witness said it would be, and in a state consistent with his father's story: The skeleton's well-preserved leg and facial bones had sustained multiple fractures.

For every success in locating isolated remains, however, most of the lab's veterans have multiple failures. One of Haugen's came on her second trip into Laos, in October 1999. Her quarry was Eugene DeBruin, an employee of Air America, a "civilian" airline owned and operated by the CIA that flew weapons and supplies to Laos's anticommunist mountain tribes — which is how DeBruin came to be aboard an old cargo plane loaded with rice and water buffalo meat on September 5, 1963, how he came to be shot down, and how he was captured by the Pathet Lao not far from Ban Alang.

Nearly three years later, he and several other prisoners jumped their guards and escaped from a jungle prison. DeBruin was almost surely recaptured, but what became of him afterwards is unclear; some reports placed him with other American prisoners as late as 1968, while others, a lot less reliable, had him living with a Laotian wife in the Khammouan Province in 1991. No trustworthy evidence of his survival has come along in more than thirty years.

Certain that he was dead, the joint task force dispatched Haugen into the jungle in search of his remains in October 1999. One witness told her that in the early seventies, he and three companions had been scouting the woods for a place to settle when they'd encountered a weasel gnawing on human bone. He'd chased off the animal and kept a small piece of mandible in which two teeth were seated. Later, he told Haugen, a shaman had advised that keeping the artifact was bad juju, and his son had disposed of the bone by wrapping it in a ball of rice and flinging it into the forest. Haugen's team spent ten days searching dense jungle where the rice ball supposedly landed. It turned up nothing.

"*Those* are tough cases," Haugen sighs. "Digging with no hope of finding even a piece of wire. Seeing nothing but sterile soil."

Posey looks over at Reynolds. "Doc's right," he says. "This ain't nuthin, sir."

6

IN PHOTOGRAPHS TAKEN before he entered the service, John Jacobsen Chubb poses beside his cherry-red Chevy Nomad on the lawn of his parents' home, the picture of hot-rod attitude — lanky frame clad in a T-shirt, jeans, and boots, hair swept in a James Dean pompadour, good-looking and careless and not afraid of a damned thing. The car, Chubb's obvious pride, his baby, is chopped and lowered and gleaming. A few feet away stands a big red Triumph motorcycle, another product of his passion for motors and machines and of all things mechanical, the passion that took him to Vietnam.

He had just turned twenty when he joined the Kingsmen. Of the four men who make up Case 1731, he'd had the most quintessentially suburban American childhood: He lived his entire life in one house, a neat Craftsman bungalow in a working-class, ethnically diverse neighborhood three blocks from the Harbor Freeway in suburban Los Angeles. He attended Gardena Elementary School, where he was liked by his teachers. He was a Cub Scout and a junior fire marshal. He made field trips to the police academy, the San Diego Zoo, and Knott's Berry Farm. In 1959, he and his parents and his half-brother Clifford vacationed in Tijuana, where they had their picture taken while wearing giant sombreros.

He played peewee football and Little League baseball, swam at the YMCA, learned judo, ran track. By the fifth grade he'd earned such a reputation as a jock that when his class produced a newspaper, he landed a front-page sports column, "John Chubb's Sports Roundup." Girls filled his junior high yearbooks with admiring notes.

At Gardena High School he joined school plays as a stagehand and electrician. He'd always been good with his hands; at home he'd carried a screwdriver the way other toddlers carry teddy bears, and had taken apart and tricked out his bicycles before tearing down his first car, a 1948 Oldsmobile, to the bolts. The Nomad was next; Chubb gave it air shocks so he could make the car pogo at stoplights, replaced the stock front seats with a Cadillac's, and — hot stuff at the time — fitted it with a stereo.

But though blessed with mechanical genius, Chubb was dyslexic, and struggled in class. An army "Report of Medical History" he completed in March 1970 asked, "Did you have any difficulties with school studies or teachers?" Chubb answered: "Had lots of problems." Frustrated, labeled a dummy, laughed at by some of his classmates, he quit school.

He worked for a rubber and plastics firm in Long Beach, then as a steelworker in L.A., bending metal rods seven days a week, saving his money for the auto shop he one day hoped to open. First, though, Chubb thought it might be wise to land some experience with engines more complex than the Nomad's. A recruiter promised that if he served a stint as a door gunner and maintenance apprentice, the army would train him as a full-fledged helicopter mechanic. His uncle Art Jacobsen was an air force lifer, and tales of his exploits in early helicopter prototypes had long fired Chubb's imagination. He reported for basic training in June 1970.

That November he completed the Aircraft Maintenance Apprentice Course at Fort Rucker, and the Helicopter Door Gunner Course the following January. He was immunized for typhoid, tetanus, cholera, yellow fever, smallpox, polio, plague, adenovirus, and influenza. Then he was ordered to Vietnam.

A couple of weeks before he left the country, Chubb attended the baptism of his infant niece in San Luis Obispo. His relatives made a fuss over him, worried about his upcoming trip, but they knew John could take care of himself. Besides, he was lucky: In October 1968 he'd hit a water-filled pothole while driving his father's old Ford pickup, a hole so deep the truck flipped and its roof crushed flat against the doors. To look at the wreck was to assume someone died. John had walked away with hardly a scratch.

Chubb reported to Bravo Company on March 6, not quite two weeks after reaching Vietnam. He did not immediately join a Huey crew. "I made it to my company about a week ago," he wrote his parents. "I work in the hanger putting inspections on helicopters. We work 7 days a week. Its not hard work but its long hours. Today I took my first shower since I've been in the company there isn't any hot water either. What really makes me mad is we don't have any sheets to sleep on it gets itchy sleeping with just a wool blanket. Its hard to get a lot of things like cameras, radios and junk like that."

Others in the company had sharper complaints. The flights into Laos had become scary, very scary, the most intense anyone in the unit had ever experienced. Once across the border, every square foot of the ground below was hostile, and the smoke and haze were so bad they couldn't see where they were going or where they were, and no approach, no altitude, was safe from antiaircraft shells that climbed toward them like fiery basketballs, and when they flared to land they'd be rocked by fire from an enemy that seemed everywhere at once. Crews could actually see the North Vietnamese shooting at them, and dodging their fire, staying alive, often seemed more blind luck than skill. Bullets thudded into metal and whizzed through the hatches and ripped through fuel cells and up through the floor. Jet fuel ran off the deck at a gunner's feet. And the hell of it was, the crews had no choice but to fly into those hot landing zones again and again and again, and every time they got hotter.

Chubb finally made his first flight as a Kingsmen door gunner on March 17, and flew again all the next day. He was back in the hangar on the 19th, when Jack Barker made a satellite call home. Dee and the kids sang "Happy Birthday" to him; the satellite links were difficult to arrange and plagued by technical difficulties, and the Barkers weren't sure they'd talk again before he turned thirty-two, three days later. Barker was tickled, especially by the singing of his sixteen-month-old son, Michael. How could it be, he asked Dee, that his baby was growing so quickly?

Dee asked him what he was doing up. The major's calls usually came at about 9 P.M. Arizona time, when it was 11 A.M. in Vietnam; this one was during the day, when it had to be the dead of night in Southeast Asia. Why wasn't he sleeping? she asked.

"I'll tell you about it later," Barker replied. "It's nothing."

An hour after lunch one day, a Squirrel circles the site and swoops into the LZ, and a few minutes later Kevin Smith, the joint task force's commander in Laos, strides across the grid with three Vientiane bigwigs, among them Done Somvorachit, the director general of the Department of Europe and Americas in the Ministry of Foreign Affairs. Done, once Laos's ambassador to Germany, the Netherlands, and Switzerland, is wearing a polyester disco shirt that strains to contain a gut the size and shape of a volleyball on his otherwise skinny frame. I leave the screens to pay my respects; I met him five months ago on a dig in Khoummuan Province, when I made the mistake of asking him a question. His answer — a monologue on how Laos had been wronged by the United States during the war and disrespected by it since — lasted for forty-five minutes.

Done seems nonplussed by my mud-spattered trousers. "You are working," he says. "I am surprised."

"Just trying to get the hang of the team's work," I tell him. The last time I saw him, he was wearing a U.S. Border Patrol cap; today, I notice, one of his assistants is wearing it, and Done's switched to a white ball cap advertising Lexus automobiles. It's a marvelous testament to the country's ongoing conversion from socialist self-denial to Western-style capitalism.

The segue isn't an entirely comfortable one, as it requires Laos to interact with the rest of the planet, something it hasn't done well since the days of its kings, who ruled for six-hundred-plus years. For the first five hundred, they oversaw a sometimes unified, sometimes disjointed kingdom unknown to the great bulk of humanity — unpenetrated by Western explorers, overlooked by merchants calling on its more powerful neighbors, not only landlocked but sequestered by mountains north and east and cascades on the Mekong to the south. Only a couple of seventeenth-century Europeans left word of their travels here; after that, more than a hundred years passed before a third set foot in the country.

With more time, the French showed up. They brought roads and modern cities and professional bureaucracy; they also imposed a foreign language, high taxes, and a harsh penal code on an unreceptive populace. When they reasserted their claim on the kingdom after World War II, the Lao chafed at the yoke and eventually achieved independence.

They might have faded back into blissful insignificance, except that Mao had emerged in China, and Ho Chi Minh was leading a war against the French in Vietnam. Suddenly little Laos, overlooked by practically everyone for centuries, was viewed as key to stanching the spread of Communism. Civil war erupted between the U.S.-propped monarchy and the Vietnamese-backed Pathet Lao. The latter prevailed, and Laos returned again to its old ways, as a place removed from and forgotten by the greater human experience.

Now, twenty-six years later, the wheel has turned anew. One of the country's top officials is endorsing a luxury car before me. "Perhaps you and I can talk later," I say. "Will you be at base camp tonight?"

"Yes," Done says. "Come over to the Lao section. We will be having dinner there." He and his party traverse the grid, eye the hole. They speak to none of the locals, and none of the site's villagers seems much interested in speaking with them. Vientiane and its representatives don't hold much day-to-day sway with rural folk, who depend on nothing from a state that has nothing to give, and whose hearts stir little for a nation that exists largely in the abstract.

I watch Mr. Done's party stride along the screening station, the ambassador nodding perfunctorily to the men and women at the head of the bucket line. The French usually get the blame for the looseness of bond between government and people in Laos: In the European tradition, they used features of the terrain to establish the country's modern borders, and in the process split highland tribes among Laos, Vietnam, China. The lowland Lao Luom, the country's ethnic majority, was split in half by the Mekong, the divide between Laos and Thailand.

To some, the result seems less a nation than a collection of ethnic leftovers, each loyal first to kin who live across a border. Other peoples have found unity in a shared purpose, rather than blood, however; what's really stymied Laotian nation building is the absence of decent schools. Without them, children aren't exposed to their country's history, or its pan-ethnic values, traditions, sources of pride. Education is essential to establishing a national identity.

As it is, villagers from Ban Chen and Ban Satum may recognize that Mr. Done is some bigwig from Vientiane, but few know who he is or what he does, and they have little reason to care — the Ministry of Foreign Affairs simply isn't relevant to their lives. Most have no firsthand knowledge of the world beyond a radius of a few days' walk. His past as ambassador to Germany will mean nothing, because few, if any, know anything of Germany — or Europe, for that matter.

The visitors return to their chopper. A minute later the machine rises from the trees at the clearing's edge, turns its belly toward us, and whisks Mr. Done away.

Early that evening, I walk Main Street to the Laotian camp, the sound of music building as I pass the last American tents. There's no mistaking Lao pop, which relies on mournful-sounding vocals and giddily upbeat melodies played in seemingly endless loops on Casio keyboards and drum machines. The songs never peak; they just cruise on emotional and rhythmic plateaus for what seems like years.

The ambassador and his entourage are seated at one of the Laotian mess tent's long banquet tables, not far from the speakers. He waves me over, and I take the seat to his right. He looks at me coolly. "We will talk," he says over the music, "and you will share a meal with us." What follows is a reprise of our conversation of months past. I ask him why the Laotian government devotes so much time and talent to the search for another country's missing. He replies that his people have agreed to cooperate "for humanitarian reasons."

"It is, as you know, at the request of the U.S. government and especially the families of the MIAs," he says. "We have sympathy toward the families, those who lost their loved ones and so forth. We put ourselves in their place. We understand their emotions, their grievances, their loss.

"The war here, it was not declared. It was a secret war, a special war. Your president, to honor your Constitution, should have declared war. But he did not." Mr. Done smiles at me. "But now we want to look beyond that, and see the future. To forget the past. We want to be friendly with the U.S. people and the U.S. government."

As he speaks, the camp's cooks, all women, carry plates of food to the table — greens, meat mixed with herbs, platefuls of animal flesh of a type I can't identify. As the spread grows, Mr. Done's colleagues fiddle with a barbecue on the table. It resembles a twelve-inch flower pot, its bottom filled with glowing coals. Across its top lies a *sin dat*, an aluminum plate that looks like a hubcap. The officials lay strips of meat on its domed middle, from which fat drains into a shallow trough around the *sin dat*'s edge. It bubbles there, cooking small pieces of vegetables.

"You can spread to the U.S. people that we are good people," Mr. Done says, eyeing the meat. "What we want to know is how we can cooperate further."

He does not raise the subject of money, which is undeniably a major incentive: The People's Democratic Republic gets a lot of American dollars in return for its cooperation, hard currency without which its government, and particularly its military, would not function. This is also true of Vietnam. The Hanoi government maintains an agency called the Vietnam Office for Seeking Missing Persons, which devotes itself not to finding the roughly 300,000 Vietnamese missing from the war, but the 1,500-odd American troops whose bodies have yet to leave the place. Its representatives at the national, provincial, district, and village levels line up workers and secure permissions for the American teams that venture into the Vietnamese backcountry four times a year.

Why? The Vietnamese cite their humanitarian bent, just as the Laotians do, but their economic health is at stake, as well: Securing open trade with the United States, which they achieved during Bill Clinton's presidency, depended on their cooperation on the MIA issue. And the Vietnam Office for Seeking Missing Persons is motivated by more immediate self-interest, because it's paid for by American taxpayers; thus, the United States finds itself in the odd position of kowtowing to a foreign agency that would not exist without it.

Whether either country's cooperation is as full as it could be is open to debate. Vietnam was pathological in its record keeping during the war, but seems to have somehow misplaced quite a few Americans who were at least briefly its captives during the fighting. U.S. officials are confident the former POWs are dead, but frustrated that Vietnam has been unable or unwilling to pinpoint their burial sites.

Not only that, but in the 1980s, Hanoi handed over dozens of remains that bore traces of chemical preservative, suggesting that the Socialist Republic had warehoused American bones with the intent of using them for political leverage. One summary prepared by American officials in January 1992 estimated that 60 percent of the remains turned over unilaterally by Vietnam and identified to that point — 161 sets out of 270 — "show signs of storage."

Laos, quite a bit less sophisticated than its neighbor, has few records to withhold, but has refused to grant U.S. teams access to swaths of its territory.

"You can try all of this," Done says, flipping a piece of meat on the *sin dat* with chopsticks. "Try this. It's very good. It's Lao barbecue."

I pincer a slice of meat with my own chopsticks and take a bite. Or try to; the meat is so tough I can't tear it. I put the whole piece in my mouth and discover that it's mostly gristle. A full minute's chewing fails to break it down. I surreptitiously spit it into my hand and flick it out of the tent and into the brush behind me.

A bottle of Beerlao appears at my elbow. I gratefully take a swig while I peruse the table's other offerings. I know better than to tangle with the fresh greens: Lao salads might be washed, but usually not with bottled water. A bowl close to me is filled with chilies and small pieces of meat. I scoop some out and find it spicy, flavorful, and tender. I have more. And more. Mr. Done, happily chewing his barbecue, nods to the bowl. "Ah, you like that. Tiger meat."

"*Tiger* meat?"

"Not really tiger," he says. "It's just called that." He points to another bowl. "You can eat that, if you like. It's cooked. Same as what you're eating now, but it's cooked."

I'm in mid-chew. "This isn't cooked?"

"No. But that is, over there."

"This is raw meat?"

Mr. Done nods. "Raw oxen." He snares another sliver of meat — barbecued oxen, I'd guess — from the *sin dat*. "This meat was killed today," he reassures me. "Not bought at market. It's very fresh."

I smile, but switch to the cooked version, while Mr. Done talks about the person he says was most responsible for bringing Americans and Laotians together on recovery missions — namely, Mr. Done. "I was the one who did that directly," he says, "because I was the one who was entrusted by the central government to do that."

I don't know whether that's true, but it's a fact that a series of 1989 meetings established most of the ground rules the two countries have followed since. Without them, Gwen Haugen's team would not now be in Laos at the height of the rainy season. Ban Alang Base Camp likely would not exist. "We have been stopped by the bad weather a few times, but that is all," Mr. Done says. "We have to have each other. When we are in need, you help. But when you need our help, we give what we can."

A pretty young Laotian woman approaches us with a tray, on which are bottles of Beerlao and Johnnie Walker Red and two shot glasses. Custom holds that we're to throw down a shot every time she circles the room. Dining with Laotian officialdom is, in this respect, a little like joining a fraternity.

Mr. Done stands and insists the woman give him a kiss before he does his duty. She demurs. He presses the point. She sticks to her position. He insists again. She finally gives him a tentative peck on the cheek, and Mr. Done swallows a shot of whiskey.

By the time she returns, I've listened to Mr. Done sulk at length about the lack of love he gets from Washington. I've also convinced him to let me travel by car to the site, which seems the closest I'll get to permission to walk.

7

A COUPLE MORNINGS LATER, Bounmy ushers me into the front seat of a Mitsubishi Pajero for our ride to work. The vehicle is a hand-me-down, one of a fleet of SUVs that Japan contributed to the allied effort in the Persian Gulf War, though it doesn't look it — it's slate-blue and fitted with shiny chrome brush guards, more like the showy ride of an American rap star than a vehicle called on to perform serious off-road duty.

Bounmy and Polo climb in the back, and with an expressionless Laotian soldier at the wheel, we roll up the camp's entrance road and onto Route 9. It has no center stripe, no fog lines, no shoulders, no discernable bed; it is simply a two-lane ribbon of asphalt laid through rice paddies and jungle, and in places it is less than that. We drive into gargantuan potholes, some eight feet across, many filled with red-brown water, the Pajero pitching violently as its tires grope for terra firma. We traverse domes of gravel that mark recent repairs. We thump over washouts. We slalom among deep bogs of disintegrating pavement and mud that reach for us from the roadside.

"In three years," Bounmy predicts from the back seat, "this road will be very nice."

For half of our journey eastward, we're in the oncoming lane, a tactic necessitated by slumping asphalt. It's not a worry, however, as we have the highway to ourselves. There's not another vehicle in sight in either direction as we pass a dejected-looking local pushing an ancient bike, a trash bag over his shoulder, and a village of stilt houses and playing little boys, their heads shaved but for the traditional small patches front and center. I ask whether I can take pictures. Polo, the district official, says no.

The Pajero lurches over a low concrete bridge spanning a creek, evidently a replacement for a bombed predecessor; I can see its ruined stone piers rising from the water. We grind past another village. A platoon of chickens wanders among its huts, and a little girl sells doughy-looking confections from a spindly roadside stand of bamboo. We steer around a herd of goats resting in the roadway and pass a hump-backed bull grazing in tall grass.

Otherwise, we see nothing but jungle — not the dense, triple-canopy forest of the mountains to our east, but charmless walls of bamboo and low scrub, the successor to a once-great woodland maimed by bombs and chemical defoliants and finished off by logging crews.

Six miles and nearly an hour east of Ban Alang we reach the small commercial district sprung up at the highway's intersection with Route 92: Ban Dong, a name borrowed from an old settlement that has long lain along the river just to the south. I roll down my window and peer at the small shops and cafes, all thatch-roofed and walled with woven bamboo, trying to imagine a war here. During Lam Son 719, this little mercantile knot didn't exist at all; this crossroads was Fire Support Base A Loui and a rallying point for incoming Hueys.

Somewhere on the road behind us, the South Vietnamese tanks bogged down, and favor shifted from invader to defender. The settlement offers no hint of its dramatic past. Today, shopkeepers smile and return my waves as the Pajero swings into an uphill right turn and onto Route 92, headed south. But right here, thirty years ago, all hell was breaking loose.

On the morning of March 20, 1971, Jack Barker and John Dugan took off from Khe Sanh in the lead of a straggly flight of the company's birds, bound for the escarpment's eastern edge, fifteen miles over the border. Their mission: to extract remnants of the Fourth Regiment of the South Vietnamese First Infantry Division, the members of which had fled downhill from Landing Zone Brown to a small, rough-edged pickup zone, or PZ, chopped into the jungle at the bluff's foot.

Behind Barker and Dugan, in Chalk 2 — military talk for a helicopter's place in line — was Alan K. Fischer, a skillful Kingsmen aircraft commander. Four birds behind Fischer, William C. Singletary piloted Chalk 6; in the cargo hold behind him, Billy Dillender and John Chubb, the latter beginning only his third day in the air, readied their guns. Four other helicopters brought up the rear.

The men of Bravo Company knew they were flying into a bad situation. Two days before, a South Vietnamese ranger unit, hundreds strong when it entered Laos in February, had been hunkered down in a crater northwest of LZ Brown, surrounded and begging for help on the radio. Of its eighty-eight survivors, sixty-one were wounded. They were nearly out of ammo. The North Vietnamese called for their surrender on bullhorns and threatened to punch through the ragged perimeter at any moment.

Cobra gunships from one of the Kingsmen's sister companies had picked up the radio plea and dived on the attackers, loosing guns and rockets on the plumes of smoke grenades the friendlies tossed at enemy positions. They'd kept it up for a good chunk of the afternoon, taking turns on strafing runs, dodging machine gun fire and airbursts, before a company of troop-carrying "slicks" arrived to pluck the defenders out. By that time, the Cobras were out of ammo, and the troops in the crater were out of smoke grenades. The incoming birds couldn't make out the crater in all the haze and confusion on the ground. One gunship crew, essentially unarmed, had volunteered to lead them in.

A spray of ground fire had blown through the Cobra, setting it afire and slicing its hydraulic lines. Struggling to control his ship, Capt. Keith A. Brandt had calmly given directions to the slick leader on how to reach the friendlies, then announced he was going to try to ditch in the Xepon, about a mile away. A few hundred yards short of the river, he'd radioed that he and Lt. Alan Boffman weren't going to make it, signing off with: "Give my love to my wife and family."

That was the sort of reception Barker and company anticipated. They knew, too, that their troubles weren't restricted to enemy fire. Seconds after Brandt and Boffman had gone down, the lead Huey had made it into the crater, only to be rushed by South Vietnamese troops. Twenty-five of them — more than three times the helicopter's regular payload — had scrambled aboard and grabbed its skids as it grunted back into the air. The crew had kicked four off in flight to keep from crashing.

The scene had been replayed dozens of times in the past few days. A Huey dropping into a PZ might be instantly mobbed by soldiers unschooled in the physics of flight and mindless that, so overloaded, it couldn't fly. Whatever order, or structure, or sensibility that existed in some of the besieged outposts evaporated: Men abandoned their posts to sprint for salvation, clawed over each other to reach the birds, surged past door gunners and crew chiefs who tried to block the way. As they did, the defenses around the zones collapsed, so that a crew struggling to lift off sometimes found itself trading shots with the enemy while it wrestled its friends.

At times the struggle in the cargo holds got so tangled that the only things keeping a crew chief or door gunner from pitching overboard were the monkey straps that anchored them to their chopper's transmission housing. It got so bad that some gunners fired their M-60s over the heads of the rushing friendlies to slow them down. Even so, they'd wind up having to punch and kick several off their straining birds before the pilots could pull up to a low hover, where they'd throw a few more overboard. And all the while, other soldiers would be jumping for the skids, trying to get a handhold.

Maintaining a grip on a Huey's thick landing skid wasn't a long-term proposition if the chopper was hovering, let alone in the fierce wind that accompanied cruising at a hundred knots. The danglers almost always fell. Some held on until the Hueys were three, even four thousand feet up.

As Jack Barker and company flew over the high mountains that marked the Laotian border, their radios crackled with calls from two flights of choppers ahead of them. They'd come under heavy fire, they reported. At least six birds were so shot-up they'd have to put down. The PZ at Brown, the Kingsmen's destination, was particularly hot.

Barker and Dugan flew on, following Route 9 down the Xepon valley, then cutting to the southwest, across the river toward Route 92. They couldn't see the pickup zone; they couldn't see much of anything. South of where Brown lay, a recent B-52 strike had kicked tons of dirt into the air, shrouding the terrain in that direction under a rusty pall. Dead ahead lay clouds of white phosphorus smoke, which cut visibility to a half-mile or less. The major flew above the smoke, using it as cover. When he popped into view on the other side, the ground below strobed with muzzle flashes. At the escarpment's base, six yellow lights appeared through the haze, bright little things, like candles — the business ends of .51-caliber machine guns, their fire blurring into an unbroken glow — and through this gantlet Jack Barker glided toward the PZ. Bullets thudded into the Huey's underside, ripped the bird's thin flanks, made sharp cracks as they passed close, breaking the sound barrier. Al Fischer, in Chalk 2, watched the lead bird continue its glide until the incoming fire was overwhelming, then roll left. Barker was going around.

Fischer swooped over the PZ. As he stood his Huey on its tail to slow down, he caught a momentary glimpse of friendlies below, crouched in the clearing, none holding a weapon. Then the cockpit's greenhouse windows shattered, and machine gun fire poured into the ship, and the guys in the back were firing their M-60s and screaming at him to keep moving. A bullet sliced through the leg of his copilot's flight suit, somehow missing flesh. Another tore into an M-16 slung over his seat. Still more came at them through the instrument panel and radio controls. Fischer banked hard and rolled out to the east, radioing Chalk 3 not to follow.

Warrant Officer Gene Haag was already headed in by that time, piloting his Huey just over the treetops, and he button-hooked to a low hover over the PZ. He stayed there just long enough for a load of South Vietnamese troops to leap aboard. Two soldiers hung from the skids as he lifted off. By this time the dust and smoke was so thick in the PZ that Tom Hill, at the controls of Chalk 4, couldn't tell where it was until he spotted Haag's rotors coming up through the cloud. He aimed for the hole the departing chopper left. Eight friendlies climbed into his machine, scared witless, and another dangled by his hands from the skids.

While Barker and Dugan circled over A Loui, preparing to lead a second run, Al Fischer's Huey was limping east, its crew chief and gunner out on the skids to look the bird over. It was in bad shape, they reported. The tail boom was full of holes. The tail rotor drive shaft housing, a delicate link to staying aloft, was punctured. Fuel streamed from breaks in the tanks.

Fischer and his copilot, Edward R. Cash, decided to risk the trip back to Khe Sanh, and steered for Route 9. They were just below the clouds when a tremendous concussion rocked the ship. Fischer blacked out. When he came to, the Huey's big windscreen was missing, and its center post with it, and most of the instrument panel, too, and wires were hanging from the ceiling control panel, sparking and crackling, and wind was howling in, and Cash was slumped in his seat, seemingly dead, and they were nosing straight for the ground. He pulled the chopper out of its dive, but found the engine wouldn't power up beyond an idle.

A 37mm antiaircraft shell, probably aimed with the help of radar, had burst just in front of them. Fischer shifted in his seat to find crew chief Lyle Smith goggle-eyed and talking to him, but the intercom was out, along with all the radios, and the pilot couldn't hear a word he said. Beside Smith was a panel that enclosed the helicopter's transmission. In it was a hole the size of a football.

They were going down, and soon; the only question was where. Through the chopper's smashed front end, Fischer saw a hill ahead, its broad crown 830 feet above the surrounding bottomland, and recognized it as a fire support base. A few hundred friendly troops were crowded in the redoubt, trying to hold off a tightening circle of North Vietnamese attackers. Fischer and Cash, now regaining consciousness, aimed for the hilltop.

As Chalk 2 fell into the base, rifle fire erupted from outside the perimeter, and as the skids hit the ground, bullets raked the helicopter's starboard side. South Vietnamese troops, unaware that they'd just witnessed a crash landing, rushed the chopper. The door gunner, Roger Perales, had to fire over their heads to hold them back. Then, with an M-60 and as much ammo as they could carry, the crew jumped from the Huey and crawled for a trench forty yards away.

Two miles to the east, Jack Barker started his second trip into the PZ.

At first, Route 92 seems a big improvement on Route 9. It is unpaved but smooth, its red-clay surface packed hard and high and out of the surrounding muck, and we glide down its middle and into a green tunnel, dense jungle on our left, an impenetrable wall of high scrub and banana trees to the right. When the road bursts from the shade, it's to cross the Xepon River on a suspension bridge, the only major span in this part of the country. It is one lane wide and hangs from rusted iron towers and cables. Wooden sidewalks straddle the roadway, their planks rotted and broken and, for long stretches, missing altogether. I ask how old the crossing is, figuring that it dates from early in the twentieth century. But the jungle is rough on all things man-made: Polo replies that it was built in 1974.

Just south of the river we encounter a mud hole that stretches beyond the road's edges; trucks trying to avoid its middle have carved deep, red-mud crescents into the jungle fringe. Our driver elects to take it with a running start. We're most of the way across the wallow before we start to fishtail, and it becomes obvious that the Pajero is floating. Its spinning tires grab hold of solid earth just when it seems sure we'll sink. We lurch onto dry ground, Bounmy and Polo laughing in the back seat.

The happy moment doesn't last. A couple hundred yards to the south another bog waits, this one far bigger, its middle a watery meringue. Its crisscrossing ruts are knee-deep and extend all the way to its edges, which have been pushed far beyond the road's normal width. There's no going around it. Emboldened by his last success, the driver floors the accelerator, and the Pajero bounds into the swamp like an eager puppy. Alas, the mud has the viscosity and adhesive properties of epoxy, and within half a second we're stuck fast, wheels spinning helplessly, engine whining. The driver eases off the gas. In the quiet, we can hear mud slurping up the truck's sides. Bounmy sighs.

Polo barks something to the driver, who slams the Pajero into reverse. We jerk backward through our own muddy wake, slewing like a canoe in a cross-current, and, accompanied by screams from the transmission and clouds of exhaust, bull our way back to the hole's edge. There's a long moment of silence while we idle there. "OK," Bounmy finally says, his tone cheery. "On foot!"

We climb from the Pajero as two long-haired teenagers approach on a smoking Russian motorcycle, crossing the mud from its far side and throwing up a rooster tail of red slop. They're ensnared halfway across, sink past their ankles when they put their feet down for balance, but manage to goose the machine through the mire.

The breezeless air smells of cow dung. Fat black flies buzz around us as we eye the mud, strategizing. I choose a path around the right side. Bounmy and Polo opt for the left. My boots are caked with about a pound of mud apiece when I reach solid ground.

We hike. The temperature creeps upward. The jungle rises around us. Cicadas screech. For a while, I can hear Bounmy and Polo chatting behind me, but soon their conversation dies, and we stride, silent and sweating, southward across the Xepon's valley. Bounmy looks particularly uncomfortable. He's clad in shiny polyester khakis, an untucked oxford dress shirt, and white running shoes, and totes his gear in a large plastic shopping bag from "Boutique de Paris."

Another motorbike approaches, and as it passes I see the two boys aboard have a baby goat wedged between them, its feet bound. I can hear its shrieks long after its captors have disappeared behind a small rise in the road. We reach another mud hole, which drives us into the brush. Bounmy stops under a tree. He points at its fruit, spheres the size of apples. *"Bombie!"* he yells. He chuckles.

"What is it?" I ask. "What is that fruit?"

"*Seng*," Bounmy says. "If you want to die, you eat."

I pass, and we walk on. Laos, I think to myself, is just stuffed with things that'll kill you.

The fire that greeted the Kingsmen on their return to the PZ was even more intense. As Jack Barker's Huey flared for landing, bullets punched through the heater compartment and out the tail rotor drive shaft, slammed into Dugan's seat, blasted a hole in the cockpit just over Barker's head and through part of the helicopter's skeleton. Chalk 1 broke off its run.

In Chalk 5, crew chief Rich Ginosky heard his door gunner screaming that he was under heavy fire and turned to discover a hole in the floor a foot across; whatever made it had missed the fuel cells by inches. Suddenly the Huey lost power, and Ginosky heard the pilot, a Kingsmen warrant named Bruce Sibley, radio a mayday. The cargo hold seemed lit by strobe — everything went black, then bright, then black. Shattered branches and blowing leaves swirled in.

Dillender and Chubb, following in Chalk 6, watched Sibley's bird crash into the trees just short of the PZ. They poured rounds into their enemy positions, and did it so accurately that for several seconds the Huey took no hits. As it dropped over the perimeter, though, pilot Bill Singletary and copilot Joe St. John heard the thumping of small-arms fire hitting the hull. They went around.

A couple of minutes later, as they climbed east of the PZ, they picked up a distress call on their FM radio. It was Al Fischer. He and his crew had reached the trench, where he'd found a South Vietnamese officer with a backpack radio. As Fischer told Singletary that Chalk 2 had crash-landed at Fire Support Base Delta, nearly ten miles southeast of LZ Brown, mortars started whistling overhead. Their explosions marched steadily toward his crippled bird.

Chalk 6 made for Delta, but its crew saw no helicopter within the perimeter there. Singletary asked Fischer to give him a "long count" — to keep his radio's mike key engaged so the airborne Huey could home in on his signal. The tactic drew Singletary and crew westward, to another fire support base, Delta One, just a couple miles east of Brown.

Fischer told the incoming crew that small-arms fire was heavy, that mortar rounds were coming in, that the fort was too hot to attempt a landing. Singletary replied that he'd be coming in low, from the north. Chalk 6 dropped out of the sky.

Back at the PZ, Rich Ginosky, crew chief of the wrecked Chalk 5, came to his senses in a bomb crater. He had no memory of how he'd arrived there. His door gunner was lying nearby, bloody and dazed, covered with shrapnel wounds. Ginosky told him to get up, then climbed into the chopper, which had come to rest on its left side. The copilot had been shot in the leg. Pilot Sibley was unconscious in the cockpit's left seat. Ginosky pulled him from the wreckage.

The bamboo around them was still for a few minutes, until Ginosky heard a faint telltale chop and looked up to see a Huey dropping toward them on an almost vertical path. It was the company's chase ship, and as it neared the treetops, the woods around the downed chopper erupted with gunfire. It sounded like a rifle range, there were so many guns firing, and the shooters were close, invisible but just yards away, all around him. As he watched, the helicopter spun in a complete circle and came to a hover directly over the wreckage. Ginosky climbed onto the crashed bird's right side and found himself eye-to-eye with the hovering chase ship's pilot, who nodded a hello.

The crew chief leaned out to pull Ginosky into the cargo hold, and as he did a bullet smashed into his shin. He toppled back onto the deck, and as others in the stranded crew heaved aboard amid a clamor of incoming fire, Ginosky crawled to the wounded man's M-60. It was jammed, a round broken in its chamber. He grabbed an M-16. It wouldn't fire, either. Somebody was screaming outside the hovering craft, and Ginosky looked around, couldn't find his door gunner, peered over the side and found the man on the skid. He pulled him in, and then they were rising out of the trees and away from the PZ. Ginosky watched Chalk 5 shrink as they gained altitude.

His machine. The cleanest in Bravo Company. He'd actually waxed it. Thirty years later, he'd still recall its quirks, and remember its tail number — 69-15505.

In 1989, while searching for Jack Barker's Huey, Pete Miller would unearth its data plate.

Two miles to the east, the crew of Chalk 2 crouched in a crowded trench alongside Delta One's garrison. Al Fischer was resisting attempts by a South Vietnamese officer to reclaim his radio. Copilot Ed Cash, a Green Beret on the ground before getting his wings, crouched nearby. Crewmen Lyle Smith and Roger Perales were firing the M-60. All the while, mortar rounds were exploding just a few yards away.

Suddenly Chalk 6 came into view, racing low toward the base, Dillender and Chubb blazing away on its machine guns. Lyle Smith scrambled from the trench and, kneeling, held his M-16 over his head to advertise the stranded crew's position. In an instant the ground around him exploded with bullet strikes. Smith flopped onto his stomach, still holding his rifle overhead, and Singletary radioed Fischer that he had them in sight.

The downed crewmen knew they had to be the first to reach the incoming helicopter. If they weren't, they'd have to fight their way through a mob of South Vietnamese, and even if they managed that, they risked seeing the bird overloaded with hangers-on, unable to escape. So as Singletary pulled his bird nose-high, braking hard, the Americans leapt from the trench and sprinted toward the place, twenty-five yards away across open ground, where they expected it to slow enough to jump on.

They fired as they ran, shooting beneath the chopper's skids at the North Vietnamese on the clearing's far side. Joe St. John watched them come, and with them, explosions that ripped the fort's red-dirt floor. The North Vietnamese were walking their mortars, getting closer with each shot.

Chalk 6 never landed, never stopped. Smith, Perales, and Cash jumped for the starboard cargo hatch while the skids were a couple of feet off the ground. Fischer made his leap as the ship started to lift, slamming his gut into the hatch's lip, and for a moment he hung half in, half out. Somebody — Dillender, he thought — grabbed the back of his flight suit and yanked so hard that Fischer skidded across the deck and had to reach for the back of Singletary's seat to keep from sailing out the chopper's far side. Then, with Dillender and Chubb firing their M-60s, and the four passengers firing M-16s, Singletary nosed Chalk 6 out of Delta One.

The battalion's daily staff journals made note of Bravo Company's losses that morning. "Acft 337 shot up at Khe Sanh 630 shop up at KS," one typo-laden entry read, adding: "492 Down at D-1 not recoverable (505) crashed west of PZ total loss; 501 shot up & is back at castle: 341 shot up & back at castle: 185 has a hole in the skip but is still flying." Ragged though its aircraft might be, however, the company had survived its sortie to PZ Brown. Against all odds, no lives had been lost.

On the ride to Khe Sanh, Fischer leaned over Singletary's seat and kissed his helmet. When they landed, the eight exchanged euphoric hugs and back slaps and told each other they'd just stared down doom, that they'd somehow cheated it, that they had to be the luckiest men on the planet. Someone gave Fischer a beer. It was warm, but it tasted great.

As it turned out, the celebration was premature.

It was shortly after noon.

The day was young.

8

THE TURNOFF TO Ban Satum is almost invisible, a narrow footpath on the road's right side, ruffed with tall grass. We climb a berm, yellow butterflies fluttering around our heads, and the village's first house comes into view, a big place on stilts. Polo stops outside it, unsure as to how to proceed, and yells a question in Lao. A naked little girl appears in the hut's doorway. From the darkness beyond comes a shouted reply, and a moment later an old man in a burlap loincloth scrabbles, hunched, onto the bamboo porch. The district official asks directions. The villager points off to our left and hollers some more, his tone and frown suggesting that we must be stupid.

We follow his gestures, past chickens and roosters and piles of goat droppings and two curly-tailed, skulking dogs, to a large, stilted building, where our path, such as it is, splits. One fork end-runs the building, which Bounmy explains is a "rice-keeping house," and disappears behind it. I assume that's the one we're to follow, because the other trail bullets straight into a bamboo thicket and is consumed instantly. It looks abandoned, reclaimed by the forest, but that, as it turns out, is the path we're to take. Polo yells back to the old man, who, shaking his head and muttering, clambers down from his porch and joins us at the fork to again point the way. We strike off into the bush.

Our corridor is less than a shoulder's width across. It wriggles around blind turns and dives down a steep ravine, into which stair steps have been hacked with *bria;* a bamboo handrail, a simple, staple-shaped affair, stands on the trail's right side at the slope's most treacherous point. At the bottom is a bamboo bridge across a stream — more a floor than a bridge, really, for murky water flows over its surface. Then the trail switchbacks back up the ditch.

Three decades after the war, the forests of Laos and Vietnam are terra incognita to Westerners, crossed by a few seldom-traveled paths, guarded by bamboo grown so close its stalks make music against their neighbors in the breeze. Perhaps it's no wonder that folks back home, in the absence of detailed information about these remote and unvisited hinterlands, speculate that Americans might still be enslaved here.

For believe it they do. The premise has fueled books and "Bring Them Home" bumper stickers, and birthed self-appointed "POW hunters," some of whom have made a tidy living by telemarketing their supposed rescue raids into the jungle. It's implicit in the black "POW/MIA" flags one sees flying at fire stations and government offices; emblazoned across the bottom of the flags' seal are the words "You Are Not Forgotten," and it's pretty clear to whom the "You" refers.

We skirt a deep crater thirty feet across. Water filling a second twinkles through the trees. We meet a worker headed the other way, back to the village to get additional help at the site, and have to turn sideways to let him pass.

The Vietnamese government has consistently denied that it held anyone after Operation Homecoming in March 1973, when it released 591 American prisoners of war. The Laotians claim that at war's end they had none to turn over; all but a few of those lost in Laos vanished in Vietnamese-controlled territory. Joint Task Force–Full Accounting was created in 1992, in part, to explore whether some unfortunate soul remained; its "full accounting" mission not only requires it to retrieve remains but also to return living Americans, if they exist, to their homeland.

The joint task force doesn't accept Vietnamese assurances as fact but says it's found no hard evidence that an American remained under guard in the region after the prisoner release. The search for such evidence has been under way for nearly thirty years and continues to employ hundreds of people in government service. It is not the joint task force's purview alone: The Defense Intelligence Agency has an operation code-named Stony Beach that specializes in interviewing Southeast Asians on the whereabouts of unaccounted-for Americans. Analysts with the Defense POW-Missing Personnel Office, or DPMO, chase leads from a suite of offices in a Crystal City, Virginia, high-rise.

Gathering reports of Western survivors has occupied officers of military intelligence, the State Department, the Central Intelligence Agency.

Down another ravine to another stream, this one bridged by a shaky-looking arrangement of three narrow logs. Polo traverses it in long, careless strides, mentioning to Bounmy that this is where the village gets its water. I tightrope across, arms out.

Every once in a while, one of the agencies involved in the vigil will get word of a Westerner in the jungle, speaking English, looking haggard. A team of investigators will take off in pursuit of such "live sighting reports," and in more than two out of three cases, find or identify the Westerners in question. None has turned out to be an unaccounted-for serviceman; they've been tourists, academics, missionaries, the occasional foreign engineer.

More than one in four of the stories have been outright hoaxes. A typical example was the story a Vietnamese man told American investigators in June 1988. A mountain tribesman, he said, had recently taken his uncle to see an injured American, the only survivor of an air crash that had killed five of his comrades. He was thin, with sunken eyes "through which he had great difficulty seeing, probably because he cried so much for his family," the source suggested. He gave investigators a dog tag allegedly corresponding to one of the man's dead colleagues. Yarns of this stripe were a dime a dozen in the eighties, and like many, this one was flawed: The tag wasn't that of an American casualty or that of an unaccounted-for soldier. Investigators concluded that the story was "a thinly disguised ploy for resettlement assistance for source's wife and child, who remain in Vietnam."

In November 1987, a source told Stony Beach interviewers that he knew of a blind, black American living with a mountain woman in a pine forest of unspecified location on the Vietnam-Laos border; he also mentioned that he was under the impression that passing on such information would win him entry to the United States. A woman told investigators she saw four Westerners picking peanuts in a field in southern Vietnam, was told by a Communist Party honcho they were captured Americans, and even overheard them speaking English; re-interviewed, she admitted that she never got closer than fifty yards to them, never heard them speak, and was never told they were Americans.

And there was this tale, of particular interest to those working Case 1731: In September 1992, a source reported that while traveling in Viet-

nam he heard of four Americans living with a tribe in the central highlands, along the Laotian border, and had been able to obtain the names
of two, along with their serial numbers and the places where they'd
been separated from their units. One of the names was "John Dugan."

Investigators instantly established that it matched the name of an unaccounted-for soldier, and that the rest of the story was bogus. The serial number bore no resemblance to Dugan's. The informant placed the
captain's disappearance in central Vietnam, not Laos. As for the second
name, it didn't belong to a missing American. "Although the source was
honestly relating what he was told," DPMO concluded, "this report is
most likely the result of a fabrication by either the subsource, or one of
the subsource's contacts."

Investigators have analyzed thousands of second- and thirdhand reports since the fall of Saigon in April 1975. Not one has panned out. Of
the 1,914 *firsthand* live sighting reports U.S. officials have received over
the same period, only 62 can't be categorized as mistaken identity or lie.
Of those, 45 have been linked to wartime sightings of military personnel or civilians who remain unaccounted for. Just 17 concern postwar
sightings that remain unresolved. Of those 17, only one describes a
sighting since 1980.

Without a doubt, the governments of Vietnam and Laos could better
explain the fates of the forty-five missing men spotted in wartime. But
are those men alive today? As the number of live-sighting reports has
dwindled to a trickle, the number of tourists to Vietnam and Laos, and
thus the pool of "outside eyes" in those countries, has exploded. And
the governments of Hanoi and Vientiane have vigorously pursued nor-
malization of their relationship with the United States — a goal that
would be the least of their worries if Washington were to uncover proof
that they'd been keeping prisoners.

The bottom line is that although American servicemen unaccounted
for in Southeast Asia are often referred to as "missing," not one of them
is officially listed that way; their government considers every last one of
them dead, and their bodies simply unrecovered. The only U.S. serviceman carried on government rolls as a captive is navy lieutenant
commander (now captain) Michael S. "Scott" Speicher, whose F/A-18
Hornet was shot down over Iraq during the Persian Gulf War.

Birds twitter overhead. As we climb back out of the ravine, their
songs are trumped by a deeper warble, a phlegmy throb that drifts
through the trees. Dingman's pump. We hike on through the bamboo,

the trail snaking, and drop into the bed of yet another stream. The water is murky, laden with silt. It's the creek below our site, choked with tailings from the screening station. We claw our way up the far side, over the mat of hacked and piled bamboo, and trudge out of the woods and into the light at the edge of the grid. Artillaga is in the hole, supervising a team of diggers.

"Look!" Bounmy yells to him, pointing at me. "I have found an American, lost in the woods!"

What happened when Bravo Company returned to Khe Sanh following its morning sortie has become, over the years, a tangle of fact, myth, and hearsay. This is known: Not long after landing, Jack Barker approached Al Fischer about making another attempt to rescue the South Vietnamese troops stranded at the PZ.

Barker knew Fischer had ditched his crippled bird at Fire Support Base Delta One and was now without a helicopter to fly. The major asked Fischer — among the company's most experienced pilots, with just a month left in his tour — to team up with him, to fly the lead ship as its left-seater.

Fischer replied that he wasn't going back. He told Barker that they'd all been sitting ducks on the morning sortie, that he didn't believe they'd had enough gunship coverage, that it was a miracle they'd survived. To go back was stupid. To go back was suicide. If American troops were on the ground, or a downed chopper crew, he'd go, no question — but he wasn't about to get himself killed for South Vietnamese who, he recalls saying, wouldn't help him help them.

Fischer says that Bill Singletary, who'd led the rescue at Delta One, told him fifteen years later that he, too, refused to fly; Singletary died in 1989, however, and thus cannot testify to that himself. Barker may have had similar exchanges with others. What's certain is that the major asked some pilots whether their Hueys were fit for another trip to the PZ, and was told they were not. Tom Hill, who commanded Chalk 4 during the morning sortie, recalls Barker approaching him and saying, "Listen, we're going to try to get back in for another sortie. Is your aircraft flyable?" Hill answered that he had rounds through his blade root — the portion of the main rotor blade subject to the greatest strain when a helicopter muscles into the air and maneuvers in flight.

"Would you be willing to take another aircraft?" Barker said.

"If you can find me another aircraft," Hill recalls replying, "I'm ready to go.'"

Ready or not, Hill didn't get another aircraft, and neither did anyone else. Army records in the National Archives indicate that a few hours later, Bravo Company notified the battalion staff that it would have eight helicopters available for duty the next day, but Kingsmen mechanics evidently had a lot of patching to do to get their birds to that level of readiness: By the time Barker had finished making his rounds of choppers and crews, there was — officially, at least — just one Huey in decent enough shape in all of the company, and that was Singletary's — 66-16185, or "185" for short, the bird that had swooped in to rescue Fischer and his crew at Fire Support Base Delta One. Barker commandeered 185 for his return to the escarpment.

Kingsmen later told Pete Federovich how John Dugan — who, like Barker, was not yet qualified to command a helicopter — wound up in the cockpit beside him: "The major asked for volunteers to go with him," Federovich says, "and nobody raised a hand. And then he said, 'Well, I'm going, if I have to go alone.' And then John raised his hand."

Fischer walked out to the bird with Dugan, pleading with him to stay put. The conversation reminded him of "talking to a guy getting ready to jump off a bridge, and you're standing across the rail, and you can't stop him." Dugan seemed conflicted about the sortie, but determined to do his duty.

While this was unfolding, several Bravo Company soldiers apparently volunteered to fly in the cargo hold. Just back at Khe Sanh after his shootdown and rescue, Rich Ginosky was loitering at the Kingsmen's operations tent when he heard the major needed a crew, and put in his name. A few minutes later, Billy Dillender turned up. "I'm going," Dillender announced.

"No, I'll go," Ginosky said.

"It's OK," Dillender replied. "I'll go."

"Forget it," Ginosky told him.

"No, it's my aircraft," Dillender said. "I'll go."

Ginosky backed down. Dillender was right: He was 185's crew chief. It was his aircraft.

An episode later in the afternoon suggests that despite his resolute bearing, Barker had questions himself about the wisdom of returning. Lt. Col. William N. Peachey, the major's former battalion commander and the man who'd given him Bravo Company, saw Barker at a refueling pad near the Laotian border. Peachey was overseeing troop rescues from a chain of beleaguered PZs north of the Xepon and was in such a hurry that his crew gassed his bird "hot," never shutting down its engine. Still, he walked over to say hello, asked Barker how his day was going. Badly, Barker replied. He struck Peachey as uncharacteristically edgy, downcast. "Well," Peachey said, trying to lighten things up, "it's good for you. It builds character." To his surprise, Barker lit into him. "What we're doing out here today," he hissed, "isn't doing *anybody* any good."

At some point early that afternoon, Barker strode over to where 1st Lt. Jon Evans was standing with other members of the Kingsmen's sister company, the Black Widows. "I'm going back out," Evans recalls the major telling him. "What do you want to do?" Evans had caught wind of the trouble Barker was having getting another sortie into the air and was impressed with the major's resolve. Here, he thought to himself, was a man who knew when he'd been dealt a bad hand, and accepted it. He replied that he'd join him, that he wasn't going to let Barker fly alone, and two Black Widow crews prepared their slicks for takeoff. As they did, Barker dropped in to speak with them. Evans's copilot, John Madden, was struck by the major's calm, and by something he said that he'd never before heard from a career officer in Vietnam: If you want to pull out, Barker told him, now's the time to do it. Nobody will say anything.

They stuck with him. With 185 in the lead, the three birds took off to the west.

The hoses again spit mud, and Dingman ventures into the ravine to tend to a problem of his own making. Our water system is circular, both beginning and ending in the creek: The pump draws from the stream and pushes water uphill to the screens, where it falls into the trough, then flows back downhill via a small ditch Dingman has carved into the ravine's side. With it goes all the dirt and rocks it's washed from the screens — which is to say, all the dirt that RE-1 has dug from the grid. The creek is now choked with roughly nine hundred cubic feet of new silt, enough to fill a small bedroom from floor to ceiling. It's running wider and shallower than when we arrived, which is making it difficult to draw water to keep the cycle going. Exacerbating the problem is the heat, which has sucked a lot of the stream's already-shallow flow into the clouds.

"Our water source is dwindling rapidly," Reynolds announces as we wait to board the chopper back to base camp. "When we started, it was about halfway up my calf. Now it's ankle-deep. So, Dingman, maybe we can go down there in the morning and see if we can figure something out. Because we *have* to figure something out." Dingman nods.

Sergeant Posey solicits comments from the rest of the team. A soldier complains that by the time RE-1 reached the hotel ice machines at Ban Alang this morning, they were nearly empty. She was barely able to get enough ice bagged to stock the break tent's cooler. "And it's not just the other teams taking it," a 92-Mike adds, indignation evident. "The Lao officials take it, too."

Krueger issues a scornful grunt. "Damn those Lao," he mutters at just above a whisper. "Why don't they get out of our country?"

RE-1 regards its linguist with silent surprise until Reynolds erupts in laughter. "Krueger," the captain says, "you're saying more shit all the time."

"Say something else, Krueger," Posey urges.

"Yeah, Krueger," Haugen says, laughing. "Come on. Out with it."

But the magic moment has passed. Krueger shakes his head.

At Mama's I share a table with Reynolds, who is suffering from a wave of homesickness. This is not the first time he's been separated from home and family in his brief Marine Corps career; that came at the Little Creek Naval Amphibious Base in Norfolk, his first duty assignment. He and Mary, his teammate on the college crew team, were engaged while he was there, and then he transferred to the North Carolina tidewater, where the marines of the East Coast ready themselves for overseas deployments. He went to Europe, and a few months after he and Mary married, in 1998, he shipped to Central America on a disaster-relief mission in the wake of Hurricane Mitch. But this is shaping up as the toughest separation: He's not only half a world from Mary but also from their two-year-old son, Matthew, and this time, Mary's pregnant.

Haugen pulls up a chair, and a minute later Doc Walsh and Capt. Mike Higginbotham, another team leader, join us. Walsh tells the group that while out with RE-2 he was menaced by a blind, six-inch worm, a shiny, black creature that terrified the locals when it appeared in the hole. "They ran from this thing," he says, "and to look at it, you'd think it was harmless. It looked like an earthworm."

"I've heard there's a snake that looks like an earthworm that's deadly," Higginbotham offers.

"Well, they say that 95 percent of the snakes here are poisonous," Haugen says, "so it's probably a safe bet to assume anything you run into is gonna be."

I get up to fetch more beer from the cooler, and when I return, the conversation has shifted to termites. Haugen says that she and other anthropologists suspect the insects might be at least partly to blame for the absence of bone at excavation sites in Southeast Asia.

Over the years, CILHI has documented that human remains don't last nearly as long in this part of the world as they do elsewhere. Sites in North Korea, opened to lab teams on a limited and heavily controlled basis in 1996, typically produce bones in far better shape than sites in Vietnam and Laos; even World War II sites two generations older than their Southeast Asian counterparts yield bones in better condition.

The lab has long explained the phenomenon as the product of acidity in the soil: The ground around here was thought so corrosive that it transformed bone to powder, the powder to smudge. But some of the places the lab could have sworn were highest in acidity have been tested in recent years, she says, only to prove unremarkable in their pH.

At the same time, she's encountered bones that have sustained damage from termites — long bones, like femurs, that on first inspection appeared complete, but which the insects had honeycombed within. "You'd see just a tiny couple of holes on the outside, maybe, where they had entered," she says, "and on the inside, they'd have eaten everything out." Perhaps, she says, termite population is inversely related to a site's potential yield in recovered bone.

This is a troubling theory, for the 1731 site is home not only to big termite mounds that rise from several places in and around the grid, but a lot of subterranean colonies. The team struck one big underground nest in the southeast corner of 512/512; some of that unit's scant ACS was found deep inside the insects' home.

They were the tail end of a flight of seventeen helicopters, 185 in the fifteenth slot, Evans and Madden in the sixteenth, and as they crossed the border and buzzed toward the descending sun it became obvious that what lay ahead was even worse than the situation of a few hours before. The radios were filled with chatter from the fourteen birds ahead of them, all reporting that the fire from the ground was intense, too hot to get past. One by one, they were turned away from the PZ.

Barker and Dugan, Dillender and Chubb flew on in 185. Evans, flying thirty seconds behind them, was surprised to find that he was taking ground fire miles from the escarpment, and it got fiercer the closer they got to the haze-shrouded pickup zone. The North Vietnamese, it seemed, had moved more guns around the scrubby, crater-pocked turf on which the friendly troops huddled. The air was thick with smoke and dust and the smell of cordite, with yellow and green tracers, with the booms and blossoms of airbursts.

The escarpment loomed high as 185 began its final approach. In the chopper's rear, Dillender and Chubb opened up with their M-60s, raking the bamboo thickets and broken forest below, and in answer the ground sparkled with the flashes of AK-47s and machine guns. Evans could see the bird taking hits, taking a lot of them. He radioed Barker to suggest that he go around. He got no answer.

The chopper was dropping fast now as it neared the PZ. Eight hundred feet. Seven hundred feet. As Evans watched, bullets from the ground streamed into it, overwhelming the meager fire that Dillender and Chubb aimed from the machine's flanks. Six hundred feet. "Goddammit," Evans yelled into his mike, "go around!"

A voice that sounded like Barker's: "Roger. Going around."

With that, 185 turned, as if heading back out, but at this point, travel in any direction put the Huey broadside to North Vietnamese gunners. They followed it through the turn, chopping its starboard side to pieces. Evans saw tracers course into its cargo hold and out the far side, then saw the Huey suddenly pitch nose down. An instant later it reared nose high. Then, it started a slow clockwise spin.

For a moment it stopped, as if its pilots had regained control of the beast. Evans could see the man in the cockpit's right seat slumped forward, but he had no time to be sure about who it was, or how badly he was hurt: The instant the helicopter straightened up, a brilliant flash consumed the rear of its fuselage, where its tail boom broadened into the cargo hold.

From 6,000 feet up, an observer in a command ship saw the Huey knocked violently sideways. From a slick a few hundred feet from 185,

Maj. John Klose, the air mission commander for the troop extraction, saw the flash, too. Then he saw the helicopter's tail boom break away.

Of all the things that can go wrong in a rotary-wing aircraft, losing the tail ranks close to the worst. A Huey's main rotor, which spins counterclockwise when viewed from above, creates enormous torque on the fuselage suspended below; left to its own devices, that fuselage would spin clockwise around its own rotor mast. What keeps this from happening is the smaller blade on the tail: Positioned on the aircraft's left side, it counters the torque, keeps the body straight by constantly pushing counterclockwise. The tail rotor thus controls the helicopter's yaw: Give a UH-1H left pedal and you increase the rotor's pitch, boosting its counterclockwise muscle, bringing the nose left; give it right pedal and you reduce the pitch, allowing torque to swing the nose right.

Without the tail, a helicopter spins helplessly. Those watching knew that 185 was now impossible to fly, and that the crew's only hope was a "J. C. Maneuver," as in *Jeeeesus Christ:* Cut the power, hope the torque drops, and brace for the coming crash.

No one cut the power. As Evans looked on, the tailless 185 again began to twirl, faster and faster, and as it did it shot skyward, arcing away from the PZ. It rose so quickly that Evans, gunning his own Huey into a climb, couldn't keep pace. Then it stopped, and its main rotor — the whirring, forty-eight-foot disk that kept it aloft — slipped from its mast and flew off on its own.

The rest of the helicopter seemed to float in place, without any means of support, for seconds.

Then it dropped.

And as it fell, Evans noticed a column of mist below it, realized it was a 200-foot trail of vaporized fuel that the bullet-riddled Huey had spewed on its breakneck climb. The instant 185 dropped back into the mist, a gargantuan fireball erupted around it, through it, in it; the helicopter blew to pieces, and fire shot down the length of the column so that the sky itself burned. The explosion seemed impossibly violent. The Huey vanished within it.

What was left of 185 fell, with a rain of debris, another 400 feet. The left underside of its nose and the leading edge of its left skid hit the ground first. On the lookout for survivors, Evans slipped his bird out of the sky and swooped in fast and low, at 100 knots and just thirty feet off the deck. The hulk was burning like a torch, completely consumed, barely recognizable as a helicopter. He could make out a crewman dangling from the cargo hatch on his monkey strap, but the man didn't move. Nothing did.

So ended a frightful month in U.S. Army history. Seven UH-1Hs were lost in Laos on March 3 and another thirty damaged, fifteen so badly they were deemed unflyable. The next day, five slicks and a Cobra gunship were destroyed; the day after that, two slicks, four Cobra gunships, and two UH-1C gunships. And so it went for weeks, only rare days passing without a chopper knocked out of the sky.

On the 20th, the day the Kingsmen flew to the escarpment, forty slicks were battle-damaged, twenty-three of them beyond quick repair. Twenty-five of the machines received their beatings within a thousand yards of where RE-1 now digs. Those statistics do not include seven UH-1Hs that were shot down outright, among them four that fell while attempting to get into PZ Brown.

The battalion recorded 185's loss with martial efficiency. A log entry for 4:05 P.M. read simply: "One bird has been hit and exploded in the air." Another entry, at 5:50 P.M., reported that the battalion operations center "rec'd word from B/101 that Maj Barker & Cpt Dugan's AC went down in a ball of flames."

PART THREE

Bone Work

∎

1

RE-1 LOITERS OUTSIDE the equipment barn, waiting for the sky to clear. There's little conversation: Long days at the site without emotional payoff, countless hours on the screens and in the hole without so much as a sliver of bone, have left the team's members drained and withdrawn. Haugen and Eagmin read silently. Dingman plays "Horse" on the basketball court with members of the other REs. Several young 92-Mikes sit among the weightlifting equipment, wordlessly drinking sodas. Reynolds paces Main Street, lost in his thoughts.

The captain moved to Hawaii just a few weeks ago — his family hadn't even unpacked when he had to leave for this mission. Mary would have her hands full, learning the lay of the land in Honolulu, looking after a toddler, completing the myriad logistical tasks that accompany a move, even if she weren't expecting; as it is, she's very much so, due to deliver a week after the team's return. And this will be the first of frequent separations they endure. Some of CILHI's team leaders spend eight months of the year "on the road."

Many relationships don't survive the schedule. I've met one team sergeant who hasn't seen his kids in a year; they're on the mainland, and when he gets home from a recovery, it's to Hawaii. It doesn't help that while they're away, teams are often without even a telephone link to home. A sailor deployed on a carrier can call Stateside for a dollar a minute, any time of the day or night. The men and women at Ban Alang get two phone calls during their stay — six minutes, total.

It's midmorning before we get the OK to take off. Reynolds calls the team together. "Everybody's getting worn down," he says, scanning faces. "So take care of yourself. If you need to take a break, if you need to sit under a tree and drink some water for a minute, neither myself nor Sergeant Posey is gonna jump down your throat."

Haugen has detected the team's listlessness, as well. "We have quite a ways to go," she says. "Just pace yourselves. We need everybody healthy to finish this site."

Posey steps up. "You heard the doc," he says. "We got a lotta work left to do. I need y'all to drink water. Drink a lot of water. You gotta stay hydrated." He eyeballs the team's youngsters. "Gotta keep watching those screens. Minute you stop watching closely, that's when that big piece of bone or tooth is gonna pop up. And you don't want to miss it when it happens. You don't want the only reason we don't send these guys home to be that one minute you weren't paying attention."

But it is difficult to stay focused. In four hours, and maybe four dozen buckets of dirt, I find only a heavy, rusted bolt and a snarled chunk of aluminum on my screen. I watch with envy as soldiers pushing dirt from a newly opened unit, 508/516, find fistfuls of wreckage in their clay. Bolts by the score wind up in Conely's collection of ACS, and slivers of curved metal stamped EDISON, and broken glass, and the links that once bound M-60 rounds into belts, and rings, springs, clumps of melted metal, chunks of instrument panel. The unit is at the ravine's lip, southeast of the debris field's center — not an auspicious place on the grid. "Were you expecting to find anything there?" a soldier asks Haugen during a break.

"Not particularly," the anthro admits.

"Because I'm finding tons of stuff."

"Good," she replies. "Now find me a dog tag."

A humid haze cloaks the escarpment, and as hours pass, and the temperature rises, the murky pool at the bottom of the big crater shrinks by half; bright green weeds, invisible when we arrived on the site, jut from the water's surface. The excavated portion of the grid, a neat, L-shaped wound, is floored in parched clay that has started to crack. The slick bog of a few days ago has turned hard. Rakes and hoes kick up clouds of yellow dust.

The dry spell has had a profound effect on the creek. The stream we could hear roaring when we arrived nearly two weeks ago is now an anemic trickle. Dingman has managed to keep the pump running by directing the screening station's outflow into a pool beside the intake hose, a strategy that has further congested the streambed with silt, but at least returns water with the rock. It is only a temporary fix, however, for the once-clear water spraying onto the screens is now an opaque sludge laden with small twigs and broken leaves, and it won't be long before we lose the last of it — and with it, our ability to sift the clay coming out of the hole.

So Dingman and Reynolds clamber down the ravine and into the shady cool of the creekbed, seeking a solution. They find it all but empty; a few small rivulets pulse weakly through the collected orange sand and pebbles near the outflow hose. Where the water trickles over a six-inch ledge, it is split by the silt into dozens of pencil-thin strands. The stream no longer runs. It seeps.

"We're just about out of water," Reynolds observes. He adds helpfully: "This is bad."

"Yes, sir," Dingman replies. The staff sergeant is old enough to be the marine captain's father. Reynolds wasn't alive for Tet, or the A Shau Valley, or Lam Son 719. He never had to register for the draft. What he knows of Vietnam, and its time, is abstraction, book-learning.

Dingman, on the other hand, grew up worrying about coming here. During his teens, every night's TV news was a montage of casualty figures and strangely named places and grainy images of skinny, shirtless GIs ducking rocket hits and shooting M-16s. John Chubb was just four years older than he was.

But like most longtime noncoms, the staff sergeant betrays no discomfort in taking orders from younger men and women. Peace in the army comes with patience and doing what you're told and keeping your mouth shut.

"It seems to me," the captain says, "that the thing to do is to try to dam it. Try to get some water collected here."

"Yes, sir," Dingman drawls. "That should work."

Reynolds shoots him a glance. "You're not blowing smoke up my ass, are you?"

"No, sir. No, I think a dam would do fine. If we could build it, say, this high" — he holds a hand at waist level — "we'd get a hell of a lot of water back here."

"Where would you build it?"

Dingman studies the streambed and points out a place where it narrows to perhaps eight feet wide. Theoretically, a dam there would create a pond upstream that, judging from the creek's vertical drop, could reach a depth of two or three feet, maybe even four. "Of course," he adds, "I don't know how strong that dam would have to be to keep that much water back."

"You ever built a dam before?" Reynolds asks him.

"Well, no, sir. Not exactly."

The captain sighs. "I don't think we have much choice."

"No, sir."

"What will you need?"

Dingman strides to the narrows and scrutinizes the breach for a long moment. "Give me four or five people working down here while you guys are up there," he says, "and we can get it shoveled out and done." Very well, Reynolds says. He calls up to Sergeant Posey for long-handled shovels and workers.

A while later, during a break, a villager passes the American tent with a baby deer on a twine leash. All the women on the team let loose a simultaneous "Awww" and scramble for their cameras. The Laotian smiles and leads the animal, trembling with fear, to where we sit. It stands a foot tall at the shoulder and looks up at us with dark brown eyes the size of robins' eggs. "What are they going to do with it?" one of the sergeants asks.

Haugen looks over to the Laotian tent, where a just-lit cooking fire is producing thick gray smoke. "I think they're setting up a battery to electrocute it," she says.

"Awww, no!" the women cry.

"Count on it," Haugen growls. "They *will* eat that deer."

"Maybe I can buy it," a soldier says. She calls Krueger over and asks him to negotiate the purchase. After a mumbled exchange with the villager, he reports that the deer's price is 50,000 kip — a little over five dollars. "OK," the sergeant says. "I'll buy it, and set it free."

"You're wasting your money," Haugen advises. "It'll die. It's too little."

"They'll just catch it again," Reynolds agrees, "and they'll eat it, anyway." The soldier keeps her money. After a lengthy photo session, man and deer stroll into the Laotian tent. We do not see the animal again.

Down in the creekbed, Dingman has his locals arrange large rocks across the stream's narrows, creating a foundation for the dam. His team fills several dozen nylon sandbags with clay from the site and stacks them carefully into a barricade about two feet high. Water slowly begins to gather behind it.

When we convene at day's end, Haugen notes that 508/516 is yielding a great deal of ACS. "As you can see, you never can tell when you're gonna start pulling stuff out," she says.

There is hope. RE-1 leaves for camp in an upbeat mood.

If CILHI's field experience has taught its anthropologists any one lesson, it's that a dig isn't over until the last spade of dirt has been turned, the last bucket has been passed to the screens, the last morsel of earth has fallen through the mesh. Any number of excavations have borne all the hallmarks of bust until their closing hours; too many teams to count have all but given up on a site, only to find a cache of bone, personal effects, or life support as they prepared to pack up their tools.

Haugen's own experience has demonstrated as much. Her first case was that of an air force pilot whose A-1H Skyraider had crashed in North Vietnam's Thanh Hoa Province, south of Hanoi. Throughout most of a difficult excavation, on a steep hillside of lava rock that broiled in the midsummer heat, Haugen came up empty. Then a near-typhoon doused the slope and wrecked her equipment. While the rest of the team reassembled the worksite, a dispirited Haugen wandered down the hill with a Vietnamese official, and stumbled across two .38-caliber shell casings and a bone exposed by the storm, the latter still wrapped in the remnants of a parachute harness. The bone, part of an arm, proved enough to enable the lab to identify the pilot.

Her eighth mission, another trip to Vietnam, offered even less hope for success. Her quarry that time was navy commander John A. Feldhaus, whose Skyraider had disappeared on an "armed reconnaissance" mission in October 1966. By the time Haugen took up the case, Feldhaus had been the focus of four American outings; her team was to finish a dig started by another anthropologist a few weeks before. So she was shocked, on reaching the site, to find that all the dirt excavated by the last team had been thrown back in the hole and that the area had been planted in sugar cane, when the Vietnamese government knew another team was on its way. Economics: The Vietnamese, like their Laotian neighbors, demand payment for any damage to crops or forest that occurs during recovery operations.

The anthro found a corner of her predecessor's excavation, reconstructed the site, and had her team sift through a lot of dirt that had already been examined once. The work, tiring and slow, turned up chunks of airplane, life-support equipment, personal effects, a piece of long bone, and a molar with a filling. Feldhaus was officially identified in late June 2001.

Haugen was not involved in the excavation that was to become the lab's most compelling argument for persistence, though Randy Posey did have a piece of it. The December 1999 recovery of nineteen marines from a tiny Pacific atoll called Butaritari was statistically remarkable; CILHI's cases have included few in which a greater number of remains have been found and identified. But the Butaritari dig holds a hallowed place in lab history more for its serendipity, for the condition of the remains that Posey's team brought back to Hawaii, and for the sheer drama of a story that began more than seventy years before.

In 1927, an army veteran, failed salesman, and Marine Corps lieutenant named Evans F. Carlson began the first of three prewar deployments he'd make to China, then a preindustrial backwater of large population and small economic means. He was entranced by the country's ancient ways, particularly its reliance on teamwork, rather than technology, to accomplish large-scale tasks. The Chinese called such unity of purpose *gung ho* — "work together."

On one year-long assignment Carlson accompanied an army of Chinese Communists, saw it use *gung ho* to gain an edge against the better-equipped, better-fed Japanese, and had an epiphany: One could marry the far-flung concepts of *gung ho* and guerrilla warfare, which he'd witnessed on a past visit to the jungles of Nicaragua, to produce small, all-for-one commando teams designed to travel light, materialize unexpectedly, take out the enemy, and fade back into the shadows.

The marines were initially cool to all this. The Corps has always resisted the creation of elites within its ranks; the service lacks special forces outfits like the army's Green Berets or the navy's SEALs because it considers itself special from top to bottom. Besides, a lot of folks were spooked by Carlson, who'd earned a reputation as a Red, a crackpot, and worse when he got into trouble for publicly urging American support of the Chinese war effort. He got so frustrated he quit the service.

He couldn't stay away. As war approached he climbed back into uniform to find that President Franklin Roosevelt's son, James, a marine captain, was advocating guerrilla units, too. The pitch dovetailed with the tactics being developed for the coming amphibious campaigns in the Pacific. Five weeks after Pearl Harbor the Marines created two

Raider battalions, one of them under Carlson. James Roosevelt became his second-in-command.

The pair promised their recruits hardship, misery, and a first shot at the Japanese, and had to turn away thousands. Encamped on pastureland outside San Diego, Carlson introduced his new battalion to *gung ho*. Decisions were reached via consensus. Officers and men ate and slept together, suffered through the same rigorous training, would fight side by side. Each man would understand his team's objectives and his specific role in achieving them. The Raiders sang songs together and discussed what kind of world they wanted after the war. They also lived outside, hiked thirty or more miles a day, became experts in hand-to-hand combat, and learned to move fast, with little equipment. Then they shipped to Hawaii, where 220 of "Carlson's Raiders" boarded the submarines *Nautilus* and *Argonaut* for the nine-day voyage to Butaritari.

Called Makin Island at the time, it was a fishhook-shaped rib of coral eight miles long and in places just 300 yards wide, at the southern tip of an atoll in the Gilbert Islands, halfway between Hawaii and Australia. A few hundred South Pacific Islanders shared its coconut groves, lagoons, and white-sand beaches with a small Japanese garrison and seaplane depot. Carlson's orders: Wipe out the garrison, creating a stink that would shift Japan's attention from Guadalcanal, a thousand miles to the southwest, where marines had landed days before. Before dawn on August 17, 1942, the subs surfaced and the Raiders started for shore on a flotilla of rubber rafts.

Five years later, Republic Pictures released a movie about the raid called *Gung Ho!* in honor of Carlson's introduction of the phrase to the American vernacular. The major, played by Randolph Scott, leads his men onto the beach and into a fierce tussle that they win through self-sacrifice and pluck. He outwits the enemy holdouts by painting the Stars and Stripes on a rooftop, prompting Japanese planes to bomb and strafe their own people. Finally, just before leading an orderly withdrawal back to the subs, he oversees the burial of the Raider dead; the camera pans across a cemetery of neat graves topped with makeshift crosses.

The movie fudged a bit on the facts. In reality, Carlson's plans fell apart in the assault's opening minutes: Strong currents and surf slowed the rafts, which landed out of sequence and far from the landmarks the

Raiders needed to orient themselves. One marine accidentally set off his rifle on the beach. Alerted, the Japanese put up a hell of a fight, bogging down the American advance across the island's middle. Lucky for Carlson, the defenders launched two banzai charges; Raider machine guns cut them down.

At that point the raid, just two hours old, had accomplished its aim; the garrison was down to a handful of men. Carlson didn't know this, however, and for the rest of the day Raider teams probed the palms, dodging occasional attacks by Japanese planes and destroying two large flying boats that landed in Makin's central lagoon. At dusk he ordered his force back to the rubber rafts as planned, leaving twenty Raiders behind to cover their withdrawal. And here's where things went really wrong. The surf had come up, and in its pounding grip rafts flipped and swamped; some turned turtle eight, even ten, times before reaching the subs, and the majority didn't get that far — about 120 men, including Carlson and Roosevelt, wound up marooned on the beach as night fell, most of them minus rifles they'd lost in the drink. In the wee hours a small Japanese patrol stumbled on the stranded men, wounding a Raider in the process. Carlson was sure this signaled that a large enemy force remained on Makin and that it was only a matter of time before it attacked his defenseless marines. So, citing the welfare of the wounded and the president's son, he surrendered. He sent a note saying so to the Japanese leadership, but again got a dose of good luck: The Japanese soldier carrying the message was killed by other Raiders before he could reach his superiors.

The next day, Carlson and the still-stranded marines, now realizing they faced almost zero opposition, blew up the island's Japanese fortifications and dragged their boats through the jungle to the placid lagoon, and at nightfall they made it to the waiting *Nautilus* and *Argonaut*. Or most of them did: One boatload was somehow misplaced, as were a few other marines. In all, eighteen Raiders were listed as killed in action, another twelve as missing. Nine of the latter surrendered in late April to the reinforced Japanese, who beheaded them on another Pacific island, Kwajalein, that October.

In 1948, a team from the U.S. Army's Graves Registration Service arrived on Butaritari in search of the unaccounted-for Americans. It found no little graveyard, no crosses of lashed tree limbs, because unlike their movie counterparts the real marines had not buried their dead; they'd paid the island's natives to do it and weren't around when the task was carried out.

Locals led the Graves Registration team to an area near the southwest end of an airbase built by U.S. forces a year after the raid, but the team's test pits uncovered no trace of the lost. They reached a depressing conclusion: So much earth had been turned in wartime bombings and construction projects that the graves were likely destroyed. The missing Raiders were deemed unrecoverable.

Decades passed, during which the raid faded to historical footnote. The men of the Second Raider Battalion, their exploits relegated to a paragraph or two in World War II histories, entered old age. Then, in the nineties, word started going around about CILHI's successes in Southeast Asia. The Raiders remained an organized bunch, and they applied pressure on the Pentagon to reopen the case of their missing comrades.

In August 1998, fifty years after the initial search, two CILHI staffers bound from Vietnam to Hawaii were diverted to the Gilbert Islands by bad weather. They interviewed four islanders who provided some pointers on where the missing marines might be — solid enough information that the lab dispatched a recovery team for another look the following May. The team was led to two likely burial sites by island natives, and spent sixteen days digging both. Like the 1948 searchers, they found nothing. They reluctantly packed up but recommended that CILHI return.

Six months later, in November 1999, Posey was part of a recovery team scheduled for a month-long dig in Vietnam when, in the weeks before, a disastrous monsoon flooded his site. The lab instead flew his team to Butaritari. The anthro was Bradley L. Sturm, a balding, goateed, serious veteran of twenty CILHI missions all over the planet.

Sturm interviewed several islanders, learning that one of their neighbors, Bureimoa Tokarei, had helped collect and bury the dead Raiders in 1942. Bureimoa, a teenager during the war, now stooped and gray-headed, led the team to where he believed the mass grave lay. It was near the end of an old cart path that ran across the island's narrow middle, from the lagoon to the Pacific. Bureimoa's father had owned a well just off the cart path's midpoint, and as a youngster, Bureimoa had traveled the path regularly. He was sure that the grave lay near the path's intersection with a road that paralleled the lagoon.

The spot he selected lay between the May dig sites; Sturm found the concrete survey markers his predecessor had left behind, used them to resurvey the area, and staked out a large grid around the new target. The sandy earth within its boundaries included property owned by several islanders, as well as their houses, gardens, pig wallows, and a stand of mature trees. To simply dig it all up didn't make much sense, so Sturm broke out a cesium magnetometer, a ground-penetrating device that detects buried metal and soil disturbances. The machine was hooked to a computer that printed out its "hits," and before long it spat out pictures indicating that debris lay under portions of the grid. The team dug until they hit water, about five and a half feet down. Aside from a few pieces of stray metal, none of them identifiable as belonging to the Raiders, they found nothing.

A conservative scientist might have concluded, at this point, that the visitors in 1948 had been right and that the burial site had been lost to the profound change that Butaritari had undergone during and after World War II. The Graves Registration team had pretty good witness testimony, after all — most of the island's native population survived the war, and despite its collective recollection of the gravesite's location, the team hadn't found squat.

Sturm wasn't ready to give up, however. He knew that the island's beaches had migrated westward, that the lagoon now met land sixty feet to the west of where it had in 1942. He could see that the road paralleling the beach — the road near which his team now excavated — had been moved westward over the years, as well. Running alongside it were vestiges of its predecessor, a route that had once clung to the water's edge, but had been abandoned as the lagoon retreated. The anthropologist wondered whether Bureimoa might be confused by the island's evolution — he might, for instance, be certain that the grave lay near the cart path's intersection with the beach road, but might be using the modern beach road as his point of reference, rather than one of the roads it replaced. The key to finding the grave, he decided, lay in refiguring the place to the way it had been nearly sixty years before.

Bureimoa was not much in the mood for another interview. He told Sturm he'd already shared all he knew on the subject. Sturm begged and cajoled him into helping one more time, and the pair returned to the one terrain feature the anthro was reasonably certain had never moved — the water well. From there, they navigated through the jungle, following the cart path's alignment. Stretches of the long-neglected path had vanished with time. Trees had sprouted from its bed. They had to use a compass.

In time they reached the remains of an intersection — not the modern beach road, nor the old one still visible near it, but the cart path's meeting with a third, even older route that once skirted the lagoon. Its surface was all but invisible beneath several inches of sandy humus. Sturm realized he may have found what he was looking for, handed Bureimoa a pin flag, and asked him to mark the intersection. The old man shuffled forward and planted the flag. They stared at it for a moment, and Bureimoa changed his mind. "No," he said. "This is not the intersection." He moved it five feet. "That," he announced, "is the intersection!"

"Do you think you can put this pin flag where the grave might be?"

Yes, Bureimoa said. He took a flag from Sturm and, with an energetic pace, walked a little over thirty yards to the spot. "It's right here," he said. The new site lay partly beneath the second of the three beach roads. Sturm staked out a new grid of long, meter-wide rectangles and instructed the team to dig out every other one, creating a series of parallel trenches separated by walls of equal width. Four crews began digging on December 6, 1999. Bureimoa watched from a thatched hut nearby. As the digging went on, Sturm asked him what he thought.

"What day is it?" Bureimoa asked.

"December the sixth."

Bureimoa was lying on a palm-leaf mat, his chin propped on his hands. "I think," he said calmly, "that you will find the marines on December the eighth."

Two days later, the team struck the edge of a grave.

The islanders of Butaritari bury their dead with time-honored ritual, placing bodies in the ground with their heads pointing to the east. As Randy Posey and his team pulled sand away from the remains in this grave, they found a skull aimed in that direction. Sturm quickly established that the cranium's owner had been non-Caucasian. As the team emptied the hole, they found no ammo, no weapons, nothing that established the grave as military. Posey recalls thinking: "Damn. We're in a local burial ground."

The next day, Sturm put his diggers to work on the second beach road, which had been laid on a three-foot bed of densely packed coral sand. They hacked through it with picks, then switched to flat-nosed shovels to skim away thin layers of earth below. Another skull appeared. Some of its teeth had fillings.

It was an electrifying moment. South Pacific islanders may enjoy relatively languid, worriless lives, but until recently, they've not received comprehensive dental care. "We kept digging and digging," Posey says, "and we hit a steel pot" — a helmet, American, of World War II vintage. Another skull was still inside it. One trench away, the diggers found foot bones and another helmet.

They worked until dark and were back digging at first light. By day's end on December 11, they'd exposed the entire grave. Shielded by the road above, filled with a benign mix of shell and pulverized coral, it had preserved the Raiders beyond Sturm's wildest expectations — and those of anyone else at CILHI, too. Twelve virtually complete skeletons could be seen from the hole's edge, and they lay just as they'd been thrown in 1942. Many still wore their helmets. The soles and lace-hole grommets of their rotted combat boots lay at their feet. M-1 Garand rifles lay beside them. Live grenades, World War II "pineapples" once hooked to the marines' now-decayed web harnesses, were scattered among the bones. "I'd never seen nuthin like that in my life," Posey says. "Each one of them still had their three-pack of grenades on, so every time we hit one we had to stop, call the EOD guy. He'd go do his thing, then we'd go back again.

"Found some logs of wood, like they tried to burn them, but they were in a hurry, so they didn't get around to it. We got boots. We found coins, money. I was so happy to be there. And Brad is so good: He would make us go so slow, so carefully, so we wouldn't disturb anything. I went and took somebody's kitchen broom, and sawed the bristles off, and we made whiskbrooms. Now I take whiskbrooms wherever I go."

Beneath the twelve skeletons lay another eight, equally preserved — in all, the remains of nineteen of Carlson's Raiders, along with that of a local apparently killed at about the same time. Sturm and his team's medic moved around the grave, removing each skeleton as it was exposed, striving to keep the bones from mingling. Some helmets had fused to the skulls; Sturm decided to wait until he was back in Hawaii to separate them. They found canteens, wire cutters, compasses. They found a hand-held radio and bandage packets. They found gas mask eyepieces, a pile of ammo for M-1s and Thompson submachine guns, and the dog tags of eleven Raiders listed as killed in action, ten still on chains looped around their necks.

On December 16, after eleven twelve-hour days in the equatorial heat, Sturm closed the site. The Marine Corps dispatched a C-130 Hercules cargo plane from Okinawa to fly its long-lost Raiders to Hawaii. After a couple of low passes over the airport's iffy-looking coral runway, the plane landed, and off stepped a marine color guard. Sturm and Bureimoa watched the four march past, resplendent in their dress blues, their Corps and American flags snapping in the breeze. And to Sturm's shock, Bureimoa, who evidently had not heard it since his boyhood, started singing the Marine Corps hymn.

Sturm's written report on the mission included a tantalizing afterthought: It could be that the Graves Registration team had missed finding the remains for the same reason that he initially had missed them — the roads had moved. In 1948, the original beach road — the one Sturm and Bureimoa discovered while walking in the woods — had been supplanted by the second road, built during the war. That road had been laid directly over the graves. The first search team may have parked their Jeeps right on top of their quarry.

2

IF RE-1 FINDS BONE, Gwen Haugen will carefully bag each fragment, recording the exact location of the find in the grid on the
Ziploc's exterior, and place the collected remains in a padded
briefcase. The case will not leave her safekeeping; she will either
have it in her possession, or locked in one of her three footlockers, for
the remainder of the JFA. When she turns it over to representatives of
the Laotian central government, she will have had legal custody of the
remains — which the lab terms "possible ossified material," rather than
bone — without break.

She will have carefully inventoried every bit of bone or tooth or flesh
she hands over, to ensure that recovered remains are not supplemented
by our Laotian hosts. A few weeks from now, after examining the team's
finds and concurring that they appear related to the loss of American
servicemen, the Laotians will turn the remains back over. They will be
packed in metal transfer cases, shrouded with the Stars and Stripes, and
placed aboard an air force cargo jet. The plane will fly first to Guam,
where, assuming the remains are, in fact, American, they will reach U.S.
soil for the first time in more than thirty years. From there the jet will
fly on to Hawaii. A ceremony of flags and salutes will welcome Jack
Barker, John Dugan, Billy Dillender, and John Chubb home.

From the airfield, the transfer cases will be driven to a single-story office building of buff-colored brick, far from the airplanes on static display and the buildings pocked and chipped by the Japanese attack on
Pearl Harbor that are Hickam Air Force Base's usual tourist destina-

tions. CILHI's polished-tile foyer, lined with offices and conference rooms and conference rooms and guarded by an inquisitive sergeant, is as unassuming as its exterior; it could be that of any small military command, anywhere in the world.

The laboratory from which the outfit takes its name is invisible behind a set of heavy doors. Pass through them, travel the length of a wide hallway, and the lab looms on the left, a brightly lit room the size of two high school classrooms combined, and separated from the hallway by floor-to-ceiling glass and a cipher-locked door. Along one edge, CILHI's anthropologists keep small offices. Along the back wall runs a workbench of microscopes and pressurized hoods, where evidence can be examined free of airborne contaminants. In the room's center are the tables.

When I visited the lab, in July 2000, the Makin Raiders lay there, nineteen complete, or almost complete, skeletons. They were arranged on their backs, their eyeless sockets staring at the ceiling, their ribs arrayed on either side of their vertebrae. The tiny bones of their wrists and ankles, fingers and toes had been painstakingly positioned at the ends of their limbs. They had been laid out as a machine's torn-down components might be, awaiting reassembly.

Some of the skeletons were stained dark by their decades underground. Some bore crusty, red-brown traces of rust, relics of helmet carefully pried from bone. Some were missing pieces — a collarbone here, a lower arm bone there, or fingers, or parts of a foot. Others were extraordinarily pristine, so complete and clean and seemingly untraumatized by their long burial that they'd not have been out of place in a biology class.

Sabrina Buck, one of the lab's anthropologists, was hunched over a Raider skull, using calipers to measure its particulars — the size and shape of its plates, the breadth of the bone at the base of its nose, the arc and prominence of its brow ridges, the angle of its lower jaw. She recorded each measurement, then straightened up and sighed. "This is strange," Buck told me, "because everything seems a little torqued. Parts of the skull go one way, and parts seem off a bit, pointing another." She picked up the skull and held it so that I looked down on its crown. I could see what she meant: Portions of the skull's front, the bones of its face, were twisted slightly to the left.

"What does that mean?" I asked her.

"Well," she said, "it means that either the skull was torqued by the pressure of the soil on top of it, or this was a pretty weird-looking guy."

If RE-1 finds bone, it will be delivered to CILHI's custody and stored in a numbered box in an alcove crowded with high shelves, alongside other boxes containing remains recovered from digs in Southeast Asia and Korea, in the islands of the South Pacific, in Africa and Europe, and the Russian Far East. Weeks, months, even a year or more may pass before Case 1731 moves to the head of the queue of bone awaiting analysis. Then, the box will be pulled from the evidence locker and carried to an examining table.

It won't be Haugen who analyzes its contents. The lab's anthros conduct blind "bone work" — the remains they examine in Hawaii are never associated with a recovery they have led, and they take pains to remain as ignorant of a case's details as they possibly can. Thus Sabrina Buck, along with several other anthros who weren't present when Brad Sturm unearthed the Raiders, performed the anthropological analysis of the island's dead.

The anthro assigned 1731 will first inventory the material Haugen has earmarked for study, then examine each fragment — under the microscope, if necessary — to ensure that it is, in fact, bone and that the bone is human. After that, he or she will measure each piece and find and record its distinguishing characteristics, aiming to describe, as completely as possible, the person to whom the bones and teeth once belonged. The anthro's descriptions are bundled with other evidence, and it's up to the lab's scientific director to decide whether it's sufficiently consistent with what's known of a missing soldier to add up to an identification.

But those descriptions can be remarkably detailed, in some cases so much so as to leave little doubt of identity. As I watched, Buck left the skull to examine the skeleton's legs. From the size of certain bones — in particular, the thigh bone, or femur, and the shin bone, or tibia — she could extrapolate the height of the deceased; even if such "long bones" are fractured, they can sometimes be reassembled to the degree necessary to estimate their complete size. The formula for determining height from these bones is not exact, but it is accurate to within a couple of inches. An anthro would be able to easily distinguish a femur of five-foot-five Jack Barker from that of six-foot-two Billy Dillender; it would be far more difficult to distinguish Barker's bones from those of five-foot-six John Dugan.

While Buck wielded her calipers, another anthropologist showed me an old black-and-white photograph of a strapping young marine, the man whose bones were now undergoing analysis. His smiling, square-jawed face looked well proportioned and absent the twisting suggested by the remains on the table before me. Even so, Buck likely would be able to use her measurements to determine his race; the skulls of whites, blacks, and Asians manifest subtle but persistent distinctions, especially around the bridge of the nose and the orbits of the eyes. A skeleton like-wise bears clues to its sex aside from its pelvis, which is an immediate giveaway. Men typically have greater muscle mass than women, and the bony knobs to which their muscles are anchored tend to be more pronounced. The male mastoid process, the bulge in the skull behind each ear, is usually larger than its female counterpart. Women's long bones are smoother, more refined-looking. Their eye orbits are sharper-edged.

An anthro can estimate age from even a modest collection of re-mains, for some of our bones don't fully form until we reach particular stages of life. The plates of the skull are slow to stitch. Five vertebrae that make up the sacrum, a triangular structure at the junction of pelvis and spine, fuse into a solid mass in adulthood. Our collarbones and the bones around our knees change. Teeth do, too — not only with wear but also in the size and shape of their roots.

Even without such telltale parts of the body represented, our skele-tons speak to our age at death. Our bones develop until we're in our early twenties and afterwards begin to slowly deteriorate; in cross-sec-tion, old bone appears a lacework of air pockets, ravaged by a decline in density that occurs at a predictable rate. Estimating age lies in gauging the degree of deterioration.

Buck examined the skeleton for scars, as well. If an anthro finds that a humerus, say, bears the telltale knitting where an old break has healed, and a missing man's medical record indicates he broke his upper arm as a teenager, the lab can further narrow its field of possible matches. If a soldier suffered rickets as a child, or had a bad hip, or arthritis, it will be revealed in his bones. And so will other, quirkier pieces of his past: A right-handed baseball pitcher will have particularly well-developed muscles in his right arm and can be expected to have unusually pronounced attachment points on the bones there. "You could spend a month," Buck told me, as she continued her measurements, "on one skeleton."

Compelling though the evidence gleaned from bone work might be, the lab cannot make a positive identification strictly on the basis of femurs and skulls. A far more surefire means of assigning a dead man's name to a set of remains is to look at his teeth.

CILHI has a staff of odontologists who perform the painstaking detail work of matching dental records and teeth recovered from the field. A tooth reveals much about a person's age, sex, and race — the chewing surfaces of Vietnamese teeth, for instance, are often cupped by the rice consumed there, which is a much tougher variety than we typically eat in the West. Dental restorations — fillings, caps, and the like — reveal even more. Their knobs and bulges, their fingers of gold or silver or platinum, are as unique as fingerprints; if an old dental X-ray of a filling in a missing man's medical records overlays precisely with an X-ray of a recovered tooth, the lab has struck forensic gold. Actually, not even the tooth is needed — the restoration alone will do.

Unfortunately, making such matches isn't as easy as it sounds. The records of those who died in World War II and Korea are often incomplete by modern standards; dental X-rays weren't the routine in the forties and fifties that they are today. The lab's dentists may find themselves with a fine set of recovered teeth, studded with restorations, but with no paperwork against which to compare them.

Vietnam-era remains pose their own brand of vexation. Not only is the soil said to be more acidic in parts of Southeast Asia, but most of those who remain unaccounted for there died aboard aircraft, and an air crash wreaks almost unimaginable havoc on a human body. In jets, the forces involved don't break bones, so much as pulverize them. Consider that in 1996, a ValuJet DC-9 nosed into the Florida Everglades with 110 people aboard. Rescuers and recovery crews reached the site within hours. Even so, the remains of only 57 people aboard the plane were identified.

A military jet crash poses even greater challenges than that of an airliner. Take the case of an F-4 Phantom shot down over Vietnam while cruising at Mach 1: Plane and pilot strike the ground while traveling at hundreds of miles per hour. The heaviest components of the jet, its engines, slam forward into the cockpit, compressing its contents. Fuel in the plane's tanks explodes. Fire consumes the wreckage. Bombs strapped to the aircraft detonate in the crash or "cook off" in the fire.

Bottom line: Not much is left of the pilot, and what little remains is in tiny pieces. Broken bone exposes more surface area to decay, and because it's light, is far more susceptible to the effects of erosion in a place that each year is swept by monsoonal rains, mudslides, floods.

Evidence of the challenge in Southeast Asia lay at the foot of the table on which Buck examined the marine's sturdy, near-complete skeleton: a cone of bone chips, perhaps ten inches wide and six high, each piece no bigger than a cigarette filter. This was all that remained of two men who'd died aboard a fighter in Vietnam.

The 1731 crash wasn't as hard as the ValuJet DC-9's, nor the hypothetical F-4's, nor that which killed the men reduced to a small pile on Buck's examining table; it was played out at much lower speeds, after all. But even if they weren't blown to bits in the shootdown, the four men aboard the Huey were broken by their chopper's fall to earth. Once reduced to bones, they'd have been in pieces. And those pieces would have fallen prey to decomposition — to the effects of climate and insects and the changing shape of the land itself. If RE-1 finds their remains, they won't be in anything like the shape of the marine Raiders recovered on Butaritari.

For years, the lab's chief compensation for the dearth of bone it sometimes found in Southeast Asian sites was deductive reasoning. A CILHI team might be dispatched to the site of a jet that went down with two men aboard, for instance, and might recover a small amount of bone there, too little to analyze for height, or sex, or race; but it might also find, buried in the impact crater, pieces of the aircraft's canopy, chunks of seat, fragments of revolver, and shards of helmet. It might find a burned but recognizable length of oxygen hose, a zipper pull. And it might find, at the crater's deepest point, the wreckage of the jet's nose cannon, and on it a data plate bearing a serial number.

Such an array of artifacts would enable the lab to identify the remains with confidence: The joint task force's analysts would trace the serial number and correlate the wreckage with a particular aircraft. The records of that aircraft would yield the names of the men aboard it when it hit the ground. The canopy and life support pulled from the hole would tell the lab that neither man aboard the jet ejected. The presence of scattered bone, the depth of the crater, and the mangled state of the wreckage would signal an unsurvivable crash. The lab might consult with the Life Sciences Equipment Laboratory at Brooks Air Force Base, in San Antonio, for its analysis of the recovered bits of seat, zipper, and air hose. With a nod from LSEL's experts, who can glean as much from tiny bits of aircraft hardware as CILHI's anthros can from bone, the case could be closed.

Deduction solved many a Southeast Asian mystery through the eighties and early nineties. Still, it wasn't enough to clear the lab's tougher cases — those in which teams found crash sites picked clean of evidence and bones in such small quantity that they said nothing of the dead; CILHI's evidence locker filled with remains from such cases, rendered dormant by a paucity of wreckage, both man and man-made. That's when science presented the lab, and the families of the missing, with an unexpected gift.

Most of our cells have a basic structure in common: Their bodies are a goop called cytoplasm, in which float organelles, specialized little miniorgans, among them the nucleus and the mitochondria. The former is a cell's control center. The mitochondria are the cell's power plants, equipped to convert simple sugars into energy. Planted in both the nucleus and mitochondria is deoxyribonucleic acid, or DNA — the chains of amino acids that make us who, and how, we are.

Newspapers are filled with stories about nuclear DNA: It's the type that decides paternity cases, links rapists to their crimes, frees the wrongly convicted from prison. We pack equal parts of our mothers' and fathers' nuclear DNA; sperm and egg each contain the genetic recipe of their respective donor, and when the two get together their contents combine to give us traits of both parents. They don't mix the same way each time, which partly explains why siblings wind up different — they may contain the same genetic ingredients, but they inherit the spices of life in varying amounts and yield similar, but unique, results. Our nuclear DNA is one of a kind.

Not so the DNA in our mitochondria. As sperm and egg collide, the portion of the sperm containing the mitochondria — and thus, the father's mitochondrial DNA — breaks off. The resulting embryo, while boasting a nucleus that contains elements of both cells, contains only the egg's mitochondria; the DNA within these mitochondria never has a chance to get together with a partner.

This means we inherit an exact copy of our mothers' mitochondrial

DNA — mtDNA, for short — and that only women pass it on to their children. If you're female, your children and your daughter's children will have your mom's mtDNA, and her mom's mtDNA, just as you do; if you're male, you likewise have your mom's mtDNA, but your children will have their mother's. Regardless of your gender, if you were to trace your ancestry back through your maternal line, you'd find that you share mtDNA with a host of folks you might not consider all that close to you: Your maternal great-grandmother may have been one of a passel of female kids in her family, all of whom inherited their mtDNA from your great-great-grandmother, and all of whom passed it on to their kids, just one of whom would have been your grandmother; your great-aunts would have passed the same mtDNA on to their daughters, and they to theirs, so that you may have scores, even hundreds of distant cousins whose mitochondria contain DNA exactly like your own.

Mitochondrial DNA has another trait that sets it apart from nuclear: It's built to last. Our cells each contain a single nucleus and just one set of nuclear DNA, but around that nucleus are scads of mitochondria — the human egg is crowded with thousands of them — and in each is a little bit of Mom. After we die, our cells gradually collapse, and over time, our nuclear DNA decays to nothing. But the mitochondria are thick-walled, sturdy little things, and there are so many of them that in even ancient remains, some mtDNA survives.

Its easily traceable ancestry and its toughness make mtDNA particularly useful to archaeologists. In 1987, American researchers announced they had traced mtDNA from 147 geographically scattered subjects to a single foremother, a woman who lived 140,000 to 280,000 years ago. Every living human carries a derivative of this mitochondrial Eve's mtDNA, and everyone's mitochondrial family tree harkens to sub-Saharan Africa, where she lived.

Geneticists used mtDNA to shed more light on our ancient past in 1997, when American and German scientists announced they had extracted it from the humerus of a Neanderthal estimated to be 40,000 to 50,000 years old — a remarkable illustration of just how hardy mitochondria can be. The bone had been found along with other Neanderthal remains — a large piece of cranium, two femurs, a portion of pelvis, two bones from a right forearm, and bits of rib and shoulder blade — in a cave in Germany's Neander Valley, near Dusseldorf, in 1856. Subsequent lab analysis showed that the Neanderthals did not evolve into modern man: The specimen's mtDNA fell outside the human range, and human mtDNA carried no genetic trace of the heavy-browed and hairy proto-Europeans.

Mitochondrial DNA earned even bigger headlines when it helped crack a more modern mystery. In 1991, close to a thousand bone fragments were exhumed from a shallow grave near Ekaterinburg, a town in Russia's Ural Mountains where, seventy-three years before, Bolsheviks had executed the country's last royal family. Anthropologists were able to group the bones into nine sets of remains, four male and five female, and tentatively identified them as those of Tsar Nicholas II; his wife, the Tsarina Alexandra; three of their five children; the family's doctor; and three servants. Investigators were sure that the tsar's son Alexei was one of the two missing kids, but couldn't agree on the other; one team of scientists figured it was daughter Marie, another that it was daughter Anastasia.

The mere possibility that Anastasia was absent from the grave was intriguing, for rumors of her survival had started to circulate within days of the executions. Her fate had ballooned into a global controversy in the early twenties, when a young woman who'd been committed to a Berlin mental institution, and who bore an uncanny resemblance to the slain royals, claimed that she was the grand duchess. A few details of her story didn't add up — she couldn't speak Russian, for instance — but she never backed off the claim, and when she died in 1984, opinion was split on whether she was the real deal.

In 1992, the remains were carried to Britain, where nuclear and mtDNA analysis revealed that five of the bodies were related and that three were female siblings. In addition, mtDNA extracted from bones believed those of Alexandra matched a sample donated by England's Prince Philip, the tsarina's grandnephew. Two years later, the grave of Nicholas's brother, Grand Duke Georgij Romanov, was opened in St. Petersburg, and samples of his bone were collected. Georgij had died of tuberculosis in 1899; an mtDNA analysis found his bones matched those of the late tsar. Eighty years to the day after their murder, the Romanovs were reburied with great pomp.

Still remaining was the mystery of whether the supposed Anastasia was authentic. Anna Anderson, as she was known for most of her life, had been cremated after her death, but a hospital in Charlottesville, Virginia, had a specimen of her intestine, removed during an operation she'd undergone in 1979. DNA analysis of the tissue proved beyond a doubt that she was not related to the tsar or his family. Further tests showed that, as her skeptics had claimed, she was Franziska Schanz-kowska, born near the German-Polish border in 1896, and a factory worker before her self-promotion to the ruling class.

The laboratory technique at the heart of mtDNA analysis wasn't developed until 1981; the Defense Department and the FBI didn't add it to their forensic arsenals until the mid-nineties. RE-1 is pursuing Case 1731 just five years after the Pentagon gave military pathologists the OK to use it routinely. It is a controversial tool in identifications, and not just because it's new. Its chief strength — that bones can be linked to anyone in the deceased's maternal line — is also its greatest limitation.

Everyone on the planet would share identical mtDNA if not for slight changes to our mitochondrial sequences that occur every few hundred years. Scientists have found that peoples from different parts of the world display bundles of mutations stereotypical of their region and have used those sequence quirks to trace the waves of migration that took primitive man from Africa.

Even with those mutations, however, seemingly unrelated people can share a particular sequence of mtDNA, and some sequences occur with enough frequency that a match, on its own, cannot be said to constitute an identification. Having one of those common sequences isn't quite akin to having the surname "Smith," but there have been cases in which CILHI has run across two or more people in the same case with the same sequence. Mitochondrial DNA is also expensive, difficult, and time-consuming to sequence, far more so than nuclear DNA.

Still, the Defense Department has found mtDNA typing a boon in picking through multiple remains. Should RE-1 find bone, it may well be commingled, the remains of the Huey's four occupants dumped in a common grave or otherwise mixed. If Barker, Dugan, Dillender, and Chubb had been found ten years ago, they might well have been buried as "group remains," the small pieces of one man inseparable from those of his colleagues. Today, the lab has a weapon to sort them out, at least partly — assuming the four have different sequences.

Assuming, too, that RE-1 recovers enough of them. An mtDNA analysis requires roughly five grams of bone, or a tooth in decent condition, from each man. That isn't much — five grams is less than a fifth of an ounce — but it can be surprisingly difficult, at the scene of an air crash, to find pieces large enough to satisfy the needs of the process.

CILHI does not perform the analysis itself. Any bone recovered by RE-1 will be studied by the lab's anthropologists, and any teeth by its odontologists, and — if it's deemed worthy of a genetic workup — at least five grams will be cut from each set of bones and shipped to the Armed Forces DNA Identification Laboratory.

AFDIL, a branch of the Armed Forces Institute of Pathology, occupies a 30,000-square-foot building in Rockville, Maryland, in the D.C. suburbs, and has grown in very few years into one of the world's most respected centers of genetic typing. When the Russians sought expertise in type-matching Nicholas II's bones with those of his consumptive brother, they came to AFDIL, and the lab has tackled a host of other, high-profile cases: helping CILHI identify the Vietnam Unknown Soldier as air force first lieutenant Michael Blassie, in 1998; putting names to the eighty-one bodies pulled from the Branch Davidian compound in Waco, Texas, in 1993; identifying the occupants of Commerce Secretary Ron Brown's downed jet in Croatia, and assisting the National Transportation Safety Board in identifying the 230 passengers and crew of TWA Flight 800, which crashed into the Atlantic off Long Island, New York, both cases in 1996; helping the NTSB in its investigation of the still-unresolved crash of USAir Flight 427 near Pittsburgh in 1994; helping the State Department identify the victims of the 1998 terrorist bombing of the U.S. Embassy in Nairobi, Kenya; and, in 1997, identifying air force captain Craig Button, whose A-10 Thunderbolt veered off course into a mountainside in the Colorado Rockies.

The Rockville lab begins its work by cleaning the samples — an important step, for everyone who has handled the bone may have left his or her own DNA on its surface. The bone is sanded, then a portion is ground into a fine powder and mixed with a chemical solution that releases mtDNA from the mitochondria. Other chemicals are added to the resulting solution, which split the DNA from any surrounding molecules. The mix is then spun in a centrifuge, which leaves the DNA floating at the top. This top layer of the solution is removed, filtered, and concentrated.

Think of the mtDNA molecule as a very long Mardi Gras necklace, its 16,569 beads made of four different colors of plastic — red, yellow, blue, green. Everybody's beads are more similar than they are different; vast stretches of every necklace have identical beads arranged in identical sequence. But in two sections — one of them 342 beads long, the other 268 — the color sequence differs markedly from necklace to necklace. It's the 610 beads in these "hypervariable regions" that are compared in mtDNA analysis. One stretch of mine might have three red beads followed by a yellow, then a green, then two blue, while the corresponding bit of your necklace might comprise three yellow, two green, a blue, and a red.

Before any comparison can occur, AFDIL's analysts must ensure that they have enough material with which to work. When pulled from old bones, mtDNA is often degraded, its chain of amino acids busted into pieces. A process called the polymerase chain reaction enables a scientist to replicate strands of DNA millions of times so that the overlapping segments of the busted strands can be identified and the pieces stitched together, in much the same way that you can overlap several photographic snapshots to form a single panoramic image.

With a goodly amount of mtDNA now on hand, the lab again purifies the sample, then prepares it for sequencing, in which it's put through a chemical wringer. The outcome is a chromatogram, a colored graph that reveals the sequence of beads in the necklace. After several runs through the process have satisfied the analysts that they have an accurate picture of the sample's mtDNA, it's compared with a reference sample — the "Anderson reference," the first complete mtDNA sequence, named for the British scientist who extracted it in 1981. Its differences from this reference are recorded and are compared with the samples collected from known donors — in CILHI cases, the maternal relatives of the unaccounted-for. If their differences from the Anderson reference sequence match at every bead, the samples are considered to have "sequence concordance," and a lost soldier takes a step on his long journey home.

Or so newspapers will say when they write of a case's resolution. Thirty-odd years after he was lost on such-and-such a mission, the stories will say, Sergeant So-and-so is finally coming home.

It's journalistic hyperbole. What actually makes its way into an American grave, after decades in the jungle, might fit into an aspirin bottle; it is in only the most abstract of senses the young man who left home in the sixties or seventies, bound for Vietnam. These are not soldiers that CILHI excavates from the Southeast Asian soil; they are fossils, no more, of lives and personalities and intersections on the great web of human relationships.

Johnie Webb, who commanded CILHI for years and, since his army retirement, has continued to work for the lab as its number two, recalls sending one soldier's scant remains home to his family, only to be confronted by the man's father. I want my son back, the man told Webb. You've sent me a handful of bones.

It was an understandable reaction: A family waiting years for some physical proof that its loved one is dead expects more than bone fragments, a few teeth. Eventually, the soldier's father came to understand that the lab's work was a triumph, that it was remarkable a team had found anything of his son at all, and he sent Webb a POW/MIA bracelet, etched with his son's name, that he'd worn for years, and which Webb keeps on his desk today.

Still, that father was right. Those bones weren't his son.

Lives don't fit into Ziplocs.

3

T HIS IS WHAT BONES won't say about Jack Barker: that he loved to read, and that he loved, most of all, to read to his boys, even thousands of miles from home; Dee would mail him children's books, and he'd sit in his hooch and read them aloud into his tape recorder and ship the tapes home.

Nor that he desperately missed his family. "Oh honey, I'm so very homesick," he wrote to Dee a month before he died, after speaking with his four-year-old son by satellite telephone. "Talking with Bryan sure did tug at my heart. You just cannot imagine how proud I was, and yet how much those few words tore at me to go home."

"I get lonesome, homesick, worried, lovesick and depressed," he wrote a month earlier. "The thing that keeps me going is love, my love for you and the boys and your love for me."

On Christmas Day, he was "so very lonesome" that he opened the family's gifts "with no one else around so no one could see the tears in my eyes." And on March 1, as momentum turned in Laos, he wrote Dee that they had only sixty-one days remaining before they'd "bed down together" during his mid-tour week off. "For sure, that will be the best days and nights I have had for a long, long time," he wrote. "Oh, the wicked thoughts that come to mind."

Then the letters stopped. Dee was reading one night, the kids in bed, when a knock came on the door. Two men in army uniforms stood on the front stoop. "Mrs. Barker?" one asked, and then he read a prepared statement saying her husband was missing in Laos, that he'd been shot down and that the army had had no contact with the major or his crew since. The men insisted that didn't necessarily mean anything — that he could well be alive in the jungle, hiding from the North Vietnamese, waiting for a chance to show himself to rescuers. The wives of other MIAs started dropping in the next day, and the wives of confirmed POWs and army chaplains, and all told her the same thing: to have faith, that he might still be alive, that the army was going back in after him.

Two thousand miles to the east, Ann Dillender sensed something was wrong before the phone call: Billy had stopped writing, which wasn't like him, and her letters had started coming back unopened. Then the army telephoned to say her son was missing, and sent two officers to the restaurant where she worked. A few days later, she received a telegram from Maj. Gen. Kenneth Wickham, the adjutant general. "Search is in progress," it assured the family. "You will be promptly advised when further information is received." The Dillenders hoped.

In New Jersey, John Dugan's family received a letter from the captain's battalion commander. "We regret to inform you that your son is listed as missing in action," he wrote. "Each member of this battalion, especially B Company, is disheartened by this report for John is regarded by his contemporaries and subordinates as a zealous officer and peerless leader." The balance of the letter gave the family little comfort. "On approach to the pickup zone," the officer wrote, "he and his flight came under intensive antiaircraft fire from all sides and plummeted blazing to the ground. There was an immediate attempt to rescue the crew but each approach to the crash site was thwarted by heavy enemy fire. No distress signals were received during the rescue attempt. At that time your son was reported missing. An investigation as to John's status is in progress and I want to assure you that as soon as more information is obtained I will write to you again.

"Please accept this letter as a symbol of our sincere concern. John is a brave and courageous soldier who occupies a very warm and special place in our hearts. Our thoughts are with you and we offer our heartfelt prayers during this time of great concern."

The same day the battalion CO wrote that letter, Jack Barker's replacement wrote to the Chubbs that their son, too, was missing. "When this was made known to the company, it brought an immediate feeling of gloom to each of us," his letter read. "John is the epitome of a courageous and outstanding soldier, as evidenced by both his cheerful attitude and dauntless determination in the face of all obstacles. His example is an inspiration to every member of his unit.

"Although with us only a short while, John's presence here has been during a most demanding time and we have quickly established a strong and special feeling of comradeship with him."

Dee Barker endured an agonizing cycle of hope and doubt. She'd wake sure Jack was dead; an hour later, she'd allow herself to hope he might be alive; just a minute after that, she'd decide that no, he had to be dead. She remembered something he'd told her before he left for Vietnam. "Don't you ever worry about me being a POW," Jack Barker had said. "I would not be captured. I could not do it."

The plain unit, 508/516, produces little beyond shards of grenade. Most of the square's ACS comes from its north side, and as the team hoes its floor smooth, gleaming slivers of metal are visible in the walls forming its northwest corner, where it meets 508/512. The debris field, this suggests, continues toward the big crater.

That crater looms as the team's best hope. In the nine units it has laid bare to the crater's east, RE-1 has found no numbered wreckage but the piece of etched Plexiglas. It has found nothing resembling human remains. If the bones of Jack Barker and his crew are here, it seems increasingly likely they're somewhere in that muddy hole.

Late in the morning, Posey is poised to begin the team's descent into the crater. He's in the blue hole, 512/508, and all that's left to dig is the unit's southwest corner, where it dives over the lip and down the crater's side. He's surrounded by a half-dozen locals, talking in Southern singsong to them, more of a cadence call, a sea chantey, than real words: "That's right, y'all." And: "Let's keep it going, y'all." And: "Come on, y'all." And: "Workin' hard, my brother."

He didn't sweat like this in field artillery, but the payoff, which he never got from his early army days, nor the classroom, nor barbering, is adventure on almost a comic-book scale, in about as distant a place as one can find from Centerville, Mississippi.

And in many ways, it's good to be far from Centerville. Growing up, he understood that the Civil Rights Act, as it was interpreted locally, came down to a one-sentence proviso: A black man might do all right for himself, so long as he stayed in his lane. Here in Laos, hot though it is, he's in charge. People depend on him. And the setting is so strange, so unfamiliar, that to a much greater degree than is true anywhere back home, Americans are Americans. To make it even sweeter, he's doing God's work, because whatever he finds will serve as a salve to the suffering. High adventure and good deeds, in one. Doesn't get a lot better.

Except, maybe, when you have to start digging out a crater in the midday sun. Posey looks at me as I pass and mutters: "I picked a hell of a time to be in the hole."

I look at the waiting dirt. It's a wedge no more than a yard on a side, but it's pointed downslope at forty-five degrees. I look at Posey. Sweat cascades down his forehead in sheets beneath his conical hat.

"God *damn*, it's hot," he pants, leaning on his shovel. "If you see me drop, come get me." I promise I will and watch as he crabwalks down the side of the crater. "OK, y'all," he tells his workers, "let's do it."

At 2:30 P.M. on April 5, 1971, the 101st Assault Helicopter Battalion convened a Court of Inquiry at Camp Eagle to determine the status of the four men aboard the downed Huey. Army regulations required that such a panel meet within ten days of an incident in which a man vanished to review all evidence associated with the case, interview all witnesses, and recommend whether the man be presumed dead or carried on the rolls as an MIA. This court, meeting nearly a week late, consisted of the battalion CO, its XO, and the commander of Barker's sister unit, the Commancheros of Alpha Company. The three received testimony from Jon Evans and another witness to the shootdown, and Al Fischer, who'd watched 185 lift off from Khe Sanh.

The court found that all available evidence suggested that Jack Barker and his crew had been killed when their helicopter "was hit by the antiaircraft fire and the main rotor system separated from the mast. The fuselage burst into flames, fell to the ground from approximately 400 feet and continued to burn." No attempt had been made to recover their bodies, the panel wrote, because the setting was "extremely hostile." The court adjourned with the recommendation that the status of those aboard 185 be changed from "Missing in Action" to "Killed in Action, Body Not Recovered." Officers all the way up the chain of command to the Pentagon concurred in the days that followed.

In the Bravo Company compound, one of Billy Dillender's fellow crew chiefs was assigned the unhappy duty of collecting his colleague's personal effects. It didn't take him long to pack them into a duffel: They consisted of two black belts, two pairs of socks, two undershirts, three sets of khakis, one infantry braid, a polo shirt, one pair of civilian trousers, a pair of swimming trunks, a small electric fan, a "souvenir statue," an address book, two hardback books, five seven-inch reel-to-reel tapes, an empty tape reel, a Sony TC-630 Stereo Tape Player/Recorder and instruction book, one New Testament, a rosary, two razors, a broken Norelco shaver, two toothbrushes, a black shaving bag, a roll of 35mm film, two large color photographs, twenty-one snapshots, a photo album containing sixty-six pictures, a portable Panasonic radio, a deck of playing cards, two rank insignias, a penny, one book and answer sheet for an extension course, a knife, seven sets of military papers, one receipt, one newspaper clipping, and three packs of negatives.

Halfway through April, green sedans again pulled up outside four homes scattered throughout the States. "By this time, I am sure that you have been notified of the death of your son," the Kingsmen's new commander, Maj. Lynn C. Hooper, wrote Chubb's parents on May 11. "I want you to know that John's death came as a tragic shock to me and all the men who knew him."

The Kingsmen held a memorial service at Camp Eagle. They polished up four helmets, and a pair of boots for each man, and the company assembled in the compound to hear the chaplain say a few words and to watch a diamond formation of Hueys pass low overhead in salute. The Dugans held a service for John in Roselle, at a Catholic church just across the street from the family's apartment. The army suggested they have a coffin present. The family chose not to.

Dee Barker took her kids to Waycross for a service there. Tom Boland, the old county agent who'd overseen Barker's 4-H projects, delivered one of the three eulogies. "Jack left such a legacy," he told those crowded into the Hebardville Baptist Church. "In the soil of Ware County. In the Georgia 4-H Club. In the Alps of Switzerland. In the jungles of Vietnam and Laos."

In late May, the army announced that each man in the lost crew had been awarded the Purple Heart. Dugan, Dillender, and Chubb were also awarded the Silver Star, their citations noting the gallantry they'd displayed during the morning sortie and their fatal return journey to PZ Brown. Dillender's and Chubb's citations for the medal described their heroics during the rescue of Al Fischer's crew at Delta One.

A month later, Jack Barker was awarded the Distinguished Service Cross, second only to the Medal of Honor in recognizing courage under fire. Its citation read: "Major Barker's extraordinary heroism and devotion to duty, at the cost of his life, were in keeping with the highest traditions of the military service and reflect great credit upon himself, his unit, and the United States Army."

Haugen closes 512/508 and opens 512/504, which is evenly divided between level ground and the crater's steep northwest slope. The screens produce little in the way of debris — a couple of large, rusty rings of metal; bullets and bolts; hair-thin wafers of green plastic; frayed cord; swatches of rotting fabric.

And two mammoth scorpions nesting in the tangle of a bamboo stump. One of them, dead and tailless, turns up on my screen — five inches long and blue-black, bristling with coarse hairs, the armor around its carapace heavy and round like the front end of a Machine Age locomotive. Its severed tail, teardrop stinger glinting, appears in another bucketful of dirt.

The locals traipse through the jungle in flip-flops, nearly naked, not even armed with so much as bug spray, while creatures like this scuttle underfoot and other, weirder beasts watch from the shadows. In the trees around the site leap flying squirrels bigger than housecats, bristly, bad-tempered creatures with half-inch claws and bright orange teeth the size of Chiclets. The Southeast Asian tiger, smaller than its Bengal and Siberian cousins, but fearsome nonetheless, cruises the teak forests that clad the mountains just to our east.

There may well be animals out there that aren't even on the books. Parts of Savannakhet Province are so closed to outside eyes that a donkey-sized antelope called the spindlehorn managed to exist in secret until 1992, when scientists identified a specimen from Vietnam's side of the Annamite Cordillera as a new species. Its presence in Laos wasn't confirmed until 1996.

As we put away the tools, one of the 92-Mikes wonders aloud where Chubby is, and several other members of the team note they haven't seen the dog all day.

"I hate to say it," Posey says, all hushed, "but I think they ate him." Several female soldiers cry out as one.

"I think they did," the sergeant persists. "Yesterday I saw some guy carrying him around, and he looked at me and did like this." He mimes eating with a fork.

Chubby wasn't much of a meal before we fattened him up. Pondering our inadvertent complicity, I wander out of the break tent, to where Captain Reynolds is talking with several team members. "You know how much Sammy got paid for this week?" Krueger is asking. The linguist squints at the marine.

"I don't know," Reynolds says. "How much?"

"Guess."

Reynolds sighs impatiently. "Ten thousand kip."

"A little more than that," Krueger says. "Double it."

"Sammy made 20,000 kip?"

Krueger nods. A little more than two bucks.

"Well," Reynolds says, "they're paying the Lao government thirty bucks a week for each worker. Somebody's getting rich."

"It isn't the workers," Artillaga says.

Will Vientiane put that twenty-eight dollars, multiplied many times over, toward helping villages like Ban Chen, where Sammy and his neighbors live in huts with no electricity, no phone, no window glass, no clean water, no medical care? Will it take the shape of a real school, staffed by a real teacher? I think of Ambassador Done in his Lexus ball cap.

"Still," Eagmin notes, "around here, that's a lot of money." The two bucks, he means.

"Yeah," Krueger says, "he's probably gonna hit the bar tonight and say, 'Stack 'em up!'"

"I heard," Dingman drawls slowly, "that if you have 350,000 kip, you're considered a rich man."

"That's probably true," Reynolds says. "Until you spend the forty bucks." He shrugs. "Then you're poor again."

Back in the break tent, Haugen stares wordlessly at the day's finds as Conely picks through them. More of the same — tiny fragments of helicopter, most too small to identify with confidence. Nothing from the crew.

"And no bone," Haugen mutters. She is standing with her hands on her hips, her lips pursed, brow creased, looking more angry than disappointed. "I still think we're probably in the right place. I just really wish we'd found something of the guys by now."

"A lot of little pieces of visor, it looks like," Conely tells her.

"Yeah." The anthro nods. "It just doesn't look like an operational loss."

While we wait to fly back to camp, Haugen pulls Captain Somphong aside to fish for anything the locals may have passed on to him, or that he might have overheard. Perhaps it's a byproduct of needing translators for even the simplest exchanges, but rural Laotians do not often volunteer information to visiting American teams; on the contrary, they tend to parse their answers to questions carefully.

One cannot make such broad inquiries as, "Is there any aircraft wreckage lying about nearby?" It must be: Have you seen pieces of airplane here, in this particular place, near this particular river, on this mountain? Haugen's found herself exasperated, at times, by how literal they can be, and by her own failure "to ask the question in exactly the right way."

On the other hand, it's not hard to imagine that a villager might have casually mentioned something to Somphong. "Do any of them remember some Vietnamese coming and salvaging the helicopter," she asks the captain, "and taking pieces of it away?"

Somphong replies that no, none of the villagers saw such a thing.

"We're hoping to find pieces with numbers on them," she explains.

"That helmet had numbers, but . . ." He struggles for words.

"What, they washed off?"

"Yes," Somphong says. "When it was first found, it had numbers." No one thought to record them, it seems. The captain hasn't the faintest idea what the numbers were.

The autumn after the shootdown, Bill Dillender requested that the 101st Airborne Division send a representative to a long-delayed memorial service for Billy. "The last six months has been rather grim for us," he wrote. "We do not have a bone to show for our son.

"My wife is sleeping (deep with tranquilizers) as I write late at night. Many times she has seen me on parade but she needs this proper ceremony for her favorite son who will not return."

The events of March 20 destroyed Mildred Chubb. She had struggled with alcoholism beforehand, but beginning in April 1971, she plunged so deep into drink that it eventually killed her.

Joe Dugan Jr. became convinced that his brother might be alive and that his government had left him for dead behind enemy lines. Dugan's mother accepted the Court of Inquiry's findings and begged Joe Jr. to let John rest in peace. He would not. Pete Federovich visited the family and told Joe Jr. that John could not have survived the shootdown. Joe Jr. could not let it go. Nor could Dillender's brother Jim, who had dreams from which he woke sure that Billy was alive. It was a year before another dream freed him to grieve: Billy appeared before him wearing a helmet and hollering, "Help me! Help me!" Then he melted away to nothing, and Jim decided his brother wasn't coming back.

Jack Barker's mother, Nettie, had dreams, as well. She told her other children she'd seen Jack dressed in rags and working in a field, a prisoner of the North Vietnamese, and was convinced for the rest of her life that he would come home.

Dee Barker remarried, but was haunted by her children's patterns of speech, by their unconscious mannerisms and the ways they moved their eyes, by gestures that made it seem Jack had stepped from the grave.

Barker's older son, Bryan, died in a car accident at eighteen. When his remaining son, Michael, turned thirty-two — and thus outlived his father — Dee gave him a letter the major had written to him on his first birthday. It was dated November 29, 1970, by which time Barker was already commanding the Kingsmen.

"Dearest Michael," it read. "Today is your first birthday, and Daddy could not be with you. I am sorry, and I pray that it will never happen again."

PART FOUR

Pieces of the Past

∎

1

A YEAR BEFORE VENTURING to Ban Alang I spent a few days in Hue, Vietnam's old imperial capital, between trips to visit recovery teams encamped in the jungle highlands near the Lao border. The city's streets were blurs of weaving motorbikes and cyclos, Chinese-built heavy trucks and bicyclists wobbly under loads of lumber and bound swine, the air thick with diesel and motorcycle exhaust. Peddlers hawked fried meats, postcards, candy. Café owners yelled invitations.

It was easy to forget the recent past, walking through the low-rise jumble of grand old colonial government buildings and tiny, unlit shops and concrete houses mildewed and crumbling in the summer's soaking heat. Hue seemed a study in high-energy mercantilism, far more capitalist than socialist, and when I happened to mention where I was from, I'd invariably earn a smile, often a shout of "USA numbah one!"

But amid all the friendly bustle were reminders of the fighting that leveled much of the place in 1968, when North Vietnamese forces captured the Citadel, the walled imperial compound at the city center. At the foot of a downtown bridge over the Perfume River I stopped to eye an array of live songbirds for sale, and stood there a full five minutes, struggling through a conversation with the old man selling them, before I realized his cages were lined up on the roof of a low concrete pill box, its gun slit facing the road. A short walk away, bullet holes and broken concrete blemished the Citadel's old palaces. And just to the east lay a wealth of mementos: Hue's military museum.

Its entrance was guarded by a phalanx of rusting American tanks and artillery pieces. Inside, the collection consisted mostly of photographs. One depicted GIs crowded around a shirtless Vietnamese. "The U.S. soldiers are using daggers to disembowel the patriotic people in their raids," the caption read. Another showed military brass congratulating a line of schoolgirls. "In the Spring 1968 general offensive and uprising," its placard read, "11 girls from the Perfume River in Hue City defeated one U.S. battalion."

This arguable claim was matched by the caption to a third photo, this one of a North Vietnamese soldier climbing from a tunnel, AK-47 at the ready: "The soldier Pham Van Khuan, by himself, defeated three counter-ambush of one U.S. battalions, in one point for one day."

Southeast Asia is crowded with such museums; every large Vietnamese city has one, and the Laotian government maintains a couple of military exhibits in Vientiane. One room of the Lao National Museum is lined with captured M-16s, which are described with the placard: "These weapons were brought by American imperialists to kill the Lao people." A photo of a GI standing among Laotian children is captioned: "The American imperialists actively suppress and threaten the people who are patriotic toward their homeland." And outside the Lao Military Museum is a big concrete statue of a Laotian trio allied heroically against the American menace. One gold-painted figure is that of a woman wielding a scythe; beside her is a soldier with rifle hoisted in triumph; and beside him is a well-muscled representative of the proletariat, a sledgehammer over his shoulder, his left foot resting on a bomb. On the bomb is painted "USA."

The Hue museum went beyond the norm in a few disturbing respects. In a glass case next to the exit was a "blood chit," a silk handkerchief issued to American aviators that bore a short message in twelve languages: *I am a citizen of the United States of America. I do not speak your language. Misfortune forces me to seek your assistance in obtaining food, shelter and protection. Please take me to someone who will provide for my safety and see that I am returned to my people. My government will reward you.* Did a downed flier ever get the chance to put the chit to use? Who was he? What happened to him? The museum provided no answers.

Next to the blood chit was a pile of military identification cards, the Americans who once held them staring from black-and-white mug shots. Only three were positioned so that I could read them. All belonged to men whose names are now chiseled into the Vietnam Memorial in Washington. Swain, Milton T., of Carthage, Mississippi, an army spec 4 killed at age twenty-two. Bush, Mark J., of Anaheim, California, another E-4, killed by small-arms fire in June 1970. McDonnell, John T., of Fort Worth, Texas, a captain. Helicopter crash.

An even more troubling scene unfolded when I wandered past a small gift shop outside, where a skinny, middle-aged Vietnamese was selling souvenirs of Hue and the war. I was paying for one — a little lead soldier in a Soviet-style tunic, an AK slung over his shoulder — when the shopkeeper fished around behind the counter and came up with a half-dozen dirt-encrusted dog tags. He held them out to me. "Real!" he said, nodding eagerly. "Real American, from real U.S. soldier!"

A dog tag isn't a piece of gear that one gives up willingly. Generally speaking, it stays with its owner — it's personal, a talisman, sacred. To see these tags for sale alongside postcards bordered on the surreal. "Look!" the shopkeeper said. He thrust out his hand, so that the tags were inches from my nose. I took a couple, turned them over in my palm. I knew they were most likely fakes; in its haste to leave Vietnam in 1975, the United States left behind some of its stamping machines, and Vietnamese had diligently cranked out tags by the bogus thousands ever since. I'd seen a big plastic bag displayed outside the doors to CILHI's main laboratory, stuffed with 1,400 dog tags, many of them artfully gritty and bent, none of them belonging to dead or missing soldiers.

The tags I examined in Hue didn't bear the usual giveaways — misspellings, first names mistaken for last, mangled religious preferences. "Real!" the shopkeeper said again, and for an instant a thought flickered: What if he's telling the truth? What if these *are* real? What if these are exceptions to the rule?

Which was exactly what he hoped I'd think. The people who sell dog tags, real or fake, do so because they rightly figure that people will buy them. But the business has not always been a quick cash-grab; it began as an enterprise in which the intended buyers weren't gullible visitors, but American officials seeking the whereabouts of MIAs.

The people offering the tags in those early days were typically Vietnamese or Laotians who'd fled their homelands and found themselves stuck in refugee camps in Thailand. They usually offered their wares in exchange for an official favor — a good word with U.S. immigration authorities, perhaps, or cushier conditions in camp. The great majority of these transactions turned out the same way: Few of the refugees had credible stories to explain how they came by the tags. Fewer still had stories that were of any value to the U.S. government.

What they usually failed to realize — and what Americans who buy the tags today don't understand either — is that even a genuine dog tag's value is strictly sentimental unless it's accompanied by four important nuggets of information: precisely where it was found, when it was found, by whom, and under what circumstances. By itself, it's merely a piece of metal, offering no clue to the fate of the man who wore it.

Just the same, the years after the war's end saw a parade of refugees approach American officials with dog tags. The Defense Department's MIA case files are fat with examples. One of them involved John Chubb.

At long last our day off arrives. Its highlight is a morning trip to Xepon, a long Pajero ride west on Route 9. I make the transit wedged in the vehicle's back seat with three 92-Mikes. The heat is overpowering, and when we roll down the windows, the chalky dust billowing off the road swirls into the passenger compartment and into our mouths and eyes.

The Xepon Market is a dark shantytown of tiny stalls, their plywood counters loaded with cheap Chinese boom boxes, toothpaste, and mosquito netting, with canned sardines and butane lighters and umbrellas and nylon cord. Weird knock-offs abound — "Timerland" golf shirts and "Pansonic" stereos emblazoned with stickers declaring them "No. 1 Hi-Fi" — and I stroll the dirt-floor aisles among "Golden Snake" and "Crocodile" bicycles sheathed in bubble wrap, bricks of anemic Vietnamese batteries, pyramids of canned Beerlao, past fishing line and nails, malaria cures, wrenches and screwdrivers, gallon jugs of MSG, and thousands on thousands of rubber flip-flops. At the market's rear is an open-sided barn of steel girders and corrugated tin, where I find more stalls crowded with fresh chilies, bananas, jackfruit and lemon grass, coconuts and fried meats, eggs from all manner of bird.

Beyond, there's little to the town. I leave the market's shade and stroll past ducks and goats listless in the heat, and greasy, stinking puddles at Route 9's ragged edge, as a government water truck rumbles by, burping black smoke and trailing a cloud of grit. From the highway's shoulder, squinting against the dust and midday brightness, I can make out a few stilted hooches and a small, concrete building, low-slung and empty. A newer, grander-looking structure, perhaps a government office, a little farther off. That's about it. This is what thousands of people died trying to seize, not too terribly long ago, and what thousands more died trying to defend. This place.

Besides the water truck growling off into the distance, the road is empty in both directions. I cross the blacktop, conscious of the temperature, which is every bit of 105 degrees. It's so hot that I might mistake what now looms through the dust for a mirage. At the road's edge is a clump of scraggly trees, beneath which is a bench sheltered by a little roof. It looks like a bus stop. Supporting two corners of its roof are the empty shells of unexploded bombs. Painted in faded white on one of them is "USA," and a crude skull and crossbones.

I take a few pictures and turn to cross back to the market, and with a start find Captain Somphong standing a foot behind me. "So, you are getting pictures of the bombs?" he asks. He lights a cigarette. "Do you know how many they are?"

"Millions of tons of them," I say. He eyes the bombs, shakes his head. "Nooooo, not millions. One ton, maybe."

"Oh, *these* bombs." So goes conversation between East and West in Laos. We walk back toward the market, stepping around ducks, leaping a fetid swamp of muddy truck ruts and crumpled food wrappers. The air smells of sewer. "So, Captain, how long have you been in the army?" I ask him.

Somphong flicks his cigarette into a rut filled with filmy water, and we turn up one of the market's alleyways.

"Ah," he sighs. "Too long." We pass a little boy making vroom-vroom sounds and pushing the bodyless, plastic chassis of a toy car through the dirt outside his mother's stall. He's not wearing pants. Somphong sighs again. "I have been in since 1974."

He doesn't look old enough to have been in the army for twenty-seven years, and I tell him so. He chuckles. "Yes, I came into the army when I was very young."

"How young?"

"Thirteen years old," he says.

In May 1986, a twenty-eight-year-old Laotian at a refugee camp in Nakhon Phanom, Thailand, sought an interview with Bill Gadoury, a U.S. Army analyst working out of the American embassy in Bangkok. When they met at the town's police station, the young man produced a dog tag that bore John Chubb's name, serial number, and blood type.

He told Gadoury that early in 1985 he'd been given the tag by a relative named Hieo, who told him he'd obtained it from "an F-105 crash site" near the southern foot of a mountain called Phou Lom, in the Savannakhet Province. The man wasn't certain whether Hieo had found the tag himself or had been given it by someone else.

The witness would not hand it over, explaining that he preferred to wait until his father, who was in a reeducation camp in Laos, was safely out of the country; he'd then let the older man decide what to do with it. Gadoury did get a good look at the tag, however, and reported to his bosses that it was "very clean and looked like new."

Hieo had also given the man a small medallion that had come into his possession at the same time. It was roughly the same width as a dog tag, but shorter — a round-cornered rectangle embossed with the stylized profile of a woman's face, eyes downcast, a polka-dotted kerchief tied under her chin. A squareish, minimalist sprig of wheat formed the image's bottom edge. "The back of the piece had two points where it had been fastened to something, possibly a belt buckle," Gadoury reported. It looked more Soviet than American — everything about it, from the babushka it depicted to its blocky artistic style, seemed Eastern bloc — but the man said he believed both had belonged to Chubb.

Gadoury was a sergeant assigned to the Joint Casualty Resolution Center, which six years later would be reorganized as Joint Task Force-Full Accounting. He sent a photocopy of the dog tag and medallion to JCRC analysts in Hawaii, who issued a report on their findings in mid-June. They found that all the information on the tag did, in fact, correlate to Chubb — his social security number, his O-Negative blood type, and his declaration of "No Religious Preference."

Nowadays, putting a bogus dog tag together is a simple matter: Bare-bones biographical profiles of every American killed in Southeast Asia are posted on a number of Web sites, and one need only surf for a few minutes to assemble the ingredients for a factually correct fake. That wasn't the case in 1986, however; Web sites as we know them didn't yet exist, and even if they had, a refugee living alongside a thousand others in a crowded Thai camp wouldn't have had access to them. Whether or not this dog tag was really Chubb's, it merited some interest.

But the story of the tag's discovery didn't make sense. The analysts noted that Chubb hadn't been aboard an "F-105," an air force "Thunderchief" jet bomber that bore zero resemblance to a helicopter. What's more, Chubb had not been reported missing anywhere near Phou Lom, which was forty miles west-northwest of LZ Brown.

Enter the man's father. Seven months later, he met with Gadoury, turned over the tag, and gave a different account of its provenance. The father said that early in 1986, while an inmate at a Lao reeducation camp, he'd been injured on a work detail and hospitalized. That spring he'd been released into his sister's care and had traveled to her village in the Savannakhet Province.

From Gadoury's report: "One day soon after his arrival at his sister's house, he noticed a dog tag attached to his nephew, Hieo's, bicycle. He asked his nephew about the tag, and Hieo told him he found it the previous year when he was gathering cardamom nuts (*mak neng*) two or three kilometers east of Route 23, on the west side of Phou Lom Mountain.

"About 50 meters away from where the dog tag was found a small medallion was located, also among the cardamom leaves. Hieo told source he did not see any aircraft wreckage in the vicinity. The only things in the area were burned-out Vietnamese trucks which were destroyed during the war. Hieo told source that the nearest aircraft wreckage was about two kilometers to the east.

"When requested to turn the dog tag and medallion over to JCRC rep, source was initially reluctant because he wanted to present the items as evidence of his assistance when he was called for his resettlement interview."

Quite a bit different from the first account. Now Gadoury was being told that the tag hadn't really been found near an F-105, but more than a mile away from the nearest remains of a downed aircraft. The tag and medallion hadn't been found together, but 165 feet apart. Hieo's discovery hadn't occurred on the south side of the mountain, but the west. And Hieo hadn't given the tag to his cousin, but his uncle.

The JCRC's analysts had trouble swallowing this shifting tale. In a memo to the Defense Intelligence Agency in Washington, they noted that even if there was a grain of truth to either account, the forest in which Hieo supposedly found the tag was indisputably "57 kilometers west-northwest of the actual location" of John Chubb's loss. The Defense Department's POW/Missing Personnel Office concurred in a 1996 report: "Although the dog tag itself does correlate to PFC Chubb," it concluded, "the rest of the information provided by the father and son is most likely false." The paperwork the joint task force gave to Gwen Haugen before this mission dismissed the affair as "a complete fabrication; the source probably purchased the identification tag from unknown individuals in Savannakhet Province and made up the story to go along with the tag."

As for the tag itself, no one can say whether John Chubb once wore it. It might be real. It might not. The JCRC sent it to Washington, from where, in 1992, it made its way to his family. His half-brother, Fred Chubb, has it today.

2

OUR RETURN TO WORK opens with motivational speeches of increasing urgency. "Just stay with it," Haugen tells the team. "Hopefully, this'll turn out to be a good site." Reynolds, up next, relies on a penchant for sports analogy shared by the military and barkeeps: "To compare this to a football game, we're at the fifty-yard line," he says. "We're not in the red zone yet, but we're close. You can smell it." Then comes Posey, with a more tough-love message: "OK, about what we've put into it is what we've got left to do," he says. "So when you get to the site, get right to the screens. Don't go hanging around the break area. Get right to work. If you do, the workers will, too.

"We're gonna get out there and move some dirt," he says, mustering a glare. "We're gonna get this shit done. Understand?"

At the site, 508/516, open for nearly four days, finally closes, and I move into the hole to start the excavation of the square to its west, 508/512. My workers include the kid who parroted me on the screens, who despite the heat has reported for work this morning in a brown cardigan and a porkpie hat, and thus acquires the nickname "Bing." The unit covers uneven, sloping ground studded with bamboo stumps; we'll not only have to stairstep its floor, to keep its depth an even twenty centimeters, but we'll also face the sweaty, exhausting task of ripping up some tenacious roots. We start at the unit's downhill edge, two locals picking the soil loose, two others shoveling it into buckets, me smoothing the hole and squaring its sides behind them. Bing supervises the movement of empty buckets into the hole, full buckets out. Before long, we're out of them; the people at the head of the line are again stacking the empties. "We need buckets!" I yell toward the screening station. "Need buck-cats!" Bing screams. "Buckets!" my helpers chorus.

The empties arrive in piles, and for several minutes we shovel wordlessly, broiling in the sun. Our buckets are crowded with ACS, and every few minutes a worker brings over a new find — transistors, broken circuit board, burnt metal, and particles of dark plastic that might be helmet material. I drop each in a bucket and send it to the screens. During lunch, thunder rumbles from the east, and shortly after, the sky becomes a steely gray blade that lops off the escarpment's peaks. The temperature drops a few degrees. We've excavated the lower third of the unit when Haugen, taking over for Posey in 512/504, yells over: "Hey, it's about that time." Our first afternoon break.

"Let me fill these last couple of buckets," I say. My team has fallen into a steady, efficient rhythm. I'm reluctant to interrupt it.

"Need two more minutes?"

"That'd be great." But even as I tell my workers, "One more bucket, then *phak pon*," I see that the bucket line's already breaking up. Our supply line disintegrates. "Never mind," I sigh. "*Phak pon* now."

"Break!" Bing yells.

"Right," I nod. I straighten up and notice that the clouds crowning the ridge have turned black. A cool gust sweeps the grid. The escarpment dissolves; a milky gray wall descends its flanks, swallowing trees and rock as it slides toward us, and with it comes a sound like the roll of a snare drum. The forest at the slope's base vanishes. The sound grows louder. The top branches of trees a quarter-mile away whip crazily, then disappear. Captain Reynolds jogs over. "Listen to that!" he says. "Let's put down a tarp." We slide a blue sheet over the open unit and weight its corners with rocks and uprooted bamboo, and as we finish the grid is doused. The rain comes so hard and so fast that it's hard to breathe.

Lightning flashes. The air is filled with crackles like balled cellophane and sounds that resemble jets whooshing low overhead. Bolts strike so close we can feel their thunder boom in our chests, prompting shrieks from some of the team's soldiers. The site turns to soup, and suddenly the ground writhes with — can it be? — *frogs*. They appear all at once, millions of black frogs, perfectly formed but no more than a quarter-inch long. Everywhere we look they cover the ground. Either they have spontaneously popped from the soil — which seems unlikely — or we're witnessing one of nature's rare and storied events, a storm so powerful that it's actually raining animals.

"You order this rain, Dingo?" Posey asks. The sergeant has been Dingman's boss from early in the photographer's tenure at the lab. The heart of any recovery team is a handful of enlisted soldiers assigned to work together on mission after mission. An RE's officer-in-charge changes from one outing to the next, as does its anthro, and of course the augmentees are different every time out. But Dingman and Posey stick together. "This keeps up," Posey says, "we'll have plenty of water to wet-screen tomorrow."

"That creek's gonna look like Lake Meade," replies Dingman, reclined on a footlocker.

"That's if the dam's still there. Dingo, you think that dam's still there?"

"That's a good question," Dingman drawls.

In September 1982, a Laotian living at a refugee camp in southeastern Thailand wrote U.S. embassy officials that he knew where the remains of "two missing Americans" could be found. He and some associates supposedly had discovered the bodies in the Xepon District of the Savannakhet Province, which included the Case 1731 crash site. "There is one identification bracelet with the name on it, but the name is not legible," he wrote, adding that the bones were in safekeeping in a nearby village. "I am write a letter to let you know."

Eleven years had passed since Jack Barker and crew had crashed. By then, U.S. analysts in Bangkok had received and translated hundreds of such letters, almost all of them from Lao and Vietnamese refugees desperate to emigrate to the United States — and angling to speed the process — or simply prowling for cash. In the region's shattered postwar economy, American bones, like dog tags, had become currency. This letter's writer got around to his point two sentences later. "Is there a reward?" he wrote. "If so, please contact me."

And so came a succession of tips, most of them of questionable value, often delivered with questionable motive. Bone dealers seemed to breed through the eighties, some of them smugglers and con men, others farmers who'd not heard that the United States refused to pay for remains, still others boat people who packed bones among their few belongings in lieu of a passport. One handed over purported American remains that had been stashed in a tube of toothpaste. Officials received another alleged bone that a refugee had ground into a fine powder, for easier transport. And among the sales pitches, offers of trade, and hearsay reports that swamped American officials were a tantalizing few with possible links to Case 1731.

Item: In 1982, a refugee wrote from a camp in northeastern Thailand that he had "the skeleton of an American pilot who was died when his jet-plane fell down in the thick of the fight," along with "the bone of three American dead from Lao-Vietnamese border in the area of Bane Dong." Ban Dong, you'll recall, is the settlement at the junction of Routes 9 and 92, three miles from the Case 1731 crash site.

The writer said he wasn't sure whether the remains belonged to soldiers or pilots, but that he had one of the men's "hat and a skeleton of his head." He added: "Now my friends keep them near the Mekong." Unfortunately, his letter didn't stop there; what followed cast doubt on his story. "I can help you to bring these from the border to you," he wrote, "but now I am in trouble in the camp. I cannot go out of the camp because (it) is very restricted there is no international organizations inside the camp so all Lao refugees there live difficultly. The have to stand in line to get water also food is not enough."

Item: In September 1988, a refugee reported that sometime the previous spring he was visited by the wife of an old associate, who told him that friends had recently dropped in on her house with remains they identified as American, found in the "Lam Son area" near Route 9. The source had no further details.

Item: In 1983, another source showed U.S. officials color photographs of jumbled bones in a plastic bag and gave them a list of the men he said the remains represented. Among the names: William Dillender.

U.S. officials were not impressed. "The alleged circumstances tied to some of the names are known to be fabrications," the joint task force advised in the background papers given to Gwen Haugen before this mission, "and it appears this was a typical remains scam. No remains were obtained from the source."

Dingman climbs onto the grid the next morning, after inspecting the ravine, and reports that floodwater has blown the dam to pieces. "Half of it is probably in Vietnam," he says. "The other half is scattered along a couple hundred yards of the creek."

He rebuilds while his teammates continue shoveling and screening

the top layers of soil from the grid. Even without the dam, the creek carries enough storm runoff to supply the screens, and by lunch, a new
wall of sandbags spans the stream. I return to 508/512, Bing again leading my contingent of workers, and we tear up all but a small piece of the
unit's southwest corner, working fast under a cool and overcast sky, uncovering ACS all the while. Haugen opens 516/508, a unit dominated by
a gargantuan termite mound over on the grid's northern edge, and
Eagmin, supervising a team of Laotians there, digs up scattered bomb
frag. But all day, nothing we find is worth a damn; none of it is anything
we haven't seen already in abundance. We make good progress on the
grid, but no progress in closing Case 1731.

Haugen is pensive throughout the late afternoon. Over the course of
a dig, an anthro has a lot of time to think about the people he or she is
seeking, the circumstances of their deaths, their families. It's beyond
disappointing to work so hard, with so many people depending on her,
and to come up dry.

"I don't know what to tell you," she tells the team. "But keep your
spirits up. We're going to be getting down into that hole.

"What I'm hoping," she says, "is that this hole was used as a trash pit,
and that the locals threw stuff in there as they scavenged the airplane."

Conely takes a turn at cheerleading, too. "Just keep thinking positive," she says. "There are a lot of pieces here. Just hope for something
bigger."

3

WHILE RE-1 AND THE MISSION'S two other recovery teams shovel holes in the jungle, the investigative element is going where no Westerners have gone before, humping it up mountains and whacking into the jungle, dodging snakes and relishing discomfort, and keeping a tally of how many leeches they've had to pry from their bodies in the course of a day.

IE members tend to keep to themselves, eating together at Mama's, tenting up in a cluster at the camp's western edge, killing time together at the Ping-Pong table and workout area. This is partly a byproduct of their jobs — these guys are trained in interviewing techniques and data analysis, not anthropology — and geography probably has something to do with it, too: They are joint task force employees, and have little opportunity to mix with the lab's staff between trips overseas.

But a lot of the team's remoteness is self-imposed. The IE cultivates an image as Ban Alang's cowboys, tougher and crazier than the rest of us. I don't know how much of this is mere self-promotion, so with RE-1 settled into stupefying routine and finding little, I climb into a Squirrel with Capt. Dave Combs and his army linguist, Master Sgt. Souriyan Collins, and take off to the west, along Route 9, to find out.

Our task is to visit a village down the Xepon where two sets of witnesses are scheduled to tell us about a pair of wreck sites. The joint task force's records suggest neither site has been visited by past investigators. What we don't know is whether the wrecks are "operational losses" — planes that went down after their crews punched out, and which are therefore of zero interest to the U.S. government — or tangles of metal that might entomb unaccounted-for Americans.

We follow the highway for a few miles, our path slicing through the necks of its loops and bends; veer from the blacktop and drop in low over the Xepon, swollen with rain and foaming through rapids of gray rock; then lean hard into a turn over a riverbank village of thatched huts and tin roofs. We carve circles so tight that the starboard-side windows look straight down on coconut palms swaying in our wash, canoes lining the river's edge, and a knot of people at the settlement's center, peering up at us. We settle slowly, palms and blowing hardwoods rising all around us, a long, tin-roofed building looming close on our left. A schoolyard. Barefoot kids scatter laughing and shrieking as the skids touch.

We're on the ground just long enough to pick up a district official, who strides from the encircling villagers with a swagger, then gingerly rise back through the trees and wheel downstream. Another village peeks through the trees on the river's far side, and in it, we can see a Lao Westcoast chopper already on the ground, rotors slowing, red stripes gleaming, other IE members standing beside it. We park nearby and clamber from the Squirrel under the gaze of squinting old men and topless mothers and naked babies.

They all move in close as Sergeant Collins confers with a clutch of Laotian officials. The discussion centers on whether the witnesses we need to speak with, and the wrecks they have visited, are in Xepon District. This is the sort of bureaucratic question to which the joint task force and the lab have grown accustomed over the years, for in both Laos and Vietnam, U.S. teams go nowhere without representatives of the national government, the province in which they wish to work, the district of that province, and often the relevant subdistrict, village, and hamlet. This protocol makes for crowded helicopters and is rarely relaxed: Should an IE have plans to visit a site in Xepon District and the weather interferes, the team can't simply fly to an alternate site — not, at least, if such a diversion takes it into another district, which in the States would be akin to crossing a county line. Lining up the necessary permissions and escorts can take days.

One official waves around a handwritten document decorated with ornate stamps in red ink. Another man, apparently the subdistrict representative, speaks in sage tones while wearing a Carolina Panthers ball cap. Whatever the issue, it's resolved quickly: One set of witnesses is waiting, the village chief tells us, and leads the way through a shady grove of thick-trunked hardwoods to his house. It is on stilts, as all homes in this part of the country are. A ladder scales the six feet to a bamboo porch that divides it into two thatch-roofed rooms. We climb the ladder, wrestle off our boots, and duck inside.

It is dark, the only light seeping in through a few narrow, glassless windows, and surprisingly cool. A couple of sleeping mats are folded in a corner. Otherwise, the room is empty of furniture. We sit in a circle on a floor of bamboo split and flattened into thin planking, on top of which the chief has laid a rug of bamboo matting. A Lao army major introduces us to our host and two barefoot witnesses, one an exceedingly thin man no older than thirty, the other in his mid-forties and wearing what looks like most of an army uniform, minus its patches and pins. The older man's right eyeball is bright red around an oozing ulcer.

Baskets and bamboo poles are stored in the exposed rafters overhead; beyond them, I can see the roof's thatching, which like every other component of the place is made of bamboo, split into a stiff straw and tied into bundles. Clothes hang in plastic shopping bags from pegs in the room's frame. The air smells of wood smoke.

The major turns the meeting over to Collins, who is cross-legged to my left. He looks to our analyst, Adam Pierce, a fit, gung-ho, smiling young Georgian to my right. "OK," Pierce says, "ask them about any wrecks they know about." The junior witness reports they know of a crash site and points the way. Combs checks a tiny compass on his watchband. "I have that as southeast."

"Ask how far," Pierce says. Collins questions the men. The younger one answers. "They say it takes about four hours to walk there, from the village."

"Ask them if they found the site or were taken there by someone else."

Collins: "They say they are the first ones."

"Ask them what they saw."

Another exchange in Lao. "They saw glass. Broken. Pieces, about that big — see how he's doing?" The men hold their hands a foot apart.

"Are those pieces of metal he's talking about?"

"No," Collins says, "I think they're glass. A canopy, maybe, it sounds like to me."

"Ask them whether the glass was flat or curved."

More conversation. "Curved. It was curved." Throughout the exchange, the older witness has spoken only to other Laotians in the room. The young guy now tells Collins they saw the wreckage about three years ago.

"What color was it?" Pierce asks.

Collins: "It was green."

"Green. Could he mean the metal, not the glass?"

Collins, after checking: "No, it's glass."

"And it's green?"

"Ah. The frame is green, the frame."

"Ask him if he saw a chair anywhere in the area." By "chair" Pierce means an ejection seat. If the men have found just a canopy, rather than an entire aircraft, the seat should be nearby, because it means the pilot punched out. The plane itself might be miles off.

"No," Collins reports.

Pierce scribbles in his notebook. "Did they move it?"

"They left it in place. Right now, he says, there's high dirt, so no one can see."

Captain Combs leans forward. "Mind if I ask a few questions?"

"Go for it," Pierce says.

"Was the wreck up on a mountain or down in a valley?"

The witness tells Collins it was in the fork of a river.

"Could they find it again?"

Yes, the younger man says. Probably. There's a clearing, big enough for a helicopter to land, fifteen to twenty minutes' walk from the site. "He says that if we land where he says, he thinks he can find it," Collins says.

Combs suggests that we hire the guy to go find the wreckage and mark the LZ, so that the IE can fly there tomorrow, adding: "I don't want to spend the day walking around in the weeds." Collins takes this up with the witnesses. They agree to try to find the site today from the air. If they fail to do so, they'll hike to the clearing they mentioned and light a fire to mark it. Either way, the IE will be able to reach the wreckage.

Combs smiles and thanks them. "I don't want to lead them too much," he tells Collins, "but explain to them that whenever you find one of these, a chair and a parachute are usually located nearby, and ask them if they know of anybody in the village who has told of finding that."

The locals eye Combs as he speaks. I wonder what they make of the captain, who led the past IE that recommended excavating the Case 1731 site, and who sports a haircut that would rate attention just about anywhere on the planet: He is shaved bald save for a short-cropped strip of hair on his crown. The result is fierce; Combs looks like a Mohican about to charge into battle. Collins translates his question. The witnesses say they've heard of no chair, no parachute. The younger man asks whether the Americans will be angry if he can't find the crash site from the air. No problem, Collins tells him.

At this point the Laotian major announces that there's been a misunderstanding — the village chief apparently knew the team wanted to conduct an interview but not that it wanted to visit a site today. He has problems with that.

"Tell him we can go by ourselves," Combs bluffs. "We know right where it is." As Collins translates, Pierce chuckles quietly. "*Great.*"

The chief backs down. The witnesses will be allowed to fly over the place they found the canopy. We all stand to leave, the hut trembling beneath us, and pull on our boots. Collins, Pierce, and the witnesses head for a chopper. I stroll through the village.

Ban La-o Khao is twenty-odd huts scattered among groves of palm and gnarled shade trees and linked by trails worn deep and wet in the sandy soil. Children run, laughing and squealing, around me. Roosters crow. A water buffalo wanders by, the bell around its neck clanking. Black-spotted pigs root in the brush at the settlement's fringe and lounge in the cool gloom under raised floors. At the intersection of two main paths I find a twenty-foot aluminum canoe made from a warplane's empty belly tank. Villagers have sawed it in half lengthwise and fastened the ends to create a flat-bottomed, round-chined boat with seating for six.

The Laotian major sidles up beside me. "Boat," he says. I smile at him, expecting him to make note of its pedigree, but he doesn't, and I'm reminded of something one of Pierce's fellow analysts mentioned. The IE has walked into villages and found wreckage recycled into tools and building materials, only to be told by the locals that they know of no crash sites in the surrounding woods. It's not dishonesty, but a reflection of how the Laotians define what they see: "You'll ask a villager,

'Do you have any wreckage from a crash site?' And he'll say, 'Oh, noooo,'" the analyst told me. "And you'll point to a piece of a wing on his roof and say, 'Well, what about that?' And he'll say, 'That's not a piece of airplane. That's a piece of my roof.'"

The Squirrel returns with the two witnesses. They've probably never been higher than the branches of the village's trees, and look eager to get out of the machine. As Collins follows them out he looks to Combs and shakes his head. The captain sighs and has him ask the pair whether they'll hike to the site to mark the LZ. The younger man tells Collins that if he leaves early in the morning, the soonest he can expect to be there is twelve o'clock. "Fine," Combs says. "Do that and the IE will rendezvous with you at about 3 P.M." The captain's plan calls for the men to light a fire in the LZ shortly before the appointed time; the IE will look for its smoke. If it's too wet to light a fire, they're to use a VS-17 panel, a vinyl signal blanket of fluorescent orange and pink, to mark the spot.

Raul Alvarez, a twenty-five-year-old marine from Brooklyn, has doubts about the plan. "You know what's gonna happen," he murmurs. "Watch 'em light that VS-17 panel on fire."

Pierce laughs. "No kidding."

"Doesn't matter," says another analyst, Greg Parmele. "It'll smoke up real nicely."

I wander off to examine the schoolhouse, which is the only structure in Ban La-o Khao that isn't on stilts. Even by the standards of the eighteenth-century American frontier, it's rough: no blackboard, no hanging maps, no books. Dirt floor. Narrow benches of hewn timber for the kids, more hitching posts than seats. For light, two squares are cut in the woven-bamboo walls. I stand at the doorway, transfixed. More than anything else I've seen in Laos, this sad little classroom fills me with a sense of how lucky I am and how mean life in Southeast Asia remains at the dawn of this new millennium. The room embodies the help a Laotian youngster will get in preparing for life. This is the ruling generation's leg-up to its progeny. This is the country's hope for the future. This is it.

How much of the millions of dollars the United States pumps into the Laotian economy each year filters its way down to villages such as Ban La-o Khao, I wonder, and to schools such as this? When our helicopters lift off later today, what will we leave behind, other than stories handed down, generation to generation, about the day the outsiders came in their flying machines?

While I'm chewing on this, word comes that a witness to the second airplane crash site has just returned from hunting and is willing to lead us there. He and Combs, Collins, a provincial official, and I climb into one of the Squirrels and take off to the south.

We climb a steep-sided ridge, just clear the top branches of its jungle cladding, and circle the peak of 2,130-foot Phou Kadoy, about ten miles southwest of the base camp. The witness points to its shoulder, to a gap in the trees exposing a puddled oval of dark rock, but before we can drop into the hole the man tells Collins he's all turned around and isn't sure precisely where the wreck is or where we are, and that he wishes he had a friend along who knows the place better.

"Let's let him get his bearings," our Kiwi pilot says over the intercom. "He's all fucked-up right now." We wander westward, circle for a minute, then slowly make our way back to the mountain. As we near the clearing Collins says the guy's figured things out. The pilot starts us down.

The hole is so tight that our blades touch branches to our right and left, chopping leaves to a green mist, splintering wood with loud cracks. Combs, sitting in the front seat, opens his door and hangs out of the chopper, looking aft to the tail rotor. "OK . . . OK . . ." Rotorwash thumps his headset's microphone, nearly drowning him out. "OK, you're touching this side but you're OK," he says. "Tail is clear."

Our touchdown comes on rock tilted ten degrees to the left and so wet and slick-looking that the pilot has Combs climb out to test the footing before he powers down the Squirrel, lest the chopper slide sideways into the woods. The captain gives a thumbs-up, and we all scramble out. It is a weird place, the rock pocked with round, foot-deep holes filled with crystalline water, carpeted elsewhere with patches of dense moss that squish underfoot. Sprigs of tall grass erupt from cracks in the stone, along with yellow flowers that resemble miniature orchids. Collins fires up a chainsaw, Combs swings a machete, and by the time a second bird arrives with the rest of the team and officials, it has enough room to settle nose-to-nose with ours.

With that, we set off into the bush. Hiking single-file, we weave among the trees down a steep hillside, the forest growing dark, the air filled with the metallic thrum of cicadas. We reach a rocky precipice, butt-slide our way down a notch in its face, and whack our way through thickening jungle below, stumbling over hidden roots, shaking loose of vines, pushing through waist-high bushes. We chop through stands of saplings and bamboo. We move so quickly that I don't have time to fret about snakes.

Thirty minutes in, we slide down a ravine to a stream studded with flat boulders. The witness gazes at waterfalls upstream and down, then tells Collins that he thought we'd find the wreck right here. "Aw, I don't like the sound of this," Combs mutters. "What's he want to do?"

"He says he'll go that way a little." Collins points downstream. "He thinks he'll find it. Then he'll come back." The villager splashes off. We squat on the rocks, slap at mosquitoes, slather on bug juice, wait. Twenty minutes later he's back, and waves us on.

Before I see any sign of a wreck, Parmele has jumped into thigh-deep water in the stream's middle and hoisted a heavy cylinder of steel from the drink. A landing gear strut. "Sweet-ass sweet!" he hollers. "Fuckin' beautiful, huh?"

Now, all along the banks, I see the shredded remains of a jet lying among stands of bamboo and the trunks of giant rosewoods and mahoganies — another section of landing gear, thick and sprouting bolts and pistons, white paint still fresh. A rusted turbine blade fused into the knotty bark of a tree. The circular guts of an engine, three feet across, combustion cans still bolted around its perimeter.

Parmele leads a group downstream while Combs and Alvarez, examining the engine, find a series of numbers in its combustion cans, hand-etched by some General Electric engineer long since retired. They record the numbers, though they're likely of limited use; they're the numbers of the cans, not the engine, and it's the serial number of the whole assembly that would be recorded in the military archives. We hear Parmele hollering, singsong, down the river: "We found the grail! We've found the gray-yell!"

"You get the engine serial number?" Combs yells.

A shout back: "Lots of part numbers."

"Shit," Combs mutters. "They didn't find shit."

"They're might be a number under this thing," Alvarez suggests, kicking the combustion chamber.

"Wanna wash it off?"

"Move out of the way." Alvarez heaves the combustion chamber onto its edge, exposing a circle of dark, wet soil in the sloping bank. A whip scorpion, a black arachnid four inches long with a stiff, antenna-like tail in place of a stinger, scuttles for cover. Alvarez doesn't even flinch. He gives the machinery a push, and the big disk thumps end over end into the creek, where it makes a tremendous splash and immediately muddies the water. He and the captain step in to their knees, fish around beneath the murky surface, find the metal. They lift it, let it flop back, lift it, let it fall, flushing red mud from its tangle of pipes and crushed skin. The effort gains them nothing: When they peer into its dripping folds, they find no number.

The team stalks through the woods lining the creek, searching for more wreckage. A few pieces lie wedged in the soil here and there, but little of the Phantom's fuselage. Combs points out the reason: The forest floor is dimpled with shallow depressions, the remains of test holes dug by scavengers. The nearest road is miles away, beyond a chain of steep and rocky ridges, but that hasn't stopped some enterprising salvager from toting big pieces of this airplane to market.

We leave after an hour, the wreck's part numbers scribbled in our notebooks, and start the long climb back to the LZ. It is far nastier than our trip down the mountain. We climb hand-over-hand up palisades of rock, grunt and sweat through broadleaf forest rising from slopes of forty-five degrees or better, cuss our way through vines bristling with inch-long spikes. I'm at the rear of the file, Alvarez behind me, and we slip, flailing and lurching, on the slick trail left by those in front. Before long the others are far ahead, invisible in the jungle.

A half-dozen times the trees thin, the slope seem to ease, and each time we urge each other on with shouts that we're about to bust out of the woods and onto the LZ at Phou Kadoy's summit. A couple times I even imagine a flash of red paint — the Squirrels! But each time, we top just a bump in the mountainside and find another slope ahead, even bigger and steeper and more snarled with brush than the last. An hour into the ascent I'm dizzy and sick to my stomach and breathing with such noisy rasps that the cicadas fall silent around us. I stop for a long drink of water, Alvarez waiting patiently as I catch my breath. It doesn't help: On my very next step, I lose my balance and topple to my left, over the lip of a small promontory, too whipped to so much as grab for a branch to save myself. A web of thick vines catches me, and holds me fast until Alvarez pulls me back to the trail.

Jack Lamar Barker
(*courtesy of the Barker family*)

Barker as a junior officer. His no-nonsense polish impressed his superiors and earned the scorn of some of his air crews in Vietnam. (*U.S. Army photo, Barker family collection*)

John F. Dugan as a newly minted army officer (*U.S. Army photo, Dugan family collection*)

A much-changed Dugan rides the right seat as a Kingsmen peter pilot. The helmet he wears, minus the visor and visor shield, is similar to that purportedly found at the Case 1731 excavation site. (*courtesy of the Dugan family*)

John J. Chubb before he quit school. Though handsome and popular, the mechanically gifted Chubb had trouble with his classes and teachers. (*courtesy of Clifford Chubb*)

Chubb poses outside his parents' Gardena, California, home with a pair of projects. Within months he joined the army. In less than a year he was dead. (*courtesy of Clifford Chubb*)

William E. Dillender practice-jumps during Airborne training at Fort Benning. He was bound for Vietnam before year's end. (*courtesy of Bill and Ann Dillender*)

Dillender, right, enjoys a cold one in Vietnam. Fun-loving and fearless, the nineteen-year-old door gunner was soon promoted to crew chief. (*courtesy of Bill and Ann Dillender*)

Dugan beside a Kingsmen UH-1H Huey, a troop and cargo carrier armed only with twin machine guns—and a fat target for enemy ground fire. (*courtesy of the Dugan family*)

This photo of a UH-1H gassing up "hot" at Camp Eagle was taken by Jack Barker and included in a letter home. The white diamond on the helicopter's tail boom identifies it as a Bravo Company bird. (*courtesy of the Barker family*)

A grim souvenir of Lam Son 719 is recycled, like so much other military gear, outside a hut in the mountaintop village of Ban Apoui.

On the lookout for American aircraft wreckage, Captain Dave Combs and his linguist, Master Sergeant Souriyan Collins, examine junk piled in a pigsty in a village off Route 9. Such piles often contain the detritus of war.

A Laotian military Mi-17 lifts off from Ban Alang for another nerve-racking flight. American teams in Laos and Vietnam depend on the Russian-built machines, as they're barred from using their own.

The tail of "Naughty but Nice," an American B-17E Flying Fortress shot down on a 1943 bombing run, rises from the New Britain jungle that hides the remains of four of the plane's crew.

Machine gun rounds, still belted to one another, lie piled amid the wreckage of a World War II dig site in Papua New Guinea.

Anthropologist Bill Belcher stands over the shredded remains of a P-38 Lightning. Belcher's team identified the plane from numbers they found painted on the twisted metal; the next day, they came upon the pilot's bones and class ring.

A minute later, we do spot red paint, and stagger onto the black rock where the rest of the team is sprawled, sucking down water. A Squirrel powers up for the first lift back to camp. I'm too weak, too comfortable lying flat on my back, to get aboard.

As it takes off, its rotorwash blows my soaked T-shirt up, baring my stomach. It's covered with blood. I find a neat round wound in my bellybutton, but the leech is already gone.

4

HALF OF ANOTHER UNIT has been emptied, its floor and walls smoothed, its clay passed moist and dark to the screens. Diggers have moved on to an unshoveled corner, and in laying it open uncovered an impressive cache of ACS, when the Americans on the screens hear a shout in Lao, see workers running from the hole. "Is it a break?" somebody yells. Reynolds strides toward the A-frame from the grid. "They think they've found a bomb."

"Let's go, y'all," Sergeant Posey barks. "Everybody to the break tent. Let's move." The team and its Laotian partners file off the A-frame and across the clearing, and near the break tent pass Eagmin, bound for the hole. Several members of RE-1 tell him to be careful. He doesn't answer, doesn't acknowledge the remarks. He's in full battle gear — camouflage flak jacket, Kevlar helmet — and staring stone-faced toward Posey and Reynolds, who are waiting at the edge of the open unit, no more than six feet from the suspected bomb.

We crowd into the tent and watch as he nears the hole, with each step armoring himself more completely in the Zen state that success in his line of work — which is to say, survival — requires. Eagmin's made this long walk many times in the past ten years — in Somalia, in the Persian Gulf, in uncountable dry runs and exercises at Camp Pendleton. But this one, he doesn't get to finish. He's still several yards away when a Laotian kid breaks across the grid, blows past Posey and Reynolds, jumps in the hole and yanks the suspected bomb out of the ground.

Before anyone has time to react, he turns the light-gray metal cylinder in his hand. "Jesus!" Reynolds cries. From the break tent, we see the captain and Posey instinctively fall to half-crouches, and time's passage slows to a near halt; in the half-second it takes the pair to drop, I feel a shriek of adrenaline blast through me, notice that the kid is only a yard from them, register that such a distance is deadly, and brace for an explosion.

It doesn't come. The kid straightens up and laughs.

Haugen reaches the hole a second later. Reynolds is bright pink and sputtering mad. "That little fucking asshole could have killed Sergeant Posey and me," he says, breathless and pointing at the kid. "Goddamn it!"

"What happened?" Haugen says.

Reynolds hands her the cylinder and takes a deep breath. The kid climbs out of the unit and, keeping his distance and watching Reynolds out of the corner of his eye, strolls off across the grid, grinning.

"Not a bomb?"

"No," the captain says, running a hand through his hair. "But it could have been."

At the next break, I sit talking with Eagmin about the close call while the kid, who looks about fifteen, squats near the grid's southwest corner with a couple of friends, laughing and pointing at Reynolds. Most of the locals seem to be keeping their distance from the delinquent. It seems they think he's as big an idiot as we do.

"I would have preferred that I removed it," Eagmin says mildly. "It'd have been nice to get in there and determine what it was, rather than have somebody just pull it out of the ground like that. Tends to save a lot of paperwork." Reynolds, sitting a few feet away, feigns indifference as the kid continues to taunt him, but calls over Krueger. "There's that little   . who picked up the bomb," he says. Krueger glances over his shoulder at the kid, who sees him do it and lets loose a loud laugh. "Listen," the captain whispers to the linguist, "this afternoon, you gotta give that guy a really shitty job."

Dig for days on end without a bad scare and it's easy to forget the manifold dangers this work presents, the many brushes with injury, or worse, that are built into the routine. The far-flung nature of the work compounds all these dangers, because to work most sites in Southeast Asia is to be hours by air from a hospital and at least one international border from anything remotely resembling Western medical care. Eyeball an open-air clinic in Laos or Vietnam — dirty, crowded with the sick, understaffed and ill-managed and poorly provisioned — and you'll never again bitch about HMOs. If you're badly hurt, you have to get to Thailand. And that brings up a risk that attends all but a few of the missions that the lab and joint task force undertake: flight.

Helicopters are essential to the recovery effort, whether in Papua New Guinea or Southeast Asia; no other craft can so negotiate insane topography to deliver teams to their dig sites and keep them supplied. But helicopters are dicey propositions by their nature, crazy choreographies of spinning parts that take to the air in defiance of nature's default modes and succumb all too willingly to the caprices of weather, mechanical failure, gravity. ABC newsman Harry Reasoner offered a perfect summation of the contraptions during a February 1971 newscast, as Jack Barker and his company braved the increasingly accurate Vietnamese fire during Lam Son 719. "You can't help but have the feeling," he told his viewers, "that there will come a future generation of men, if there are any future generations of men, who will look at old pictures of helicopters and say, 'You've got to be kidding.'"

On practically every helicopter flight I've made — and I suspect I share this trait with a good many passengers — I've thrilled to the machines' speed and vantage, all the while almost unconsciously picking out flat shelves on the ridgelines, breaks in the jungle canopy, gravel bars in the rivers, strategizing: If the engine quits, where in God's name can we set down? It's little comfort that a falling chopper will usually autorotate, the upward rush of air spinning its rotor and braking its descent, for the adventure won't end smoothly; an emergency landing, even a good one, most likely will suck.

Pile up all the risks that accompany the missions and you have to ask: Are they worth it? As the years pass and the lab's cases in Southeast Asia get tougher — the sites more remote, the witnesses older and less reliable, the effects of decay and erosion more destructively complete — we draw ever nearer to the point where the risks outweigh the results. Will we acknowledge that point when we reach it? One has to wonder, because the joint task force and its mission have become political sacred cows with which no elected official dare interfere. But just how much peril should the living face in recovering the dead?

*   *   *

Four months before RE-1 arrived in Laos, the worst day in the history of America's search for its unaccounted-for servicemen — April 7, 2001 — brought those questions front and center.

That Saturday a CILHI sergeant, a navy corpsman, and six members of Joint Task Force-Full Accounting's Vietnam detachment, in Hanoi, conducted advance work for a JFA the following month. With them were nine Vietnamese, including some of the Socialist Republic's top officials on the MIA issue. They flew in an Mi-17 owned by Northern Service Flight Company, a Vietnamese government-sponsored operation that had flown thousands of sorties on behalf of recovery expeditions. Its helicopters were the only ones available for the job: Like its Laotian neighbors, Hanoi did not, and does not, allow American teams to use U.S. helicopters within its borders.

The weather started going bad as the chopper flew south toward Hue, in central Vietnam, and it eventually got iffy enough that the crew requested a landing at the Dong Hoi airfield, a stainless-steel strip just north of the former DMZ. The Vietnamese lieutenant colonel at the controls — with 3,300 flight hours, one of the country's most experienced helicopter pilots — dropped the Mi-17 into thickening fog as he made his approach, apparently decided he'd descended too far, and was pulling back up when the back end struck Am Mountain, a hill in Quang Binh Province. The chopper broke into pieces. The pieces burned. All aboard died.

Many blamed the Mi-17 for the accident; news reports centered on the state of Vietnam's fleet, on reports that in its final moments the craft rocked oddly in midair. The U.S. Pacific Command, of which the joint task force is a part, suspended American use of Mi-17s throughout Southeast Asia while the Vietnamese researched the accident's cause.

The outcome was moot to the critics back home; what mattered to them was that lives had been lost on what they viewed as a mission of increasingly debatable merit. Two weeks after the accident, *Time* magazine opined that "these operations should be wound down," that the countries involved "have other areas of common interest, such as commerce," that "the remains of those Americans likely to be found have already been located." It labeled the mission "mortally expensive," concluding: "The time has come to let the ghosts of Vietnam rest in peace."

The Defense Department disregarded that advice, as well as those who argued that the price, in monetary terms, was too high — that spending $100 million a year on recovery and identification made far less sense than spending the money on economic development or health care in the countries involved. To the men and women of the U.S. military, giving up the mission was tantamount to violating the sacred contract. At the memorial service for the seven Americans killed in the accident, held in a chapel at Fort Myers, adjacent to Arlington National Cemetery, Undersecretary of Defense Paul Wolfowitz recommitted the Pentagon to the mission. Later in the year, a succession of military brass promised the families of unaccounted-for servicemen that they'd press on with the effort to find the lost.

The Vietnamese investigation into the wreck, along with a "collateral" inquiry by the Pacific Command, found the evidence suggested pilot error: He failed, the American report said, to "properly react as the aircraft descended from a scattered cloud level into an unforecasted, rapidly forming thick layer of fog." Satisfied that the Mi-17 wasn't itself at fault, the Pacific Command lifted the moratorium on its use.

Even so, the accident looms large at Ban Alang. In the days since our arrival, word has spread of the white-knuckle journey from Savannakhet, of how our Laotian crew appeared to be lost, of how, with all our wanderings above and below the clouds, it took us close to ninety minutes to reach Ban Alang, rather than the usual hour. Perhaps our experience would not be so discomfiting had it not occurred on the first American flight since the Pacific Command lifted its ban. No doubt many aboard the chopper were silently drawing parallels between our blind ascent through the clouds and what we knew of the Vietnamese helicopter's fogbound end. I know I was.

So it's a lucky break that I've had a bracing shot of rice moonshine when I climb back aboard one of the Russian machines a few days later. Again, I'm with the IE: While I'm eating breakfast at Mama's, Dave Combs stops by my table to invite me along for what promises to be an interesting day of interviews. I've wakened with dread at the prospect of returning to the screens. I leap at the offer.

Our travels begin aboard a Squirrel. We land on the escarpment three miles south of camp, on a sloping shelf of rock just outside the village of Ban Taht Kong. It is a prosperous place, by Laotian standards. The houses are built on stilts of stout timber, rather than bamboo. A couple dozen cows wander through the settlement. Tiny black piglets scurry among stacks of firewood, and goats chew their cuds in the shade of low, spindly trees.

Striding through the village, we pass an airplane bomb canister, the sort that once dispersed *bombies,* turned into a feeding trough. On one porch is an array of stew pots fashioned from pieces of aircraft aluminum. Beside them is the snout of a bomb or belly tank, now a large bowl.

Four witnesses wait at the chief's house, which rises from the bank of a sluggish stream. We sit, shoeless, as water buffalo trundle past outside, roosters crow, children giggle. The men tell of a crash site they say they first encountered in 1973 or 1974, about the time the village was established, near the top of a mountain little more than a kilometer to the northeast.

Captain Combs unpacks a laptop computer, turns it on, and searches a database of known losses in the vicinity, his face glowing green in the hut's shade. The records show the mountaintop is called Phou Rep, but it's probably better known by its wartime label: LZ Lolo. Two helicopters and a jet were left there after going down, the database says. All were operational losses. We'll find no bones in their wreckage.

We set out for another village, Ban Apoui, a half-mile to the west. The principal highway linking the burgs is a skinny trail that corduroys down steep ravines and over bamboo-clad ridges, and in a few muddy stretches shares its route with a streambed. We're spattered with red clay when we reach the rocky, shadeless settlement of thirty houses.

Combs points out a GI's plastic helmet liner hanging upside down from one hut, an aloe plant growing within, and another bomb-canister trough. Two teenage girls are grinding rice beneath the chief's house, driving a stout, six-foot log into a mortar of stone with loud thumps. As we step inside, we pass the metal sleeve of a 105mm artillery round lying outside the door.

The hooch's main room is crowded. Besides the chief, the team, and four witnesses, we've attracted a gallery of young boys, who whisper to one another as we take seats on the wood-plank floor. The house is sturdy, far more finished-looking than the others I've visited. Its frame is hewn timber, and the walls are of woven bamboo mats lashed to wooden frames that are hinged along their tops so they can be tilted open. A cool breeze wafts through the place.

We are the first Americans to visit Ban Apoui since the village was settled in 1978, the chief tells us. He introduces the first witness, who says that on his hunting trips he has come across lots of metal.

"Ask him how far."

"Not far," Collins says. "A few *lak*."

Combs and Pierce exchanged pained glances. A *lak* is a Lao unit of measure without a hard-and-fast Western equivalent. It seems to stretch or shrink to suit the person using it, and this elasticity, while understood by the locals, has long flummoxed visiting Americans. Some of the IE's members reckon it equals about six hundred meters, others half a kilometer; others are equally confident that it's close to a full click. "Have him tell us without using *lak*," Combs suggests.

"About three times what we just walked over here," Collins replies.

Pierce tells him to ask the other witnesses what they've seen, and a second man speaks up. "He say he thinks it's a jet, because of the pointy nose," Collins says. The first witness now reports that he knows of this metal and that during the war, he saw a "rocket ship" there.

Combs: "Did they scavenge the site? Did they go there to get metals?"

Collins: "He says yes, everybody. Even the kids."

Pierce: "What's left at the site now?"

Collins: "An engine."

Pierce: "Ask how big the engine is."

Collins points to a flat, round rice-drying basket stored in the hut's rafters, about thirty inches across. "About that big." Several villagers nod agreement.

"And how long?" Pierce asks. The first witness stands and paces out roughly eight feet.

"Ah," Combs says. "A whole engine." Collins asks if the object "has teeth." Yes, the man answers. Pierce records the engine's location. At the mission's conclusion, the IE will pass it along to analysts at the joint task force, who'll go through their files to correlate it with a known aircraft loss. If they fail, or if they find that an aviator went missing in the area, they'll send a future IE to the spot to gather more information.

But for now, a more immediate challenge looms. Throughout the interview, a tall glass bottle containing a clear liquid has been positioned at the room's center, a shot glass beside it. *Lao-lao*, the aforementioned moonshine, is the liquor of choice in rural Laos, and when you're offered a shot — usually during a visit to a friend's house, a wedding or other celebration, or at the conclusion of business — custom requires you to down it. To refuse is to insult your host.

The village chief picks up the bottle, shows it off to us, smiles. An appreciative murmur ripples through the crowd. Pierce mutters, "Oh, no." It's not yet 10 A.M.

We hike back out in a light rain, *lao-lao* gurgling in our guts. Pierce's work is done for the day; Alvarez will be the analyst on the cases we'll chase in the afternoon. So Pierce and I take the Squirrel back to Ban Alang, where I'll meet Alvarez and board an Mi-17. The Squirrel will return to the ridge top for Combs and Collins, with whom we will rendezvous on Route 9, just west of the Vietnam border.

It would be a heck of a lot easier just to zip Pierce down to camp and pick up Alvarez on the return so that we could fly to our remaining appointments together; the Squirrel has plenty of room for four Americans and our Laotian escort. But the Mi-17 didn't fly yesterday, and word is that the camp's Laotian army officers, mindful that the United States will be billed more for a flying chopper than a parked one, have insisted we use it.

A half-hour later, when Alvarez and I strap ourselves in, the big machine's crew outnumbers its passengers, two to one. It is not an especially good-looking piece of hardware: The red and blue stripes of the Laotian flag that run down its flanks are faded and oil-stained and blackened with exhaust. Bare metal gleams brightly through chips in the paint. Its tires are so low on air that it nearly rests on its rims. We're alone in the cabin save for a Laotian official dozing at the rear and a small pile of gear — a lawn chair, ice chest, some bottled water, a soccer ball, a large gourd, and a dozen pumpkins. Alvarez looks at me and shakes his head.

I do not enjoy the absurdity of the moment nearly so much as he does. Despite the calming effects of the *lao-lao,* my mouth has suddenly dried. My stomach churns. I can hear my heart thumping over the turbines, which start with a low grumble and steadily build in pitch and in volume to a sustained scream. We take off in a steady shower and speed east along Route 9, the cabin's portholes fogged and streaked with rain. As on my last Mi-17 ride, the cockpit is crowded with aides to the pilot, and as on that ride, they seem to do a lot of pointing. We stay low, dark clouds just above us, the pitted highway below. Villagers peer skyward as we race over them. Some wave. Some are so close I can see their smiles.

The Mi-17 banks left and slows, a shiver running its length, and as the ground rises toward us the branches of nearby trees whip crazily, even thick-trunked rosewoods sway, and the air becomes a whirl of blowing leaves and twigs and dust. The Russian bird is so windy that it can't fly into most villages without lifting roofs and shredding bamboo walls.

The crew chief opens the cabin door and jumps overboard as we hover over a weedy, rutted hollow just off the highway. There's a thump as we touch down, a hydraulic sigh as the machine settles, but it lasts just a second, because we lift off again and wheel in a slow 180. Again we ease to earth. This time the whine of the chopper's turbines drops in pitch. We're spooling down. But no — we power back up, jerk to a two-foot hover, and creep forward ten feet or so. I see the crew chief dart past the open door, heading aft, then again a moment later, headed for the nose. The Mi-17 cautiously drops once more. This time, it stays put. I'm tempted to kiss the ground when I deplane.

The Squirrel arrives with Combs, Collins, and our Laotian major, and with the rain easing to a light drizzle we hike east on Route 9. Its asphalt surface has worn through completely here, leaving a bog of mud, gravel, and deep holes. We crunch along at the head of a parade of thirty kids, their parents and grandparents bringing up the rear, and stop at a roadside hut that has a pile of scrap in its front yard. Cast in the heap with sections of railing and rusted car parts are white-painted aircraft components.

At the village chief's house, an old U.S. ammo box serves as a doorstop, and a bottle of *lao-lao* and two shot glasses wait on the floor. The bottle's neck is plugged with a wadded plastic bag. It looks like a Molotov cocktail.

The team asks old-timers about a jet lost while bombing North Vietnamese tanks on March 22, 1971, two days after Jack Barker's crash and the day he would have turned thirty-two. The locals tell us that only one wreck was still recognizable when they returned to the area in 1973 or 1974 after several years in hiding. At the time, Route 9 was littered with tanks, "too many to count." Then outsiders showed up, chopped up the tanks, and carted the metal away.

A large beetle falls down the back of my shirt. I lean back against the hut's doorjamb. It crunches flat, spiny, and leaking, as Alvarez asks whether Americans have visited before. Yes, the elders reply, seven or eight years ago. What did they do? Interviews, the men say. A little digging. Combs grimaces. His team is duplicating old efforts. "I don't like that answer," he mutters.

A better one doesn't come along. Back on Route 9 and bound for the Squirrel, we pass a neat round hole in the road, and beside it, a heavy, riveted rectangle of metal. " Combs cries, "that's the hatch from an armored personnel carrier!" We surround the hatch, which is in remarkably good shape and which, it seems, has just been exhumed by a couple boys we can see farther down the highway, digging another hole. Just what Route 9 needs: a little freelance road destruction.

We reach them a minute later. One is hard at work with an entrenching tool, chopping at a hole a foot wide and twice as deep. The other is wearing headphones wired to an ancient-looking metal detector. "That thing probably works better than anything we have," Combs says. Its handle is only a foot long; its head is an enormous plastic bowl. The digger pauses, and his partner passes the bowl over their excavation. He nods. More dirt comes out.

Combs takes a slow step back. "Maybe," he whispers, "we ought to put some distance between us and whatever that kid finds down there."

5

I N THE SOUTHWEST CORNER of 508/512, the workers again pull all manner of small items from the soil — more transistors, pieces of red and clear glass, slivers of metal, striped wire, bolts. Bing is beside me, having assumed the role of my chief helper, and he's recruited some of his village's hardest workers to take up shovels — Fred, so nicknamed because someone on the team thought he resembled Fred Flintstone; Sammy; Charles Bronson; Ringo; and a malarial young man who wears an oxford button-down fastened at its neck but otherwise open, in the style of a barrio gang-banger. Eagmin, digging in the other unit, yells over: "Hey, how'd you get all the good workers?"

"Reputation," I holler back. "The word's out about my hole." My workers burst into laughter, and a guffaw travels up the bucket line. I hear several villagers repeating something that sounds like, but not exactly like, "out about my hole." Eagmin and I stand there as the laughter continues, looking at each other. "God knows," I mutter, "what I just said in Lao-Theung."

Halfway through the morning, Bing leaps away from a bamboo stump at which he's been hacking with a trowel. The workers near him scatter, a couple stumbling in their hurry, and out of the ground corkscrews a centipede ten inches long, horns sprouting from its head and tail, its segmented body a clownishly bright orange, its legs yellow. I chop it in two with my shovel. Both halves desperately try to crawl away, but Haugen scoops them onto her trowel blade, and we watch as they clasp one another in a poisonous embrace.

Wildlife sightings continue after lunch when, while digging around the last of the unit's stumps, I'm passed by a Laotian official carrying the roasted carcass of a spaniel-sized animal. For a horrified moment I mistake it for Chubby, but then see that it has a long, whiplike tail and a snout that narrows to a sharp point. I wave the official over, and he shows off what Haugen later identifies as a "bamboo beaver," a large indigenous rodent. Its fur has been burned away, its skin blackened and split, the fat beneath turned to crackling. The official smiles, runs his tongue over his lips, and pats his stomach, then lugs it across the site to the officials' tent, where he hangs it from the bamboo frame. A little while later, when flies gather around it, we see Captain Somphong spraying his evening meal with a liberal dose of insecticide. Chubby, alive and well, reappears on the scene at about the same time.

We finish 508/512, at long last, in the early afternoon. As I walk the last bucket to the screening station, Haugen approaches with what appears a black worm on her trowel, slender, eyeless, and about six inches long. "I think it's one of those worm-snakes that Doc Walsh was talking about," she says, as the villagers in the bucket line back away from her. She rolls it onto my trowel and saws at the creature with the edge of hers, trying to cut its head off. As she presses the blade into its surprisingly tough skin, the animal opens its mouth, a tiny, whitish half-moon no more than an eighth of an inch wide. "That thing's poisonous?" I ask her.

"Supposedly," she says. "Although I don't know how it could bite a person."

"How can it open its mouth wide enough?"

"And I don't see any teeth."

Still, we don't put our skepticism to the test. As the workers watch apprehensively, I fling the wounded worm-snake into the ravine.

Haugen opens a new unit, 512/500, on the crater's northwest side. The team rakes it shortly before the day's end but doesn't start pulling dirt from the hole until the next morning. We get a late start: Rain sweeps the Xepon just after dawn, and with its passing, the crater, drained just yesterday, has two new feet of water in its bottom. Planted in the muck in a pair of high rubber boots, the anthro directs two dozen locals in baling the water and dumping it into the smaller crater behind the break tent.

The unit proves unworthy of the hassle: It yields almost nothing. Later in the morning, however, another unit — 508/500 — opens beside it, and two soldiers digging in its northwest corner unearth a clump of metal that Eagmin identifies as the rear end of a rocket-propelled grenade. Its significance is plain. As Haugen notes in her field diary: "Interesting, as the REFNO 1731 aircraft was allegedly hit by an RPG in the tail rotor."

At first, it seems a lucky break, another nugget of evidence that we're close to finding 185's lost crew, that a cache of bones waits somewhere below the grid. But while screening I discuss the RPG's implications with Eagmin and emerge from the conversation with a perplexing question. If this is, in fact, the rocket that struck Jack Barker's helicopter, we can expect to find pieces of the Huey's tail not far away, but the rest of the bird reportedly spun up and away from its tail after the explosion. How likely is it that when the bulk of the aircraft fell to earth a few seconds later it landed in the same place it started?

After lunch, Haugen enlists Reynolds and me to join her on a walkabout: Having dug up less debris than expected in the units that held the most promise, she wants to explore the ravine's floor, on a hunch that some wreckage may have slid into the creek.

Her intuition has paid dividends through the years. In October 1997, Haugen flew to a site northeast of Hanoi, where an air force F-105B Thunderchief had crashed in 1966. Vietnamese witnesses reported its pilot, a lieutenant colonel, had been pulled from the wreckage, buried, and later exhumed and reburied, a common practice among people given to ancestor worship, and to caching their forebears' bones. A while later, the Vietnamese said, the remains had been dug up and reburied again.

Haugen was the second anthropologist on the case; her predecessor had found nothing identifiable of the missing man. The Vietnamese directed her to a couple of possible burial sites. She put diggers to work there, but counter to local advice, also opted to excavate the crash site. The graves yielded nothing. The plane's point of impact produced bone fragments and a tooth — enough, with the circumstantial evidence present in the hole, for the lab to make an identification; pieces of life support established without a doubt that he'd been aboard the plane and could not have survived the crash.

We descend the gully's steep bank on a course that takes us away from the path that villagers have used on their trips across the creekbed and come across surface wreckage hidden among the untrod tumps of grass a few yards below the grid's lower edge — frayed white cloth, tri-angular fragments of seat armor, bits of wire. "Well, this is interesting," Haugen says, crouching to flick soil away from a nugget of aluminum. "We might have to open another unit or two."

We move farther down the bank, slipping on its loose soil, and nego-tiate the steepest few feet on all fours before dropping into the creek. Dingman's dam spans the waterway a few yards upstream, its sandbags stacked chest-high, a pool of black behind it. We head the other way, slogging through ankle-deep water and shoe-sucking mud, on the look-out for anything man-made.

A little ways downstream we pass beneath the stacks of bamboo dumped on the ravine's slope when our site was cleared. The piles loom high overhead and in places have slumped onto the branches of spindly trees rising from the creek's edge in the bottom of the gully, so that they overhang our path, partially roofing the waterway. Haugen claws up the bank beneath the eaves to trowel at the soil. She finds no wreckage, but plenty of evidence that the ditch's sides have been shaped by abundant flows of water: They're scoured smooth and striated with the stains of past floods. "When this place gets a lot of rain, the water must really run through here," she says. "It must fill this whole ravine." Overhead, we can see splinters of bamboo and brown sprays of displaced shrub snagged in the branches of the ravine's slender young trees. Some of the stuff is ten feet up.

We splash farther downstream, ducking beneath an arbor of vines. Reynolds, wearing a machete on his belt, pulls the tool from its scab-bard and tries to clear the way. He takes two, maybe three whacks at the dangling wood before slicing a finger. "Shit!" he mutters. "I'm bleeding! Smart one, Reynolds." Beyond the vines, bamboo leans almost horizon-tally from the banks. We shove it aside, alert for snakes. Along the right bank, sunlight pushing through the trees illuminates a web, and we stop to admire the spider in its center — a pale yellow bundle of horns and spikes, black spots forming the image of a face on its carapace. It looks like a Pokémon character.

A little farther on, in a bank of fine silt alongside the water, we find a chunk of seat armor, and a yard away, a small aluminum disk. A path cuts up the ravine to our right, and Haugen climbs it a few yards, stop-ping to examine more evidence of past floods; then she announces she needs to hit the latrine and continues up the path and back to the site. Reynolds and I struggle on, our boots sinking deep into the soft mud on the stream's flanks. The water is five feet wide, murky brown, clouded with sand and sediment from the screening station's outflow, now fifty yards upstream, and in places widens to occupy the entire ravine bottom, leaving us no choice but to splash through the shallows. While we're leaping from rock to rock across one knee-deep pool, a neat set of steps comes into view, chopped into the shale on the left bank. We climb it to the gully's crest and follow a path into a grove of young hardwoods, where it peters out. A side trail plummets back down to the water's edge. "I'm walking a path that North Vietnamese soldiers may have walked, during the war," Reynolds muses. He sucks on his finger wound.

One hundred yards below Dingman's dam, the creek takes a hard right turn; the bank on the outside of the bend has been carved away, revealing a wall a dozen feet tall and striped in different shades of brown. The little canyon's depth, and the stratified sediment we see in the wall, testify further to the power of past floods. In the bend's crook we find two of Dingman's sandbags. Both are nearly buried in sand and gravel.

More troubling questions: If the bulk of the helicopter's wreck did slide down the ravine over time, how far would the creek have carried its aluminum and plastic? If one rain could wash heavy sandbags this distance, how far might thirty years of rain have swept the bodies of the Huey's crew? And how many rains would it take to bury them deep, beneath layer on layer of sediment from the fields and forests upstream?

Haugen closes 512/500, which has produced just a smattering of ACS, and opens 504/508, southeast of the crater. Its eastern third, not an especially promising piece of ground, immediately yields a long green hinge — not the beefy fitting that would have anchored the Huey's front doors, but perhaps part of an engine access cover, or an onboard toolbox. The hole is littered with light aluminum sheeting. Helicopter skin.

Invigorated, Haugen tells the team that she plans to open two new units at the eastern end of the grid, where she, Reynolds, and I stumbled on the surface debris en route to our exploration of the ravine. "We won't do that until we're finished in the crater, though," she says. "We've got two or three days of work ahead of us down there, first."

By late afternoon, diggers have almost finished 508/500, the eastern end of which reaches the crater's bottom; its northeast corner is within inches of the spot Mr. Talin said he found the helmet. Progress is slow, the hole a slick, stinking bog. When one of the 92-Mikes working at its bottom tries to climb up its sides, her mud-caked boots fail to grab, and she slides back down. Her second attempt gets her no farther. "I can't get out of the hole!" she cries.

"Get out of the hole," Posey intones from the crater's lip.

"I'm trying!"

"Get out of the hole, Sergeant."

She claws halfway up the slope, and again loses her grip. She makes a running start from halfway across 508/504, and still can't reach the top. "Is this the best the U.S. Army can do?" Reynolds hollers.

I watch from the crater's lip, my eyes drifting to the spot Mr. Talin planted the pin flag. Despite the site's dearth of wreckage and the questions the RPG fragment raises, the helmet remains a source of hope. If there really was just one crash in these parts that brought death, that helmet suggests this has to be it. Surely, I think to myself, the man wearing it couldn't have survived whatever caused those holes.

PART FIVE

Answers

∎

1

HALFWAY THROUGH the next morning, Victoria Conely is directing excavation in the southeast corner of 504/508 when one of her diggers hits on a small rectangle of aluminum. It comes up mud-caked and bent, but she recognizes it at once for a most valued piece of evidence: a data plate. It measures perhaps two inches by an inch and a half and bears two numbers — a part code, "204-040-012-13," and a serial number, "ABC-3392."

It isn't stamped with a helicopter tail number; even the space printed on the plate for an aircraft model number is blank. But it was once bolted to a specific piece of mechanical or electronic gear aboard a specific helicopter. It should be possible for the joint task force's analysts to trace the part number to a particular component, and to find, somewhere deep in some military log, an entry that links the serial number to the individual aircraft on which that component was installed.

Haugen slips the plate into a small Ziploc bag, which she labels in black ink:

REFNO 1731, 8/30/01
504/508 (SE QUADRANT) ~10CM DEPTH
DATA PLATE

"We can't right away correlate it, that it's our aircraft or isn't our aircraft," she tells the team. "But we'll put in a request for information." When RE-1 reaches Ban Alang, she heads for the commo shack and types an e-mail message to the joint task force.

The team's members are excited by the development, and it dominates conversation that evening at Mama's. But the nearly three weeks the soldiers have spent at the site are beginning to show. Everybody slouches at the restaurant's tables. Faces are drawn. Conversations segue into exhausted silences, blank stares. "I just can't look at those screens anymore," Reynolds whispers.

"It does get pretty damn tedious," I admit.

"I can't keep working the screens and getting nothing in return."

"You give and give and give, and get nothing back."

He shakes his head sadly. "I just can't have a relationship like that."

RE-1 is whipped. Haugen observes in her field notes: "Monotony of screens is getting to everyone."

While we sleep, CILHI teams are four thousand miles to our east, wrapping up work at two World War II sites that illustrate how difficult, by comparison, the lab's Southeast Asian cases can be. That's not to suggest that the excavations afoot on New Britain, a large, mountainous island to the north of Papua New Guinea's main landmass, are easy: Digging in the jungle there presents dangers every bit as perilous, and worksites equally rugged and remote, as those of Vietnam or Laos. But next to the Case 1731 site, the wrecks that await teams laboring in the South Pacific are akin to time capsules of events sixty years passed.

To reach them I took a detour on my way to Laos, flying from the States to Sydney and on to Port Moresby, Papua New Guinea's crime-plagued capital. From there a small jet took me to Rabaul, New Britain's largest city and until recently one of the cheeriest, most colorful burgs in Oceana. Today it's a wasteland of tree stumps and skeletal ruins: Around the city and its harbor loom five active volcanoes, two of which blew their tops on the same day in September 1994. Several feet of black ash fell on the city, crushing houses and commercial buildings under its weight, destroying the town docks, burying entire neighborhoods, and smothering the lush tropical vegetation that sprouted from every cranny. All is now packed under cinders layered chest-high over the streetscape. The team was encamped in an ash-stained, cinderblock hotel, one of the handful of buildings in central Rabaul to survive the eruptions, and these days a lonely outpost in a weird, windswept desert of piled ash and blackened wreckage.

Early one morning I drove with some of the team out along the rutted coastal highway that linked Rabaul with the rest of the island. We passed the rusted skeleton of a Japanese harbor crane, and caves in which the empire's soldiers dug in as Allies swept north in 1943, and eighteen miles from the hotel pulled into the East New Britain Historical and Cultural Centre, and a lawn crowded with old weapons pulled from the island's woods and water: a Japanese 37mm gun; the rusting and curled casing of an American 2,000-pound bomb; a big antiaircraft gun, its gray barrel gouged by bullet strikes that looked like thumbprints in cake icing; the smashed cockpit of a Japanese "Betty" bomber. We wandered past a P-38 Lightning's huge twelve-cylinder engine and the mangled remains of a U.S. Navy F-4U Corsair.

The grounds were sunny, quiet, fragrant with hibiscus, ringed by mango and casuarina trees, breadfruit and balsa. Coconuts littered the grass around an old Zero fighter, metal skin peeled to expose its aluminum ribs. Geckos darted and hopped across the husks of old bombs.

From there I ventured to a CILHI dig led by Bill Belcher, the pudgy, bespectacled thirty-nine-year-old anthropologist who'd shown me the silk survival map from his English excavation. When his team had arrived on New Britain three weeks before, its members did not know exactly who or what they were looking for: The wreckage they were to unearth was unidentified. Buried deep in the bank of a dry riverbed they found two engines that identified the plane as a P-38 Lightning, a fast, twin-tailed American fighter. One hundred yards away, in a grove of hibiscus, they found more wreckage, ripped and balled beyond recognition.

So it seemed, anyway. One of the team's augmentees, an amateur aircraft enthusiast, thought he detected a tail boom in the mass of twisted metal. "I took one look at it and thought, 'There's no way we'll get an ID off that,'" Belcher told me as we walked, sweating, through the trees to the pile. "But we bent it back into shape." And lo, at the end of the suspected tail boom was a crushed tailplane — and painted on it, a number.

"We could read part of a '2,' part of an '8,' and part of a '4,'" Belcher said, as we squatted beside it. The numbers were flaking, but intact enough to read. "We did a search of P-38s that had that number sequence, and there was only one that was lost." The fighter in question had gone down in November 1943. Its pilot's fate was unknown.

Within a day of that discovery, a team member cleaning the plane's recovered .50-caliber machine guns and 20mm cannons found a serial number, and just after that, the team pulled a number off one of the plane's buried engines. Both correlated to the same plane. "So we now had the identity of the pilot we were looking for," Belcher said. "The day after that, we found his high school ring. It had a date of 1936 on it, and on the inside were his initials."

The soldier who found the ring recovered a finger bone with it. Other bone turned up, too: On the morning of my visit, two teeth and a sliver of possible humerus, or upper arm bone, had been picked off the screens, and as Belcher and I slugged down water in the break tent, a team member hurried up to the anthro yelling, "Temporal bone! Found a temporal bone!"

"You did?" Belcher asked, taking it from him. He turned the dark yellow, inch-square plate over in his hand. A suture — the zigzag seam between two sections of skull — crossed its center.

"Oh," Belcher gasped, "you *did!*"

That was near the end of Belcher's dig; he wrapped up the site a few days later.

Gwen Haugen has a third of her excavation to go at the Case 1731 site. Anything can happen.

It is an overcast morning, with a cool breeze from the south. Flies are thick at Ban Alang, signaling an approaching storm. Haugen mentions that atmospheric trouble is brewing in the South China Sea. As skinny as central Vietnam is, and as close as we are to the border, it won't take long to reach us. We face a hard rain.

Pete Miller's team, facing the prospect of getting stuck at its site a half-hour south of ours, is staying put for the day. Our morning meeting thus stars a new player, a 92-Mike sergeant from Miller's team. He's a loud character and on joining the huddle informs us that today is RE-1's lucky day.

"You ain't found bone yet, because you ain't had *me* to find it!" he says. "We're finding bone today. I can *feel* it!"

I'm standing beside Krueger, who glares at our guest. "Somebody's gonna wind up in the ravine today," the linguist growls quietly. "That's what I can feel."

On the flight out, strong winds sweep down the valley to buffet our Squirrel, and we sway drunkenly in the especially fierce gusts at the escarpment's bend. I can see another Squirrel far ahead and above us, fishtailing as well. To the east, over Vietnam, the sky is the color of eggplant. I look over at Don Guthrie from the front passenger seat. "Don," I say into my headset's mike, "do you know what the forecast is?"

Guthrie shakes his head, keeping his eyes on the sky. "No idea."

"I heard there was some big system moving off Vietnam."

"Maybe there is." he shrugs. "We're gonna fly anyway, aren't we?" A large hawk cartwheels past us, blown out of control by the wind and upended by our downwash. "The reality is that we're flying short distances in remote areas," the pilot says, "so any weather forecast we could get wouldn't be very bloody helpful, would it?"

The site is sodden. Puddles fill the footprints crisscrossing the grid, and the big crater's bottom is under two feet of water. Haugen sets up a baling line, and Guthrie and I watch as the locals pass water a bucket at a time up the hole's slope and across the site to the crater tucked in the trees behind the break tent.

Once the hole's emptied, Haugen opens the unit that occupies most of its base, 508/504, the square of earth in which Mr. Talin supposedly spied the helmet. It is the seventeenth unit to open in the grid; in its three weeks on the site, RE-1 has dug, bucketed, and sifted roughly 2,700 cubic feet of material, enough to fill a backyard pool. ACS has accounted for maybe — just maybe — 6 cubic feet.

Two hours into the day's digging, as our visiting sergeant works a screen and continues to trumpet his bone-finding prowess, Conely steps off the A-frame with a balled-up piece of aluminum, unearthed in the new unit's southwest quadrant. She folds it flat; it's another data plate, painted olive drab and torn into the shape of Massachusetts. A thin strand of gleaming metal corresponding to Cape Cod partially encircles a machined hole, above which are embossed the words "TYPE" and "SIZE." Over the latter, the plate has been stamped "1"," apparently a reference to the hole, which must have once accommodated a plug of some sort. Conely is more interested in the plate's middle, for there — near, say, Worcester — is a number, "15562E."

Haugen closes 504/508, the unit that dips into the crater's southeast corner, having recovered the large data plate, a couple of hinges, and a spray of ACS from its soil. She decides to excavate half of the unit directly to its south, 500/508; if it produces, she says, we'll extend the dig into the whole square. A work party rakes it bare, then begins carving at its northern edge. A few yards away and fifteen feet below, Dingman slops around in the crater's gooey floor, his knee-high rubber boots swathed in mud. His barefoot workers keep moving, lest they sink past their ankles, as they pour ooze from the southeast corner into buckets. Each step they take sounds like a wet kiss.

By mid-afternoon, the eastern half of the unit has been dug twenty centimeters deep, and the workers' mud-weighted shovels and picks are marching steadily toward the northwest corner, where the helmet reportedly lay. As I watch from the crater's lip, I see a giant water bug, a leaf-shaped creature with a snorkel in its tail and evil-looking pincers for front legs, scurry out of the diggers' path and take cover among a few hardy sprigs of water grass. A tiger-striped wolf spider trundles through the mud beside me, hauling a marble-sized egg sac. Refugees, struggling to escape a war zone.

During a break, one of the 92-Mikes pointedly observes that we've found no bone. The visiting sergeant objects that the day isn't over. "The bone man is here," he tells the team. "I'm telling ya, I can *feel* the bone." Most of RE-1 just stares at him. Krueger grunts, "I'll bet you can."

Conely and Haugen compare notes. "There's a lot of material coming out," the navy chief says.

"Yeah," Haugen says. "Which is good. I'm just surprised we haven't found any zipper pulls."

"Or zippers."

Haugen nods. "Pretty unusual. When you're finding flight suit pieces, you can usually expect to find zippers, or pieces of zipper."

Across the break tent, Krueger is called to the grid's edge by Sammy and a couple other locals, who gather around him, speaking quietly as they eyeball the team's enlisted women. Krueger says something in Lao, and the group erupts in laughter. "Krueger, what are you saying to them?" one of the women asks. Krueger looks at her and chuckles. The locals ogle. She yells over to Reynolds: "Sir, I think we need a new linguist. Krueger's trying to trade us!"

Krueger does not deny the charge. "Jesus, Krueger!" an indignant female soldier hollers. Reynolds, lying on the equipment platform, his eyes closed, says sleepily: "Krueger, stop trying to trade the women."

One of the villagers, looking self-conscious, asks Krueger a question. "They want to know," he dutifully translates, "whether you like a Lao-Theung man."

"Who, me?" one of the women asks.

"All of you."

As the women weigh this question, the rain eases. "Let's go, y'all," Posey says. "Let's get out there. If we move, the Lao move." Eagmin rises heavily from a bench, sighing. Posey shoots him a glance. "Ain't it time to make some doughnuts?"

"Let me tell you something," Eagmin replies. "I'm never going to look at a doughnut again."

The wind blows strong and wet from the southwest. It offers little relief from the heat. Dingman and his team wallow in the crater's gassy slime, as Eagmin sweeps the already-excavated portion of 508/504 behind them. He scores several hits and stops at each, roots around beneath the soft crater floor with his trowel, uncovers a gnarled piece of aluminum, and a thick, curving plate of metal. And something else, bright green, about four centimeters below the floor. "This," he says, "is something from the incident."

Haugen clambers into the hole, where the EOD hands her a bright teal cylinder — an M-60 shell casing. "Has this been fired?" she asks.

Eagmin nods. He is beaded in sweat, which drips steadily from the tip of his nose. "Yup. This was fired in anger."

"How do you know?"

He points out a small dent at the center of the cartridge's base, where a machine gun's firing pin started the chain reaction that propelled a .30-caliber round down the weapon's barrel. "I also got a really big hit over here." He indicates a rectangle of ground almost three feet long. Haugen chops into the mud with her trowel, going down four or five inches. The EOD follows her with a shovel, and several inches further down pries up a large slab of heavy metal.

Haugen turns the metal over in her hand. Bomb frag, by the looks of it. "Sergeant Dingman," she calls across the crater. Dingman, hacking away at the unit's western edge, freezes his pick in mid-swing. "Ma'am?"

"That area you're in? We're getting a lot of metal and other stuff out of here, so maybe you could take it a little deeper for me."

"Yes, ma'am."

"And we'll need you to backtrack over this part of the unit, and bring it down another ten centimeters or so." Dingman, too winded and overheated to say much, his face a deep pink, merely nods.

Eagmin continues his sweep. He locates another underground anomaly. He can't say what it is but declares it the most powerful hit he's picked up at the site. He points out its center, and Haugen digs in with her trowel. A minute later, she's opened a hole four inches deep

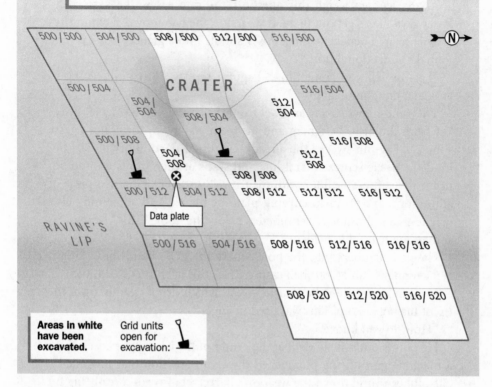

500 / 500   504 / 500   508 / 500   512 / 500   516 / 500

→N→

500 / 504   CRATER   516 / 504

504 / 504

508 / 504   512 / 504

500 / 508   516 / 508

504 / 508

512 / 508

508 / 508

500 / 512   504 / 512   508 / 512   512 / 512   516 / 512

Data plate

RAVINE'S LIP

500 / 516   504 / 516   508 / 516   512 / 516   516 / 516

508 / 520   512 / 520   516 / 520

Areas in white have been excavated.   Grid units open for excavation:

and six wide, but revealed nothing unusual. Eagmin sweeps the hole and the surrounding dirt. "Still there," he announces.

She scrapes deeper into the crater's bottom, takes the hole eight inches down — roughly sixteen inches below the crater's original bottom. She looks up at Eagmin. "Could you check it again?" she says. "I don't see anything here." He sweeps it once more. "Still there."

I take over for Haugen, using a full-size shovel. Eagmin again sweeps. "Still there." I shovel on. "God," Haugen mutters, "there goes my unit's beautiful floor." Archaeologists are an anal bunch, fond of neat work sites. When Haugen eats ice cream from the carton, she scrapes her spoon across the top, excavates it in smooth layers. I stop digging while Eagmin sweeps the area yet again. He shakes his head, mystified. "Still there." I switch to a trowel. "Is this thing big?"

"I have it on the lowest sensitivity," he says, "and all I have to do is sweep it by really fast and I get a ping. So yeah, I would think so." I lift more dirt out of the hole, wait for his sweep. "Still there." I probe with the trowel's point, reaching underground past my elbow. "Brian, I'm several inches farther down, and I just don't feel a thing."

Eagmin creeps the detector's head around the edge of the hole. "Try to shovel a little this way." He points a few inches to the east. I plant the shovel and immediately hit something hard and big enough to stop the blade, six inches down. When I turn it to lift the dirt away, it makes a loud, metal-on-metal scrape. "Ah," Eagmin says, "there it is."

With the dirt lifted away, a big slab of dark metal confronts us. "Jesus," I mumble. "What is that?" Haugen squats beside it, gives it a poke with her trowel, and looks up at us. "Aircraft," she says.

Could this be it? Have we found 185? Does the chopper's crew lie just below this ragged section of fuselage? We slip the shovel's blade beneath the plate and pry it loose from the mud. It measures nearly two feet long, and the ground in which it's lain for thirty years is unwilling to part with it; it takes us a minute to uncover enough of the Huey's skin that we can yank it free.

Haugen turns it over in her hands as I peer into the hole. At its bottom, shielded all these years by the metal, is more mud.

A variety of interesting ACS comes off the unit's screens, including four pieces of a black plastic knob, roughly circular, that once read TO EXTEND PEDAL PUSH DOWN AND TURN. It certainly suggests that some of the helicopter's cockpit wound up in 508/504, but other units have yielded shards of the instrument panel, as well, so it's impossible to say whether the discovery really means much.

At day's end we pull tarps over the open units and straggle into the break tent. A large, green-brown snake crosses the plastic on 500/508, which creates a commotion among the locals, but most of RE-1 is too spent to pay it much mind, and besides, its attention is demanded by the visiting sergeant, who promises that we are on the cusp of a major discovery. "Maybe I should come back again," he says. "Help you guys out."

Krueger looks as if he might require restraints, but Posey smiles kindly at the sergeant. "Brother, we'll take all the help we can get. You want to come back, we'll find work for you."

Haugen ducks into the break tent, and the team closes around her.

"The crater will have to go a little deeper, so we'll spend longer in the hole than we expected," she says. "But we're finding a lot of stuff there, so let's get it done.

"We have to push really hard to get that dirt through the screens," she adds, "because we really are on a race against the clock now."

At Ban Alang, Haugen and Conely step into the communications shack, and when they emerge a minute later, announce that we have a reply to Haugen's request for information about the first data plate we found: Its part number identifies it as the label from a UH-1's tail rotor gearbox. The analysts in Hawaii can say little more about it than that, Haugen says. "They can't correlate it to a particular helicopter."

"The tail rotor?" I say. "Well, that might be something, considering the tail boom broke off."

"It *was* only eight meters away that we found that RPG part," she says.

"Yeah."

She nods uncertainly. "If it's the right helicopter."

2

THERE COMES A TIME in every excavation when a recovery team's motivation shifts from achieving success to simply finishing the job, and the reply to RE-1's request for information seems to provoke such a shift. At its meeting the following morning, a cheerless resignation grips the team, as if all its members have had the same unhappy epiphany during the night: We haven't found anything yet, there's little reason to expect we'll find anything today, and time is running out.

Little at the site lifts our spirits. The routine on the A-frame is no longer numbing; it now approaches torture. We're sifting dirt loaded with small pieces of ACS and bomb frag, picking some man-made object off every screen, and still the rhythm of it and the sound of it and the look of it — of seeing little but pebbles and lumpy clay and wire mesh for hours on end — grows maddening. Even our unswervingly tireless Laotian helpers seem sapped of energy: My screen partner, a middle-aged village woman, spends the morning looking around and conversing with her neighbors, rather than pushing dirt. I demote her to the bucket line at lunch and try to draft Sammy to replace her. Even cheerful Sammy is in no mood to work. He insists on remaining in the bucket line.

Haugen closes 500/508 and opens 504/512, a unit southeast of the crater. The squares to its east and west have been fully excavated, and because their southern halves produced few artifacts, she elects to dig only the northern half of the new one. Late in the afternoon, in the unit's northwest corner, the team unearths a decal that has pulled away

from some component of the wrecked helicopter. Printed in block cap-
itals on the strip of clear, skin-thin plastic are the words TAIL BOOM.

"It looks like that area over there is where the tail hit," Conely tells
Haugen, "because we're pulling all this tail stuff from right there." The
data plate from the tail rotor assembly was found one unit to the west,
in 504/508. It does, indeed, appear that a helicopter's tail once lay there.

"Or that's where somebody scavenged the tail boom," Haugen says.
"Or that's where they drug the tail boom." She sighs. "Things are often
not what they appear, unfortunately."

Conely, Dingman, Artillaga, and I share a table at Mama's. It is one of
the few times we've dined together; the team has been split by the limited size of the restaurant's tables into cliques, and we haven't been in
each other's. RE-1's three young white women have become a unit.
Conely, Dingman, and Posey, of similar age and experience, have often
formed another. Posey is also part of a clique of black sergeants, and an
occasional member of the knot of bosses — Reynolds, Haugen, Doc
Walsh — that convenes most evenings. The team's two black women are
inseparable. Eagmin and Artillaga are free agents, each floating among
several circles. Krueger speaks most readily to Reynolds, but has defied
membership in any club.

Our meal is a muted affair. "It's just so frustrating," Conely says, "to
find so much ACS, and nothing else."

We all murmur our agreement.

"So what do you think?" Dingman asks, leaning back in his chair.
"Are we gonna find any remains?"

"I don't know," Conely says. "I'm just going to keep hoping for the
best. But it's hard not to be discouraged."

We again murmur agreement. "If we don't find any," I ask her, "will
you consider the trip a waste?"

She answers without hesitation. "Oh, no. This has been a great experience."

"Even if you don't find anything," Artillaga says, "it's a good mission."

Conely nods. "If I were one of these guys," she says, "I'd like to think
people would come looking for me, and would work as hard as this
team has worked."

Another round of murmurs.

"We gotta stay positive," Conely says.

Dingman leaves. A few minutes later, Conely announces she is going to turn in early and heads for her tent. Krueger pulls up a chair, Beerlao in hand, just ahead of the similarly equipped Doc Walsh. Right behind comes Mike Crosgrove, an aide at the joint task force's detachment headquarters in Vientiane.

"Did you hear the news?" he asks. Crosgrove is a wiry, bespectacled air force technical sergeant, smart and gung-ho about the JTF's work. He's on a weekend visit to the field.

"What news?" Artillaga asks.

"RE-3 found some bone."

"They *did?*"

Crosgrove nods, smiling. "Found a piece of rib."

Those of us from RE-1 stare stupidly at him. It occurs to me that I should toast the mission's successful recovery of human remains, that I should feel happy a family may be able to lay a loved one to rest after a three-decade wait. I should feel bittersweet satisfaction at an end finally achieved.

Instead, I feel a twinge of jealousy. Where are *our* guys? Artillaga looks at me, his expression glum, and shakes his head. "Just gotta get out there again tomorrow," he says. He, Krueger, and Walsh leave. Crosgrove and I drink our beers.

"Same old shit?" he asks.

"Afraid so." It seems an act of betrayal, of faithlessness, to voice doubts about RE-1's prospects to an outsider. "I hate to say it," I tell him just the same, "but I don't think we're going to find anything."

Crosgrove takes a swig of his Beerlao. He's the expat who in no time figures out where to eat, find American cigarettes, change currency; how to haggle with the natives; whom to see to get things done. "Listen," he says, and I do it. He leans forward over the table. "You never know. You can be digging right to the end, and suddenly find the whole thing. *You never know.*"

The rain comes. It starts that night, falling in drops that would each fill a teaspoon, and hard enough that it drowns out the TV in Mama's. By the following morning, the ground outside my tent is under an inch of water. The deluge does not ease. RE-1 gathers for the morning meeting, Main Street a shallow river outside the barn, the temperature rising, and still, it falls.

The escarpment remains invisible behind a caul of vapor. The helicopters stay on the pads. Shortly before midday, Haugen and Reynolds decide to attempt a trip to the site. They find the grid completely swamped. The anthro calls off digging for the day.

The rain continues throughout the afternoon, stops briefly, then resumes after dark. It's still drizzling the next morning when we again meet in the barn. "We're gonna have a swimming pool in that crater," Haugen says. "We get out there, we'll be bailing — hell, there might be enough water to use the pump." She looks around at her team, sapped rather than energized by the wasted day in camp. Eagmin and Conely, both typically talkative and chipper, stare at their feet. The 92-Mikes are bleary-eyed and sucking coffee from Styrofoam cups. A couple look close to tears. My arms ache and my hands are blistered and I feel as if my skin is basted in a sticky paste; it's just after seven, and despite the rain, the day is already impossibly hot.

"Just go out there and do what you've been doing," the anthro says gently. "We're very close. We have just a few hours left."

The crater is thigh-deep in water. Rather than drag the pump across the site, Haugen has a half-dozen villagers bail out the hole, passing their filled buckets up two lines. Chubby and another dog, teeth bared but soundless, wrestle among them. The men and women in the line are absorbed in the fight when there's a shriek at the crater's bottom: One of the bailing teenagers has been bitten by a slender, foot-long snake in the water. As the Americans in the hole back away, the injured worker traps the creature under his flip-flop, grabs its skull between thumb and forefinger and squeezes. I can hear it crack from thirty feet away.

Fifteen minutes later, another snake pops up in the water. In a blur a villager snatches the animal up by the head, gives its body a twist, pulls it taut, then pinches its head flat. He flings it west across the site. I watch it land on the ravine's lip and writhe, crazed, down the slope.

Despite the excitement, the crater is drained by midmorning. Its bottom is a fetid brown glue into which Eagmin sinks with his metal detector. He uncovers small knots of aluminum, wire, screws, and a few chunks of bomb frag, while three enlisted women supervise the destruction of a defiant clump of bamboo in 504/500, on the crater's southwest slope.

Eagmin, moving to 516/504, an unexcavated unit on the crater's far side, gets a hit, digs with his trowel for a moment, then walks to the break tent for a shovel. "Going to China?" Haugen asks him.

"I'm not sure," he says. He opens a hole a foot wide and six inches deep, then sweeps his detector's head over it. "It's big, whatever it is." He takes up the shovel again, and as I watch I recall Mike Crosgrove's words, that we could work right up to the last day without finding much, then hit a trove of remains.

It turns out to be bomb frag. A couple feet away, under a bamboo stump, he pulls up another chunk of heavy metal, orange with rust, and on the unit's south side, he finds an M-60 tracer round. No trove.

Lunchtime. We gather in the break tent. The conversation centers on what the team plans to do in Savannakhet, where we'll spend a night on our way to Thailand and a military jet home. Reynolds is eating another can of cold chunky soup. "When we get out of here," he says, "I'm never eating this shit again. Ever."

I walk to the cooler to grab a bottle of water. Krueger is standing beside it, humming to himself. "I'm definitely coming back here in a year," he says, looking around.

I look around, too, to make certain he's speaking to me. Every conversation we've had, I've started.

"What, so you can visit Vientiane and stuff?" I ask.

"Fuck Vientiane," he says. "I'm coming back *here*."

"Here? To this village?"

He nods. "Stay with the chief."

Fair enough: Krueger's become enamored of village life, of stone-age simplicity. Of hard, honest labor performed in the name of subsistence, rather than the acquisition of status or luxury. Of reliance on a *bria* and a crossbow for all one's needs. Of sitting on the ground and cooking over fire. I can appreciate it, myself. To live in Ban Satum is to forego the myriad stresses that grip most Americans, like credit-card debt and promotions at work and whether the kids will get into a top-tier college; to be free of such inconsequentials as the latest fashions, as celebrity gossip, as the goings-on in Washington, in London, in Paris — in any settlement beyond Ban Satum.

It's not an easy existence, reliant as it is on nature's kindness. When it rains, you get wet. When a snake bites, you might die. Get sick and you'll probably have to beat your illness without modern medicines. Break a leg and you're hobbled for life. Plow or plant in the wrong place and you blow to smithereens.

Ban Satum doesn't even have a schoolhouse, rough as they are hereabouts. Life doesn't get much better, or much worse, from generation to generation. In fact, life hasn't changed much in five hundred years.

"You gonna bring your girlfriend, or something?" I ask Krueger. I figure that he might want to share his next visit with someone close.

He replies, matter-of-factly: "I'm gonna get married here."

"Oh," I say. "You gonna bring somebody with you?"

"No," he replies, "I'll marry somebody here."

I haven't noticed any romance bloom in the grid or on the screens, haven't seen Krueger conversing with any of the local women. On the few occasions I've seen him speaking with anyone, it's been with the officials, a village chief, or the young guys that work the hole.

I'm digesting his news when a large rhinoceros beetle flies noisily over our heads, legs spread oddly, its hard outer wings swiveled forward, and bounces off the underside of the tarp. "That thing'll be coming in for a landing soon," Reynolds observes, as the insect struggles to escape the break tent. A soldier prepares to swat it with a T-shirt but is shouted away by several team members; we watch it carom off the nylon, urging it on, until it seems sure to reach open sky. Just before it does, a Laotian boy darts to the tent's edge, snatches the beetle from the air, and immediately breaks off its legs with loud snaps. He slips the helpless creature into his shirt pocket.

"That beetle is *so* bumming," Haugen groans. "Keep watching. Sometimes they'll break off the back end and suck the juices out." We wait expectantly. The kid fails to suck the beetle.

"They'll eat anything," Krueger murmurs. There's admiration in his tone. "Bugs," he says. "Mud."

I stare at him, wondering how he'll cater his wedding.

Low, swirling clouds sweep in from the north, the temperature drops into the eighties, and a stiff breeze develops. A twilight falls over the grid. For all this bluster, we get only drizzle. Just the same, the team in 508/504 works quickly, striving to wrap up the unit before the weather's inevitable turn. The rough circle dug into the crater's bottom is now sixteen inches deep.

Haugen and Artillaga are working the unit when a third snake materializes in the mud. From the screens I can see the Americans and several Laotian workers retreat while a sole villager lunges for the serpent. He snares it by the ends, twists it, and snaps it taut — and keeps pulling.

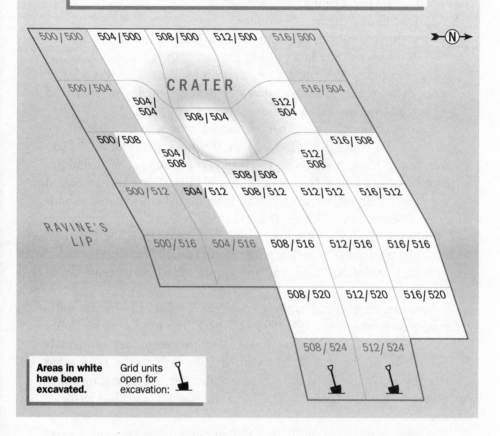

The snake stretches. "Aw, noooooo!" Haugen cries, and as she does the snake rips in two in a fountain of red, dousing Artillaga in a spray of blood and shredded muscle. A cheer goes up from the bucket line. The local hoists the snake's dripping halves overhead in triumph.

Not long after, 508/504 finally closes, having yielded nothing of consequence. Haugen and I watch the last of the locals clamber up the crater's side. "I hate to see that," she mutters. "I hoped that even if the wreck wasn't in the crater, maybe the locals had used the hole for stuff they didn't want."

"It's pretty damn disappointing," I say. "Especially after that helmet."

"Yeah," Haugen sighs. "Assuming Mr. Talin really found it there."

"You don't think he did?"

"I don't know," she says. "I wonder."

"You think somebody told him to say he found it there?"

"I don't know." She kicks at the ground with her boot. "A village makes out pretty well when an excavation happens. They get a lot of money. And it doesn't really matter whether any remains are recovered — they get paid, no matter what."

I turn the thought over. There is, indeed, money to be made off the recovery effort, and the longer it takes, the more there will be. "If you were them," Haugen says, "and you could get a team to come in and pay everybody in a village for a month, wouldn't you?" We silently regard the site's seventy workers. The locals have turned out in some memorable T-shirts today. "Three Times Three Are Nine," one announces. "Mercedes, Symbol of Relatives," reads a second. And: "Be Like Us!" And: "Baseball 2000." Another villager wears a dark blue shirt sprinkled with little American flags, and the words "Land of Liberty" on its placket.

Some are clearly handouts from past teams; some of the rattier shirts might even date to the IE's 1994 visit here. The others are no doubt knock-offs from the Xepon Market. Western images are immensely popular in Southeast Asia: Last year, at a site in Vietnam, I saw a kid wearing a "Titanic" T-shirt. It was a match for the American movie poster, except that Leonardo DiCaprio and Kate Winslett had jet-black hair.

As the wordless seconds pass, I mull our expedition's genesis. A team visits in 1994 and finds so little it recommends against an excavation. Another team visits seven years later with the same result — except that this time, a helmet figures in the story, a helmet that no one thought to mention during the first team's visit. Without Mr. Talin's helmet, we wouldn't be here.

Haugen has been turning this over, too. "If you want to get a team in to excavate," she says, "you tell the IE that you've found a helmet, or flight suit, or zipper. Those three things are almost guaranteed to get a response, because you're talking life support." She squints at me. "I think the Lao have figured that out."

"But if they've figured that out, surely they're smart enough to know that the gravy train's gonna dry up if they keep having us dig where they know we won't find anything."

"Maybe." She shrugs.

"So what happens to the helmet? Do you think it'll turn up again, at some other site?"

"Could," she says. The joint task force has no evidence that the Laotian government has knowingly engaged in evidence planting, though the years have seen many episodes that have injected doubt into the postwar rapprochement — one being that mysterious report of bones at Pete Miller's 1989 site.

But deception has certainly been part of Vietnam's style of business on the MIA question, and for years after the war, the Vietnamese mentored the Laotians on all manner of things. The Vietnamese not only have warehoused bones but have further tested American patience by apparently planting evidence on several occasions.

One 1989 example saw Hanoi officials turn over two dozen bone fragments they represented as the remains of a navy A-4 pilot shot down over Haiphong twenty-two years before. The Vietnamese said the remains had been recovered in a unilateral excavation, performed without independent observation, along with a few pieces of material evidence. The artifacts included a five-dollar bill, an immunization card, and a faded military ID card, all "in remarkably clean condition," and a parachute, "remarkable and clean beyond comprehension for a chute which was said to have been removed from a crater some 12 meters deep more than 20 years after the incident." U.S. investigators concluded that the pilot had ejected from his plane before it crashed and that his life-support materials and personal effects had been collected shortly after he hit the ground and stored since. A life raft was recovered, too. The experts suspected that the Vietnamese soaked it in jet fuel to bolster their story that it was pulled from a wreck.

The lab was eventually able to identify the pilot from the turned-over bones, but where and when they were recovered remains a question.

Even if the Laotians are squeaky-clean in comparison, their casual handling of the helmet is a worry: A piece of material evidence, linked to one case but bearing no identifiable markings or numbers, remains in private hands in a region busy with unresolved cases. Mr. Talin could trade the helmet away. It could travel several provinces from here. It could reappear in Vietnam.

Three feet of water lie in the crater's bottom when we reach the site. Dingman hauls the pump to the hole's edge and drains it within a half-hour. Posey leads a team digging the last corner of 504/500. He's finished by 9 A.M., and RE-1's focus now shifts to the grid's eastern edge, where Haugen strings two new units, 508/524 and 512/524, on the ravine's thirty-five-degree slope. The squares encompass the ground on which she, Reynolds, and I found surface debris at the start of our exploration of the creekbed. They almost immediately yield some promising artifacts: Eagmin pulls a chunk of zipper from his screen, in which he's pushing dirt from 512/524. "An interesting development," Haugen calls it. "Unfortunately we're out of land. Any farther down and we're in the river."

Indeed, solid ground ends abruptly at the units' downhill edge. The final ten feet to the creekbed are vertical, the ravine's flank having been chewed away; it was here, on this scoured and stratified bluff, that Haugen found evidence of regular and violent flooding when we hiked the creek. Much of the cut bamboo piled beyond the lip is resting on the small hardwoods below. If we were to tread on this dank thatching, we'd fall straight through and into the water. "It's a bummer," Haugen says, "because if any wreckage was down any lower, it's . . ." She sweeps her arm downstream. "It's gone."

A half-dozen local men work in the hole, one of them in dressy women's sandals. The site bakes dry. Puddles vanish. The smooth floors of the excavated units parch hard. One of the team's enlisted women pulls off her soaked T-shirt and works in a tank top. The sight of her muscular shoulders and arms prompts an impressed murmur from the bucket line.

Lunch. We assemble in the break tent. "Not to scare anybody," Posey says, "but we had three snakes jump out at us yesterday. If anybody goes downhill to help move that bamboo, be aware of what might jump out at you, that you're disturbing something's home — and whatever it is, it ain't gonna be too happy about it."

Conely dumps artifacts from the morning's dig into a clean screen. "When we're done with 512/524," Reynolds says, "we can have everybody work that last unit, bang that out. Have all twelve screens working the dirt from that one hole."

Haugen nods. "It won't be long before we're ready."

Conely holds up a swatch of green fabric, the stuff she identified days ago as Nomex. "I don't think that's flight suit material," she says uncertainly. "Now that it's drying, it looks rougher, more like a cotton — like a kit bag, or something."

"Have you ever seen flight suit material that's been in the ground for thirty years?" Reynolds asks her.

"Well, no."

"Me, neither," the captain says.

"I just keep going back to the '94 IE report," Haugen mumbles, more to herself than to the team. "The villagers told those guys that within two months of the crash they were here, and they found no bodies, they saw no personal effects, no clothes, no boots — and they always came looking for clothes and boots. They really wanted that stuff. They mentioned no blood."

"It burned, though," I say. "Maybe there wasn't any blood."

"Still, I'm surprised we haven't found any personal effects," she says. "No pieces of wristwatch, for instance. Those guys seemed to like those big, chunky, metal Seikos, and they leave lots of pieces. There's been no dog tag chain — not the dog tags, just the little metal balls." She shakes her head.

Across the tent, Krueger confides that he's decided not to marry a villager he's had his eye on. "She's already married," he explains. "I confirmed it." I follow his gaze to the Laotian break tent, where a beautiful young girl, waist-length hair tied in a purple ribbon, is staring back at him. She drops her eyes when she sees me looking. "How old is she?" I ask him.

"Thirteen," he murmurs.

"Let's go, y'all," Posey says. "Let's get back out there."

Haugen asks for five volunteers to hack away the bamboo stacked below the open units, and nine villagers scramble bare-footed into the tangle, swinging *brias*, unfazed by the almost certain presence of snakes in its depths. One of them climbs onto the pile and bounces up and down until it collapses under his feet, and he drops into the creekbed. Unhurt, he tugs at the pile's underside while his colleagues slip bamboo poles beneath its uphill edge and pry it up and over the ravine's lip. It ascends in a single mass, matted and wet and heavy. Under it, a cobalt-blue scorpion crouches, every bit of six inches long. A local promptly splits it with his blade.

In 508/524, an old villager wields an axe to chop up a huge bamboo root, which resembles an asterisk of thick, yellow wire more than anything living. His blows glance off the fibrous stalks, and when he scores a solid hit, it only chips their skin. Two younger locals join in with picks, and one finally works the head of his tool under the root's massive center. It takes all three workers, pushing on the pick's handle, to rip it loose from the soil. Beneath it are a sliver of glass, a swatch of black fabric, and an inch-square piece of flat rubber. A few feet to the west, another worker uncovers a large rectangle of olive-drab cloth.

Haugen, troweling at the unit's edge, shows off a strip of metal stamped with numbers, and a thick chunk of painted glass, apparently part of a backlit instrument panel display; its unpainted portions form the word CAUTION. "We found another piece of fabric," she says, "but it looks like cotton, with an over-and-under weave. Nomex is a polyester, so I don't think that it's flight suit. We found a piece of what looks like seat belt, too."

"Seat belt?" I say, excited. "Doesn't that count as life support?"

She crinkles her nose. "I wish it were," she says, "but with helicopters, it's really discrete, what's plain wreckage, what's life support. A helicopter has troop seats."

"Wouldn't troop seats have seat belts?"

"Well, yeah, they would. But that's why it doesn't really mean anything," she says. "In a jet, finding a seat belt says the seat was still in the aircraft when it hit. It tells you whether the pilot ejected.

"In a helicopter, with so many seats — and with no ejection seats — it's just wreckage."

When the day's work is done, Conely's buckets are filled with pieces of seat armor, with red and green and clear glass, with shards of aluminum and torn pieces of fabric. The holes have yielded instrument panel warning lights that read 20 MINUTE FUEL and ENGINE OIL PRESS., and washers and wires and stainless-steel disks, and ragged squares of metal screen. But today, as on every day, no bone. No identifiable personal effects. Nothing that directly connects the site with Barker, Dugan, Dillender, and Chubb.

3

THURSDAY, SEPTEMBER 6, 2001, 7 A.M.: "Isn't it amazing," Brian Eagmin says, as RE-1 gathers in the barn beside the mess tent, "to think that today might be our last day pushing dirt?"

As usual, all the team but Haugen is wilting in the early-morning humidity. Reynolds pauses between gulps of bottled water to glare at the EOD. "Thanks, Eagmin," the captain says. "You just jinxed us."

"Watch us find bone," Eagmin says, unfazed.

"God," a sergeant sighs, "I hope so." The team responds with a chorus of Amens and No shits.

But the morning passes with few artifacts unearthed; the only item of real interest is a broken black handle, a double for the piece of plastic that Conely identified early in the mission as part of the helicopter's cyclic. This fragment is larger, and its identity obvious to Eagmin. "That's no cyclic," he tells Conely. "That's a bayonet grip." American, he judges, of the type that mounted under the muzzle of an M-16, and evidently left here by soldiers on the ground, not by the crew of a crashing helicopter.

At lunch, the team distributes a trash bag full of hand-me-downs to the villagers, clothes that its members carried to Laos from Hawaii. They pass out blouses, shirts, skirts, women's pants, even a silvery thong from Victoria's Secret. God knows where the stuff will end up: Perhaps some of it will be traded with peasants from elsewhere in Savannakhet, or travelers on Route 9, and make its way to a village far from here, where months or years from now an American team will land to dig for the dead and encounter this little slip of underwear on a worker — worn who knows how — and wonder: How the hell did *that* get *here?*

The team also hands out magazines, which are rarely seen commodities in the borderlands. During a break, a soldier flips through an issue of *Cosmopolitan* with a gallery of village youngsters, who gasp at the magazine's ads and fashion spreads. Its cover is splashed with a headline they can't read: "Sexify your look."

And there's another piece of business that Haugen brings up before the break ends. The joint task force in Hawaii has relayed a request to RE-1, via cable to Vientiane and radio to Ban Alang, from John Chubb's family, which has been apprised that an excavation is under way. The door gunner's survivors have asked that the team gather some mementos of the site — pebbles, or earth, or bits of the wreckage — and bring them back.

"So what I was thinking," Haugen says, "is that everybody could collect four rocks, one for the family of each guy on the helicopter, and we'll send them back to the States. Does that sound like a good idea?"

Several soldiers answer that it does. We fan out across the site in search of rocks.

At 2:15 P.M., Randy Posey finds a small piece of green fabric on his screen. He rinses it under his hose. Two letters, printed in black, appear on its surface. He carries it to Haugen. "Doc," he tells her, "I found me some name tape."

Every American soldier in Vietnam wore his surname on the tunic of his fatigues, on a strip of cloth sewn over his right breast pocket. Posey's find is torn at one end, burned away at the other, but the letters "BE" are clearly visible, along with a portion of a third. Judging from the empty space off to the left of the "B," it looks to be the leftmost portion of the tape, the beginning of a name.

Conely examines the strip during the team's final break. "B-E-R?" she murmurs. "B-E-B? B-E-P?"

"Whatever it is," Haugen sighs, "It doesn't correlate with our four guys."

"Maybe it's not the beginning of a name," Conely says, hoping. "Could it be from the middle of one of their names?" Several team members silently run through the surnames of the missing crew. It takes just a moment to dismiss the theory.

"Of course, it could be somebody on the ground," Eagmin suggests. "It may be one of the guys they were going in to pick up."

"It could be," Haugen agrees.

"Doesn't help us much," Posey says.

"No," Haugen says. "It doesn't do anything to correlate this site with 1731." We stand sweating in the break tent, passing around the name-tape, reaching no consensus on the third letter. There is no wailing, no cursing, no display of any emotion beyond fatigue. As disappointing as the discovery might be, we're all too whipped to hurt much.

As it turns out, the site has waited to within an hour of the excavation's end to cough up this final relic. Haugen, working in 512/524, sends the last bucket to the screens at about 2:45 P.M.; Dingman turns off the pump twenty-five minutes later. We gather the tools, wash them, carry them to the break tent. We fold the tarps that have shielded the open units. The team says nothing to the Laotians to indicate that the site is closing, and to look at it, there's work left to be done. Six complete units and half of two others remain unexcavated, Haugen having deemed them outside the debris field's boundaries. We leave the screening station in place, the shovels and picks, the radio; the team will swoop in tomorrow to pack them up. The locals can sense the end has come, just the same. Sammy, Bing, and a passel of kids hover nearby, watching us closely.

"Well," Haugen says, when we're ready to board the Squirrel, "we finished. You guys did a great job." She smiles sadly. "Of course, the big news of the day was that we found a piece of name tape. That might be the most important thing we found, because it might mean that this isn't the helicopter we thought it was.

"You shouldn't feel, though, that this has all been for naught. This team did excellent work. And finding that piece of name tape may allow us to remove this site from the list of possible locations for the helicopter."

Reynolds thanks the team for its efforts. "I'm sure everybody has learned something on this little expedition of ours," he says. "We're coming out of the tunnel now. Let's get everything done we need to get done. Let's stay smart, and get home safe."

We leave for Ban Alang having excavated twenty-two full units and two half units, having carved away some 368 square meters of jungle floor, having shoveled and sifted roughly four thousand cubic feet of dirt.

Something like twelve thousand bucketfuls.

A thousand buckets a screen.

Every one of them empty of what we came for.

4

Two days later, Haugen and Reynolds fly to Savannakhet with the mission's other anthropologists and team leaders to meet with the joint task force's analysts and to file their reports, and those of us left at Ban Alang pack up the camp. The team's gear is stowed in footlockers and loaded onto trucks, which lug it down Route 9 to a warehouse in Savannakhet. It'll be stored there for a month, awaiting the next mission. The hotel ice machines are loaded up, too, and the mess tent and the propane stoves and the Ping-Pong table. The Laotian workers at Mama's break down the restaurant's kitchen and pack up its tables and chairs. The showers are stripped of their tarps. The commo shack is emptied. Finally, the tents come down, one by one, until Ban Alang Base Camp is a windblown waste of concrete slabs and trampled grass and whip scorpions uprooted from their nests.

Most of the remaining Americans leave on the Mi-17s, which buffalo into the sky in a thunder of rotorwash and skim westward over the jungle ringing the camp, the sound of their thwacking blades audible long after they've disappeared from view. I climb into Kevin Smith's Squirrel, the last bird out. As we spring into the air and swivel toward the Mekong, I get a final glimpse of our home in the Laotian woods.

The residents of nearby villages have swarmed the camp. Eight or ten kids creep into a fenced trash compound at the LZ's edge, where a thick helix of greasy smoke rises from our burning garbage. Several reach into the fire to salvage our scraps.

*   *   *

We spend that night at a motel run by a Savannakhet businessman who owns the warehouse in which the joint task force's gear is stored, and the trucks that transport it to and from Ban Alang, and the bottling company that supplies the American effort its water, and the Mekong ferry that links Savannakhet with its Thai neighbor, Mukdahan. His daughters were schooled in the States. He drives a Lexus SUV.

The next day we climb into a couple of his buses — actually flatbed trucks with bench seats — and ride out to the old Air America hangar at the Savannakhet Airport, where we board an air force C-130 cargo plane. Its Alaskan crew flies us first to Vientiane for passport checks, then to the U-Tapao Royal Thai Naval Air Station, south of Bangkok. We expect a two-day wait in nearby Pattaya for another air force plane to take us home.

That night, our first on the town, some of us are in an Internet café, catching up on a month's worth of e-mail, when a member of RE-3 suddenly gasps and tells Reynolds and me to check the CNN Web site. When we do, we see a just-posted news bulletin.

Back in the States, it's the morning of Tuesday, September 11, 2001.

It takes us more than a week to reach Hawaii; our air force jet is diverted to the Persian Gulf, and the mission's fifty troops are split among several commercial flights. A few of us fly to Osaka, then to Honolulu on a jumbo jet that carries just fourteen passengers.

I have a two-day layover before the first available flight to the mainland, and Haugen offers to take me on a tour. She pulls up outside my hotel in a red Jeep Wrangler, and we tool through downtown Honolulu and around Diamond Head and down the beaches of Oahu's southeast coast. In mid-afternoon, we aim for the Punchbowl.

The National Memorial Cemetery of the Pacific is nestled in the crater of an extinct volcano, Puowaina, rising from a residential section of central Honolulu. A narrow road ascends its cone, slips into the crater through a narrow pass, and bisects its floor. Among the more than 38,000 graves in the lawns that flank the road are those of unidentified men and women who lost their lives in World War II, Korea, and Southeast Asia.

At the road's end stands a platoon of marble obelisks, each the size of a shipping container, on which are chiseled the names of the unaccounted-for who lie on the grounds and those whose remains have not been recovered from the battlefields on which they fell. There are 28,788 names carved on these "Courts of the Missing." A broad, white staircase rises from among them. It ends at a thirty-foot statue of Columbia, a laurel branch in her left hand. Behind the statue stands a pergola decorated with large maps of mosaic tile, depicting the combat theaters in which the United States lost these honored dead.

Puowaina's rim encircles the grounds completely, sealing out any sight or sound of the busy city beyond. Haugen parks the Jeep, and in the Punchbowl's peaceful hush we climb to the maps. A placard reveals that the obelisks near the foot of the stairs commemorate the unrecovered dead from the war in Southeast Asia. We walk back down the stairs, past a monument engraved: "In these gardens are recorded the names of Americans who gave their lives in the service of their country and whose earthly resting place is known only to God."

At the staircase's bottom we split up. I wander among the obelisks, reading the names, running my fingers over the carved letters, and near the corner of one I find Jack L. Barker. Just around the corner, within a few feet of the major's name, I find John J. Chubb's. A row of names away are William E. Dillender and John F. Dugan.

I sit on a low wall around the obelisks, staring at the names. I have witnessed the dedication and sweat of young soldiers, sailors, airmen, and marines who never knew these men, but who've spent an uncomfortable and hazardous month in the Laotian jungle in search of them. I have seen the technological might of the American military, and millions of American dollars, devoted to finding them. I have been part of a quest that has demanded the skills and brainpower of countless analysts, linguists, logisticians, statesmen, and scientists for decades.

And none of it has brought these four men home. All that effort, expense, and expertise, and not so much as a bone to show for it.

Were we in the right place? Were we at the right helicopter? If so, what happened to the crew? Who took their remains, and where are they now? And if we weren't in the right place, where is it, where are they? Could the Huey's midair explosion have scattered it so thoroughly that there's little left to be found? Could it be that 185's wreckage lies half buried in the jungle floor beyond the edge of our site, undiscovered by even the locals? Do the Laotians know where it is and choose not to share the information?

The joint task force will send another IE out in the coming months, beating the bushes for new leads on Case 1731. And if that IE fails to turn something up, another will follow, and another, as they always do. Will they have better luck?

Haugen walks toward me, having inspected an obelisk on the far side of the stairs. "I found some guys I've sent home," she says quietly. "It's kind of strange, seeing the names."

I nod toward the Huey's crew. "Our four are right there." She scans the marble. "Three of them are on this side," I add. "Barker's just around the corner."

She finds the names, one by one, and runs her hands over them, then walks slowly to the wall and sits down beside me. We stare at the obelisk in silence for a minute.

"I sure wish we'd found these guys," she murmurs. I nod. It's a beautiful day, warm and breezy. Leaves rustle in the trees around us. Sunshine bathes the stone.

Haugen breathes a long sigh. "I hate that we didn't find them."

Across Honolulu, on a mountainside overlooking Pearl Harbor, in Joint Task Force–Full Accounting's windowless offices at Camp H. M. Smith, analyst Bill Forsyth is still at work on Case 1731. He drafts a letter to Ron Cribbs, chief of military technical support at Bell Helicopter Textron Inc., in Fort Worth, Texas. "I am the Lao analyst at JTF-FA and I once again request your assistance in our mission to account for Americans missing as a result of the Vietnam War," Forsyth writes. "On our just-completed mission in Laos, a Recovery Element (RE) excavated a suspected UH-1H site believed to be associated with UH-1H 66-16185 . . . which was shot down near Landing Zone Brown on 20 March 1971, in the final days of Operation Lam Son 719, with four unaccounted-for Americans. The RE recovered no remains from the site and there is some question if in fact we excavated the right site, since four UH-1Hs were lost that day. . . .

"The RE did recover one data plate from the tail rotor gear box with a serial number. I am hoping you can match the serial number to the assembly on one of the four helicopters when they left your factory. Of course, I understand the assembly might have been swapped out after it left the factory, but there is always hope."

Forsyth faxes the letter to Texas, along with the tail numbers of the four helicopters lost in the area. One, of course, denotes Jack Barker's Huey. Another is 68-16492, the chopper Al Fischer crash-landed at Fire

Support Base Delta One. The third is 69-15505, Bruce Sibley's bird, which crashed into the trees short of the PZ and which Pete Miller dug up in 1989. Last is 69-16654, a helicopter on which Forsyth has no information beyond a few bare-bones records indicating that it was shot down without fatalities a few hundred meters from the 1731 site.

Cribbs replies with an e-mail to Forsyth on Friday, September 21, 2001. "Our records indicate that the subject 90-degree tail rotor gearbox . . . was installed on 69-16654," he writes. "Looks like it was not your target ship."

PART SIX

Perseverance

■

1

IN THE MONTHS after RE-1's return I track down the Kingsmen who flew into Laos during Lam Son 719, seeking their memories of the four for whom RE-1 searched. To a man, they recall the date and circumstances of the shootdown without prompting, remember where they were and what they were doing when they heard that their commander and three of their company were gone.

The Kingsmen were lucky in Laos. The men aboard 185 were the only troops they lost. Regardless of whether they loved Barker or hated him, trusted Dugan at the controls or couldn't wait to set down, got along with Dillender or didn't — and regardless of whether they'd even had so much as passing words with Chubb — the men of Bravo Company remember.

I call Al Fischer, who's living in the Midwest and is still haunted by his refusal to fly the second sortie — not because he thinks he should have done otherwise, he tells me, but because he was tragically vindicated by what transpired a few hours later.

"That has probably dominated the memory banks of my mind," he says. "That day is always there. It's not just getting shot at. It's also losing people, and the fact that I made a decision that changed my life." If he has any regret, Fischer says, it's that he couldn't talk Barker and Dugan out of it.

He had a mild stroke a few years ago, he says, but it hasn't much affected his memory of those days in Laos, and that morning sortie, that later conversation with Barker, in particular. "That March 20," he says, "it's still a big thing in my life."

I track down the pilots and crews from other companies that were at the escarpment that day, and John Klose, who oversaw the extraction at LZ Brown. He tells me he can still picture Barker's chopper "out of the right front of my helicopter" as it swooped over the jungle, and how he swung his own bird to keep Barker in sight as "the last third of his tail boom came off right before my eyes."

He relates how, after 185 went in, he broke off the extraction, radioed the South Vietnamese below that they'd have to hoof it east, toward Route 92, if they wanted a lift out. Hundreds were picked up the next day on and near the road.

"We'd never broken one off," he tells me. "That was the only mission we failed to accomplish, that extraction out of Brown." For a long minute he says nothing; then: "It was your worst nightmare." Another long silence. "I have tears in my eyes right now," he finally tells me. "And I don't cry. I never did go see a psychiatrist or anything like that, and I've probably suppressed a lot, carried it around.

"That's why I probably have such an affinity for Jack Barker," he says. "It's unfinished business."

Among the last veterans I find is Jon Evans, the closest eyewitness to 185's crash, now living in Huntsville, Alabama. He's made a career of army helicopters, as a pilot and, later, a teacher at Fort Rucker.

He thinks of Barker often, he tells me, his voice a deep, steady rumble, his tone one of competence, directness, and zero tolerance for bullshit. Evans replays the conversation he and the major shared before the second sortie. "He knew," he says. "You can look in a man's eyes and see that he knows. He knew a goat dance when he saw one. And he was just professional enough to take responsibility and to serve what he believed was a larger purpose.

"To me, bravery is like that: To know what sort of calamity, what sort of catastrophe, can be visited upon you and still make an honest effort. In my book, that puts you in the tall trees with the big dogs."

I ask him to recount what he saw and heard as the choppers approached LZ Brown, and how he reacted to it, and he does, in admirable detail: He can recall how much torque his helicopter pulled as he tried to follow Barker's tailless Huey in its final climb, along with air speeds, altitudes, angles of attack.

"For a couple of low-time guys, they didn't do too bad," he says of

Barker and Dugan. "They had tracers flying through their goddamn airplane, just coming through that bird, left and right. And they didn't go around until I told them to the third time."

He describes his pass over the burning chopper, the bird's barely recognizable state, its total consumption — and his realization that the area was far too hot to risk a landing to pull the bodies. "That was the first time I ever left anybody lying," he says quietly. "It took me years to reconcile it, and it's something that still bothers me.

"But it was fucking insanity. It was really bad. As it turned out, it was the worst day in aviation history for the whole damn war.

"I'll tell you this," he says, taking a deep breath. "If there had been American soldiers on the ground, somebody that day would have got the Medal of Honor."

In those same months I speak with the families of the men who died aboard the Huey. Dan Dillender, Billy's little brother, actually seeks me out even before I've had a chance to find him. He was a kid when his brother died and thirty years later has embarked on a quest to learn more about him, and having exhausted the sources who knew him best, he's turned to those who knew him most intensely — the people with whom he flew in his final four months.

What can I tell him? Nothing, beyond particulars of the terrain in which his brother's life ended. I do my best to describe the escarpment, the jungle, the landscape of craters and rice paddies into which the Huey fell. He devours the information: Although most made some effort to extract details from the army during the war, the families of those lost aboard the Huey have only a vague understanding of what transpired at PZ Brown and little insight into the heroism their sons, husbands, or brothers displayed in trying to reach it.

Dan Dillender puts me in touch with his brother Jim; his uncle, Bill Quarles; and his parents. He sends me his brother's service record, which profiles the lost Spec 4 almost mathematically: He was earning $249.90 a month as a crew chief; he spent 361 hours in the air before he died. He tells me he looked on his Billy as "my hero, the guy I wanted to be like, the guy who I always looked up to, and then, *poof* — he was gone."

The army's Casualty Affairs Office in northern Virginia clears the way for me to call John Chubb's brother Clifford. He has all of the medals Chubb earned in his brief army career framed in his California home, and a portrait of his brother on proud display. Still, he struggles to describe a kid who was still waxen, unformed, a work in progress when he made his third and final combat flight.

He sends me Chubb's boyhood scrapbook, filled with ribbons from YMCA foot races and Dodgers ticket stubs and newspaper stories that mention his Pop Warner football teams. He sends me Chubb's yearbooks from Robert E. Peary Junior High. Reading their scrawled inscriptions, so everyday, so familiar, is akin to viewing the preserved forms of children and dogs dug from the ash at Pompeii. One girl brands Chubb "the cutest guy in the 9th grade." Another says that keeping his company was a "panic." A third note is from his steady, Regina. "It's really been a blast this semester sharing each others troubles and most of all, all the fun we've had this semester," she wrote. "You know how I feel about ya, at least by now you should. I can't really think of anything else to say except that I love ya!"

I ask Clifford Chubb whether it would mean much to him to have his brother's remains repatriated after so many years, so long after it became clear to him that John was dead. He is unequivocal. "He didn't belong there," he answers, struggling for composure. "Laos was the wrong place to be. It was wrong, wrong, wrong. And he should come home."

"That's why I really appreciate what these guys are doing, looking for him, because he shouldn't be there," he says. "He had no business there then, and he shouldn't be there now."

Dan Dillender tells me the same thing. He wants Billy "home, on the ground he died for."

Dillender's mother, Ann, says that only her son's remains will quell her fears that he might still be alive in Southeast Asia. "I still have my doubts, even right now," she says. "I still have my doubts. I cannot accept the fact that he's gone."

Dee Gowin, long remarried, says that she, too, waits for the day when Jack Barker's remains are returned. "Even though I'm married and I'm very happy, he still was a part of my life and I loved him, and I really want to know, I really want to hear," she says when we talk by telephone.

"I would have loved to know that they'd found something, though I don't think they ever will. I hope they do, because even though there's probably not much there, it's a final thing."

Others aren't so sure that the appearance of remains, at long last, will amount to much. "Would it make a difference to me?" Barker's older brother, C. W., says. "All I know is we've done accepted that the Lord was ready for him, and he's not here. I really don't know how we'd react to the news if they were to find his remains."

John Dugan's older brother, Joe, suggests we speak face-to-face. He invites me to dinner at his home near Flemington, in northwestern New Jersey, and arranges to have Michael, the youngest Dugan brother, drive down from New York City. We sit around the breakfast table with Joe's wife, Naomie, who's known her husband since the fourth grade and knew John, as well. On the table before us are some of the family's few mementos of Capt. John Dugan's military service, which I pick through as we talk — letters of condolence from commanders and politicians, a program from the dedication of New Jersey's memorial to its Vietnam dead, a menu from Dugan's commissioning dinner at Fort Sill, saved through the years by his mother.

In strong Jersey accents, they tell me about the family's life in Roselle, about crowded apartments, Yankees games, and Dugan's collection of British Invasion 45s. We dig into Naomie's terrific meatloaf and talk about Dugan's elopement, his travails behind the wheel, his cars. We drink coffee. We get to what happened in Laos.

"I'd been in the service," Joe says. "I didn't trust the system, at all. And here we knew very little about what had happened. Nobody could tell us anything, and we had no body. We had no evidence, really, that John was dead.

"So I made a decision," he says, "that I wasn't going to believe that my brother was dead until I spoke to some of the people who'd been there."

"Did the rest of the family feel the same way?" I ask.

He and Michael shake their heads.

"Pete Federovich felt obligated to come see my mom and dad," Joe says. "I think this was right after Pete left Vietnam, he came to see us. Pete gave us the information we needed. I knew I could take him at his word when he said there was no way John could have lived."

"So you accepted that he was dead?"

No. "I think I gave up hope of ever finding my brother alive maybe around 1990," he says, "so I kept that hope alive for about nineteen years." He looks at his wife, his brother, then back at me. "Then I hoped he wasn't alive."

"What would it mean to you if his remains were identified now?" I ask. "Do you think it would bring you the 'closure' people always talk about?"

"The only thing it could do for me," Joe says, "is say that John was killed at Point X — he wasn't killed in Hanoi. He wasn't held a prisoner somewhere."

I turn to Michael. He is slow to answer. "It is beyond the point," he finally says, "of meaning anything."

Finally, I call Jack Barker's son.

Barely walking when his father died, Michael Barker is thirty-two years old now and has a family of his own: He lives in Columbia, South Carolina, the city where his parents met, with his wife, Jenny, their five-year-old daughter, Jane Anne, and a boy, James Grady, who's three. Michael is a project manager for a big contracting firm and is wrapping up a lengthy and complex restoration of the Columbia federal courthouse.

I recognize his voice when he answers the phone. It is his father's voice: At five-foot-nine, he's a bigger man than Jack Barker, and is not so round-faced as the major, but his voice — quiet, soft-edged, musical — is a match for that I've heard on tapes made during Lam Son, cockpit recordings of the radio chatter during the invasion.

He tells me he can conjure up no firsthand image of his father. He has this in common with many children of the unaccounted-for; many have lost their mothers in the years since the war's end and are now their fathers' next of kin, left to stand vigil for men they never knew. But Barker had a stepfather early enough in childhood that he does not recall feeling Jack Barker's absence. After the shootdown, Dee took the kids to Allendale, South Carolina, her hometown, where they stayed with her family; Michael was still a toddler when she met her second husband, James John Gowin, whom Michael grew up calling "Dad." The major became, and remains, "Jack."

He remembers consciously thinking about his biological father's death in the first or second grade. "It's not like it was hidden from me. We had his medals and some of his flight paraphernalia," he says.

"On display?" I ask.

"No. They were maintained, but they were stored away in the attic."

"Did your mom tell you about him? That he'd been a hero and everything?"

"She had explained to me from early on about his 4-H project, about his going over to Switzerland," he replies. "He was almost a celebrity type, almost a mythical figure — you know, 'You had this dad who was a great man.' She elevated him that way. But very little specific. It was mostly general.

"It was not a taboo subject in our house, but it just wasn't discussed. I think my mom's decision to try to carry on, to get on with life, was paramount with her, and so it wasn't discouraged, but she never initiated it."

And so Michael and his older brother, Brian — whom Michael says "would have looked exactly like Jack," had he lived — grew up with a stepfather they loved, Michael never missing the father he never knew. The family moved to suburban Atlanta. They visited Jack's kin in Waycross for a few years, but the time between trips gradually lengthened, and eventually they stopped going altogether.

Then, well into adulthood, Michael started feeling a tug. "My stepfather, I love him," he says, "but we're different. I couldn't have explained why until I learned more about Jack's character. Jack was guided by a deep sense of integrity and personal conviction. I respect him for the decision that ultimately cost him his life. I'd like to think I'd have the same strength of character and courage to follow my convictions, even if I were faced with losing everything.

"There was a night I'd had a really bad day, and I found myself for the very first time thinking to myself: 'I wish I knew how Jack would respond to this.'"

He was in his late twenties when he decided to try to find out. He sent e-mails to some of the dozens of Web sites maintained by Vietnam helicopter pilots and crews. "I got an overwhelming response," he says. "And to be frank with you, some of them were a little scary in their responses.

"Some of them were very generous. But some of the others, they were a little strong, and they were using some strong military lingo — 'If you're ready to lock and load, we're going to go in deep,' things like that. There were some guys who wanted my address so they could send me stuff. And I realized that I didn't know any of these people, and here I was, potentially exposing my family to the unknown."

Barker backed off. He did not share his address. He made no further solicitations on the Web. He hoped for more information about his father, but wasn't sure how to go about getting it. Then came word from the army that RE-1 had been to Laos. Like the other relatives of the crew, he is hungry for information about the dig, about the setting for the helicopter's shootdown, and for any new details I might be able to offer about 185's final seconds.

Like the others, he's also grateful. Regardless of whatever ambivalence they might express about having bones to bury, the relatives are thankful and impressed, to a person, that the U.S. government is going to such extremes to find them.

The joint task force's detractors have their case; the recovery effort is wildly expensive, and it's dangerous, even deadly. But for the families of Case 1731, and nearly two thousand others, it serves as their government's acknowledgement that the lives lost in a problematic war were more than statistics. It makes good on that sacred contract.

"So if they were to find your dad's remains, would it mean much to you at this point?" I ask Michael Barker. "This is someone you never knew." There's a pause, so long that I'm beginning to wonder whether he's still on the line. "I can't answer that in a simple yes or no," he finally says. "I have lived my life without my natural father. It's just the reality of my life. Since I was a young child I've never known anything different.

"But would it be significant? Oh, yeah," he says. "It would be significant. To me, recovery of something, recovery of *anything* — even facts about Jack — they provide me with a glimpse of who he was, my dad. Any little piece of information, anything I can get from excavations — what it would really do, maybe, is tell me more about *him*."

2

FOUR MONTHS AFTER leaving Laos I decide to dig out the history of the Huey that RE-1 so carefully excavated. It proves difficult: Bill Forsyth is able to dig up little on 69-16654 in the joint task force's records; the "Gold Book," a compendium of history and statistics on most army helicopters in Vietnam, has nothing on it. I make inquiries of the Vietnam Helicopter Pilots Association, which maintains its own database on Vietnam-era choppers. I get nowhere.

But Texas Tech University keeps a large Vietnam War archive, and in its collection of Lam Son 719 records is a thick report prepared by army major general Sidney B. Berry on air operations during the invasion. Attached to the report are appendices on combat damage, and there I find 654. The records show that it was shot down within two hundred yards of our excavation site at 1 P.M. on March 20, 1971, and that it was a slick attached to the 174th Assault Helicopter Company, one of the many units that, along with Jack Barker's company, pulled South Vietnamese troops from LZ Brown.

Veterans of the 174th maintain a Web site, which I examine for any mention of the helicopter. It is not listed in a roster of the company's machines. With fading hope I troll the rest of the Web site's pages, and on one devoted to the war stories by and about the 174th's veterans, I find a link titled "The Shootdown of CPT Peterson and his Crew." I click on it. An April 16, 1971, story from *Southern Cross,* a military newspaper, appears on the screen:

QUANG TRI, (23rd Inf. Div. IO) — "I broke the ship to the right and pulled in pitch to get more power and speed and, as I did that, my rotor pin [RPM] just slowed down, and I knew we were going down," Captain Donald A. Peterson recalled.

"The next thing I remember, the ship was on its side in a heavily-wooded area on the slope of the hill, and I remember thinking, 'Got to get out of here, maybe there's a fire.' I grabbed my M-16 and crawled out of the ship and saw the ship was intact, and my crew was in good shape."

Captain Peterson, of Cut Bank, Mont., recounts the crash of his UH-1H (Huey) helicopter, a crash that left him and his three-man crew stranded on a Laotian hillside fifteen miles due west of the giant American base at Khe Sanh for more than three tension-wracked hours.

Units of the 1st ARVN Regiment were being moved back across the border from Landing Zone Brown and helicopters of the 14th Combat Aviation Battalion (CAB) had been called in to complete the extraction.

"We had all the troops out when the last chopper out radioed that a litter patient had been left behind," Peterson, an aircraft commander, recalled.

"I was about a half a mile behind the lead chopper, and I rolled in and called our air mission control chopper to tell him we were going down to get him."

The pick-up zone (PZ) lay in a thickly-wooded area along a bluff at the bottom of a ridgeline.

"When we started down, everything went real fine until we got to the edge of the PZ and I threw the ship into a flare maneuver to come to a stop," he continued. "That's when we started to receive very heavy AK-47 fire."

"There was a big explosion underneath the ship just before we started to go down," noted the door gunner, Private First Class Jimmy L. Graham of Houston.

"We took hits in the transmission and there was hydraulic fluid and transmission fluid pouring all over me. With all the red liquid running down my flight suit, I thought I was hit."

"When we went down I wasn't really thinking about anything, because my M-60 had jammed and I was working on that," said Specialist Four Darold A. Berger of Waukon, Iowa, the crew chief.

"When I saw we were going to crash, I reached for my M-16 and the next thing I knew, we were surrounded by green. I climbed out of the bird without much difficulty because I had my seatbelt unfastened since Graham and I were going to have to jump out of the bird to get the wounded ARVN we were after."

The crash had twisted the barrel of Graham's M-60 into the shape of a pretzel.

"If I had my seatbelt fastened, I probably would have been pinned in," the door gunner mused.

"The four of us laid low outside the chopper for a few minutes," Peterson said. "Then I reached inside and switched off all the electrical equipment and we made our way through the trees and bushes to within 50 feet of a dried-up creekbed at the bottom of the slope.

"We didn't want to go down to the creekbed because we thought if we could use it, the NVA could just as well be using it."

"I turned my survival radio on and called for help for about ten minutes," he continued.

"I told him we didn't know our exact location and they radioed that they were trying to get a dustoff (medical) chopper for us, and then we broke off commo."

The Americal chopper crew tried as best they could to remain concealed in a thicket. As they silently lay there, Berger spotted an NVA soldier walking down the creekbed about 50 yards from them with a brand new AK-47 slung down from his shoulder.

"He walked by us," Peterson explained, "but when he was some 20 to 30 feet from us, he turned around and looked up, and it was quite obvious he realized things weren't quite right."

"When I saw that NVA soldier walking down the creekbed, as far as I was concerned, he could keep on going and I'd keep on minding my own business," commented Warrant Officer Chester C. Luther of Brockton, Mass., co-pilot.

But the enemy troop did not budge, and the American helicopter crewmen kept their rifles trained on him all the while. When he started to raise his weapon, they opened fire on him.

"He had a weird, sort of resigned look on his face just before he caught the first rounds," remarked Graham.

"After we killed him, we moved back up to the aircraft and sat there for a couple of hours while I continued to call over the radio," Peterson said.

The whirl of approaching helicopter blades lifted the crew's spirits as Peterson picked up a call from the pilot of a 223rd CAB chopper requesting him to pop a smoke grenade so he could get a fix on their location."

"All I had were some pin flares," Peterson explained, "so I popped one and they spotted it and radioed that we were about 115 meters from the original PZ (pick-up zone). The ship came in and took some hits as he was making his final approach, and had to get out of the area fast."

"After what seemed like an eternity," Peterson continued, "the chopper came back and I popped another pin flare."

"The chopper came in low level, which is a normal maneuver in that type of situation because the sound of the engine is deceiving and the bird just whizzes by anyone trying to zero in on it," Luther explained.

Cobra gunships accompanying the mercy craft worked over suspected enemy positions with rockets and mini-guns as cover while the ship hovered three to four feet over the downed helicopter and Peterson's crew scrambled onboard.

"As we came out, we started catching more small arms fire, so we all opened up with our 16's." Peterson noted.

The dustoff chopper stayed at tree-top level for about a mile as it moved down into the valley, and gained altitude very slowly for the ride back to the Leatherneck Pad at Khe Sanh.

"I was never so happy in my life as when we touched down back here," Berger said. "We never did get the names of the crew that pulled us out there, but if they're ever in trouble someday, I hope we're around to pay them back."

My attention fastens on the story's description of the crash area, particularly the presence of the creekbed so close to the wreckage. It's only on reading it a second time that I recognize that the crew chief's name — Berger — matches the nametape that Randy Posey pulled out of the ground.

I find Berger still living in Waukon, Iowa, where he runs a masonry company. He is mystified that someone should have tracked him down to ask him about a frightening but ultimately inconsequential afternoon thirty years before; he recalls the incident, of course, and nails its date when I ask him for it, but though he was his chopper's crew chief — and thus, the only member of the crew unfailingly attached to that bird — he can't recall his wrecked Huey's tail number.

I ask him about the lay of the land where they went down. "We were on a wooded slope," he tells me. "It sloped down and then it got steep and went into a ravine."

"Were any of you hurt?"

"Banged up," he says. "Sprained ankles, light wounds. I do remember that the copilot had his mustache shot off."

"That sounds like it would hurt," I offer.

"Yeah," Berger chuckles, "I think it did."

"Do you recall whether you left any articles of clothing in the helicopter, or near it?" I ask not only because we found nametape that presumably was once attached to a shirt, but because the locals who spoke with the IE back in 1994 reported seeing a shirt when they first visited the site, two months after the shootdown.

Berger doesn't remember. "It's been a while," he reminds me. "A long while."

It takes me several days to track down a second crewman. I post a query on the Vietnam Helicopter Pilots Association Web site, and another veteran passes on a number for Chester "Chick" Luther, the copilot of Berger's downed bird, the man who lost half a mustache in Laos.

Luther still lives in Massachusetts. I get his machine, and he calls me back a few days later. He doesn't remember the tail number, either, but in open New England vowels he recounts that afternoon in detail. "That whole mission was a nightmare," he says. "If it were on TV, no one would believe it."

His crew had made a run into PZ Brown in the late morning, he tells me, had successfully picked up a load of South Vietnamese troops and dropped them off. The air mission commander asked for a crew to head back in to pick up one or two wounded men on stretchers. Captain Peterson, the aircraft commander, replied that his crew would do it.

"I briefed the crew as we got close," Luther says. "I told them, 'We're gonna go in hot, we're gonna do a hairy flare, and you've got five seconds to get out and get the guys in here. If you can't, leave 'em, because we're getting out.'

"So we go in, and we do a hairy flare, and the (North Vietnamese) just stepped out, in uniform — I think it was the only time I saw them in uniform — and stood there, shooting at us. They were right *there*. We started taking some hits, and Captain Peterson said, 'OK, we're going around, we're getting out of here,' but by that time, sirens were going and lights were flashing, and we got a mile away, maybe, before we settled into the trees."

The helicopter rolled onto its side, and they scrambled out of the wreck and into the bushes on the sloping flank of a ravine. "I took my helmet off and put it down, and picked up my weapon," Luther tells me. He noticed he was hurt — he was cut across the bridge of his nose and across the right side of his face, a wound that required stitches when they returned to friendly territory. The doctor's work claimed half of his mustache. "So I didn't get it shot off, exactly," he says, "but yeah — I went into the PZ with a whole mustache, and at the end of the day I had half a one."

Hunkered down in the brush, they watched the North Vietnamese soldier walk slowly down the creekbed. "That poor son of a bitch," Luther says. "I'm a liberal Democrat, and basically I was a pacifist. I really wanted him to just keep walking."

But he didn't. "He looked up, and it seemed like he looked right at us for what seemed like a full minute. And my crew shot him.

"When we got back, we were all talking, and it was Don Peterson, I think, who said to me, 'Gee, it's too bad you didn't get your helmet before we left.'"

I feel the hair on my neck stand on end.

Luther is on a roll. "And I said, 'Who cares about that? I lost better stuff there — I lost a camera, and I don't care about *it*. I'm glad to have got out with what I got.'

"And he said, 'Yeah, but still, it would have been neat to have the helmet.'

"And I said, 'Why? What's so special about the helmet?'

"And he said, 'Didn't you see? Your helmet had an entry hole and an exit hole in the back of it.'"

NOTES

ACKNOWLEDGMENTS

NOTES

Most of *Where They Lay* is based on events I experienced or witnessed during Joint Field Activity 01-5L, the fifth recovery mission undertaken in Laos by Joint Task Force–Full Accounting in fiscal year 2001. The JTF and I used five criteria in choosing Case 1731 from among the pending excavations in Vietnam and Laos: It offered a reasonably good prospect of success; the missing had enjoyed interesting lives before their disappearance; the circumstances surrounding their disappearance were compelling; the setting for the search was spectacular; and the families of the vanished soldiers were willing to speak to me.

I met the incoming teams in Savannakhet on August 10, 2001, flew to Ban Alang Base Camp the same day, and remained with them until we broke camp and returned to Savannakhet a month later, on September 10.

PART ONE: IN THE LAND OF THE LOST

CHAPTER 1

My description of the shootdown is based on telephone and e-mail interviews with eyewitness Jon Evans, who was piloting the Huey directly behind Barker's; with John Klose, the air mission commander at LZ Brown, who was hovering in another helicopter several hundred feet overhead; and on written testimony submitted to the Court of Inquiry into the incident, convened at Camp Eagle, South Vietnam, on April 5, 1971. The court's paperwork is available on microfilm at the Library of Congress and was included in the personnel files of the four unaccounted-for crewmen, all of which were afforded me by their families.

The readiest sources of background on Laotian history and politics are probably Andrea Matles Savada, ed., *Laos: A Country Study* (Washington: Federal Research Division, Library of Congress, 1995); Grant Evans, *The Politics of*

Ritual and Remembrance: Laos Since 1975 (Honolulu: University of Hawaii Press, 1998); Evans, ed., *Laos: Culture and Society* (Singapore: Institute of Southeast Asian Studies, 2000); and Martin Stuart-Fox and Mary Kooyman, *Historical Dictionary of Laos* (Metuchen, N.J.: The Scarecrow Press, 1992). Others I consulted include *Laos: Its People, Its Society, Its Culture* (New Haven: Hraf Press, 1960); and Wilfred G. Burchett's *The Furtive War: The United States in Vietnam and Laos* (New York: International Publishers, 1963).

The figures for unresolved cases from America's various wars are from Joint Task Force–Full Accounting and the Central Identification Laboratory. The $100 million price I've ascribed to recovery operations is from the JTF.

CHAPTER 2

The JTF supplied the breakdown of what's happened with the 2,583 MIA cases since Saigon fell.

The decorations earned by Jack Barker and his crew are detailed in their personnel jackets. The judgment that the Huey was on "basically a suicide mission" is that of Bill Forsyth, the JTF's Laos case analyst, and was included in the "Laos Excavation Lead Sheet" of background information supplied to Gwen Haugen when she left Hawaii.

My account of the Ho Chi Minh Trail's development and the American attempts to destroy it rely, in part, on March 2001 conversations with Al Teel and former members of the navy's VO-67 squadron. Teel, at the time a staffer at the JTF's Detachment Three in Vientiane, flew C-121s during the war — Lockheed Constellations loaded with electronic gear designed to home in on the sensors I mention. VO-67, a secret unit of modified antisubmarine planes, was responsible for dropping the sensors on low-altitude runs over the trail. I interviewed squadron veterans Adam Alexander and Larold W. Gire, and several relatives of deceased VO-67 members, as part of my research for a *Parade* story on the JTF's search for a downed VO-67 crew, published in the magazine's July 22, 2001, edition. I also relied on Gire's *Wings of Gold Over the Ho Chi Minh Trail*, a monograph published to limited circulation in 1999.

Details of the Lao Aviation crash are from a lengthy report, dated October 19, 2001, in which Greg Berg answered questions I'd put to him by e-mail.

Posey's history is from an August 21, 2001, interview.

CHAPTER 3

The Point Pleasant reference is based on a description of the Shawnee dead, or lack thereof, in John A. Stuart's *Memoir of Indian Wars, and Other Occurrences* (New York: The New York Times & Arno Press, 1971).

The histories of the JTF and CILHI are drawn from numerous interviews with principals in both organizations in 2000 and 2001, among them CILHI deputy commander Johnie Webb and the JTF's public affairs officer, Lt. Col. Franklin Childress. I also relied on Susan Sheehan's *A Missing Plane* (New

York: Putnam, 1986); Deborah Funk, "Final Journey," *Army Times*, April 2, 2001; Elizabeth Sullivan, "The Long Road 'Home,'" *The Plain Dealer Sunday Magazine*, April 20, 2000; and Mick Elmore, "The Hunt for Those Missing Gets Harder," *U.S. News & World Report*, Feb. 21, 2000.

Case 1731's long past is distilled from a pile of documents on microfilm in the Library of Congress. Authored by Joint Casualty Resolution Center workers in Bangkok, in Honolulu, or in the field, the papers include planning papers associated with a Laotian delegation's visit to the JCRC and CILHI on October 24–28, 1988, during which the Laotians first agreed to permit an investigation of 1731; memos analyzing that meeting; a detailed account of the December 10–16, 1988, recovery operation in Savannakhet Province, during which the 1731 site was first reached by an American team and a Lao official reported the presence of bones amid the wreckage; a summary of the January 2–3, 1989, summit between U.S. and Loatian officials in Vientiane; "talking points" papers prepared for the American participants in negotiations scheduled for later in January 1989; reports from the recovery trip of March 18–26, 1989, during which the Laotians refused a visit to the 1731 site; a May 17, 1989, memo announcing Laotian approval of a 1731 dig and proposing that such a mission start May 26; the June 1, 1989, message that Pete Miller's team had dug up the wrong chopper; the full report of that mission, written a few days later; and the full report of the January 1994 site investigation, led by army captain James Stanley and the JTF's Bill Gadoury. I also relied on the report describing Capt. David Combs's IE visit of March 2001, not yet filed at the Library, which I obtained from CILHI officials.

CHAPTER 4

My descriptions of the grid system and of wet and dry screening are based on conversations with Gwen Haugen and CILHI anthropologists Dave Rankin, Bill Belcher, and Ann Bunch.

Under the Universal Transverse Mercator grid system, Pete Miller's 1989 dig was centered at 48QXD 515 352, and Gwen Haugen's at 513 350.

Major Khampheui, the Laotian official who mentioned the bones, is quoted in the December 16, 1988, report by the first American team to visit the reported site of the Case 1731 crash. The major apparently made the remark three days before. Numerous subsequent JCRC and JTF documents cite the incident.

CHAPTER 5

A fast-reading, fascinating explanation of what happens to the body after death can be found on a forensic entomology Web site built by University of Oslo graduate student Morten Stærkeby, at http://folk.uio.no/mostarke/forens_ent/forensic_entomology.html. Also instructive is William R. Maples and Michael Browning, *Dead Men Do Tell Tales* (New York: Doubleday, 1994), a casebook of some of the world's most celebrated forensic anthropology cases, related by a scientist who helped solve them. The history of the University of Tennessee's "Body Farm" is described by Daniel Pedersen in "Down on the Body Farm," *Newsweek*, Oct. 23, 2000; Robert F. Service, "Where Dead Men Really Do Tell Tales," *Science* 289, No. 5481 (Aug. 11, 2000); and by Knight Stivender in "Bass Studies Science of Decay," a (University of Tennessee) *Daily Beacon* story posted at http://dailybeacon.utk.edu/special/bodyfarm/.

Col. Dave Pagano, then CILHI's commander, told me of the World War II dig in Papua New Guinea at which soft tissue and an ear were recovered. Haugen consulted her files to relate the story of the B-24J crash site in France. Bill Belcher told me of his B-17 recovery in England in conversations at CILHI in July 2000, and in New Britain in August 2001. He showed me the survival map during the earlier exchange.

Data on the scope of Laos's UXO problem and the bombing that created it varies by source. Laotian officials repeatedly told me that 3 million tons of ordnance was dropped on the country during the nine-year campaign; U.S. sources, both official and not, tend to put the figure at around 2.1 million tons. I relied especially on Stuart-Fox and Kooyman's *Historical Dictionary of Laos* and the Mennonite Central Committee (www.mcc.org). The former put the cost of the bombing at more than $2 million per day for nine years. The latter, one of the first nongovernmental organizations to address the UXO threat, was my source on the number of bombs; the province I mention was Xieng Khouang, where church experts figure 300,000 tons of bombs fell.

PART TWO: THE MISSING

CHAPTER 1

My childhood having unfurled during the war, I can recall sound bites of Southeast Asian geography from those years — the DMZ, Quang Tri Province, the Citadel, the A Shau Valley — but none pertaining to ambitious and disastrous Lam Son 719.

One of history's largest-ever airborne assaults is a blank to most Americans, little more than an exotic tag on an operation distant in time and space. Part of the reason, no doubt, is that it happened in Laos, which then, as now, was a name without a corresponding image to folks in the States. On top of that, the troops on the ground weren't GIs, but South Vietnamese, which dimmed the invasion's relevance back home even as Hueys were falling from the sky.

I owe my education on the invasion to dozens of interviews with Lam Son veterans, particularly the Kingsmen and members of their sister companies; to conversations with Jim Williams, the army aviation historian at Fort Rucker; to Williams's "Lam Son 719, January–March 1971: A Baptism by Fire for Modern Army Aviation," written in March 2000 for publication in *Army Flier;* to Mike

Sloniker, the historian of the Vietnam Helicopter Pilots Association; and to Bill Forsyth and Lt. Col. Kevin Smith at the JTF.

I consulted a number of books and official reports. Most helpful were Maj. Gen. Nguyen Duy Hinh's *Lam Son 719* (U.S. Army Center of Military History, 1979), one in a series of monographs written by indigenous commanders on various facets of the war; and "Airmobile Operations in Support of Operation Lam Son 719," prepared in 1971 by Maj. Gen. Sidney B. Berry, then the 101st Airborne Division's assistant commander for operations. Its appendices include a roster of every helicopter lost in the fight. The three-inch-thick report is part of the Vietnam Archive at Texas Tech University.

I also corresponded via e-mail with retired army brigadier general Samuel G. Cockerham, the top aviation officer in the army's XXIV Corps, which ran the American part of the show. Cockerham put the total number of army aircraft involved at about 650. At one point, he wrote, some 256 Hueys were airborne in a daisy chain stretching from Khe Sanh to Xepon.

My account of Jack Barker's childhood relied on telephone interviews in the fall of 2001 with his siblings, Eloise Murray and C.W. Barker Jr.; his 4-H advisor, Tom Boland; and his high school classmate, Marie Young; on e-mail exchanges with his friend Christopher Boyd; and on several 1956 and 1957 newspaper clippings from the *Waycross Journal-Herald*. The Class of 1957's choice of Barker as Boy Most Likely to Succeed can be found in the newspaper's May 16, 1957, edition.

Details of his time at Stetson come courtesy of his siblings and Esther "Dee" Gowin. Not surprisingly, Dee was also the primary source for my account of Barker's first encounter with his future wife, the couple's first date, and their early courtship. I found a chronology of his army assignments and copies of his performance appraisals in his military personnel record, which was provided to me by his son, Michael, and his nephew, Steve Hinson.

The quote about Vientiane's "bomb blast problem" is from the November–December 2000 embassy news bulletin. "The basic problem," the bulletin explained, "is that our country was liberated only 25 years ago, and there are people who still want to destroy peace and order in the country, hoping to harm the country. They want other people to believe what is not true, that there is still fighting in Laos. The real situation is that our country has democracy and peace."

CHAPTER 2

Details of Barker's first Vietnam tour, including quotations from his letters of commendation, are from his personnel record. Dee Gowin related the circumstances of his proposal, his homecoming, and the couple's life in Europe.

Reynolds recalled his past to me in two August 2001 interviews at Ban Alang. My description of the ridgetop camp is founded on firsthand observation, during my visit to an excavation for the remains of army master sergeant

Ralph J. Reno (REFNO 0383), in July 2000; likewise the passage about the pup tent campsite, in which I stayed in a March 2001 visit to the REFNO 0982 dig site on Phou Louang, in Khammouan Province. The other miserable scenarios rely on the memories of Randy Posey and Valerie McIntosh, respectively.

CHAPTER 3

Conely's history is the product of a lengthy interview we conducted at Ban Alang. My biography of John Dugan is based on interviews with his brothers Joe and Michael, family friend Kenny Lavolpe and army colleague Pete Federovich, and on Dugan's service file.

CHAPTER 4

Sources for William Dillender's biography included his service record and interviews with his parents, Bill and Ann Dillender; his brothers, Dan Dillender and Jim Leathco; and his uncle, Bill Quarles.

My description of Barker's reception in the Kingsmen compound is a distillation of interviews and/or e-mail exchanges with former Bravo Company members Gene Haag, Joe Kline, Tom Hill, Dave Whiteley, Gerry Morgan, Al Fischer, William T. "Tom" Robinson, Danny Elzie, Bruce Sibley, and Rich Ginosky, and with Barker's first battalion commander, Lt. Col. William N. Peachey.

Barker describes his promotion to CO in a November 8, 1970, letter to Dee, and describes the challenges of running the company in another dated November 29. He mentions giving up his army career in a January 1, 1971, letter and alludes to it again on March 5: "Honey, it's not worth it. This being apart is just no good."

CHAPTER 5

Pete Federovich described John Dugan's efforts to land a place in the Commancheros and his fondness for Alpha Company's hooches. My summary of Dugan's strengths and shortcomings is the product of interviews or e-mail exchanges with former Kingsmen Joe Kline, Gerry Morgan, Gene Haag, Tom Hill, Al Fischer, Danny Elzie, and Dave Whiteley. Tom Hill, in particular, was a great help in explaining how aircraft commanders assessed apprentice pilots. Kline described the nighttime repair episode. Barker wrote of his lack of flying time on January 17, 1971.

The story of Haugen's OP-2E dig is based on her own notes from that mission, which she shared with me in October 2001 telephone interviews.

My portrayal of life at Camp Eagle is a composite of interviews with the above-mentioned Kingsmen and with Joe St. John, Rich Ginosky, and Tom Robinson. Barker described the VIP mission in a January 22, 1971, letter. Bravo Company's flight up Route 1 was reconstructed via e-mail by Dave Whiteley.

Barker's letter on the episode was dated January 30. In his letter of the following day, he not only told Dee that the Kingsmen had returned to Camp Eagle but also urged her not to mention his January 30 letter to anyone until news of the Laos invasion broke in the States.

Dingman's history is based on telephone interviews in August 2002.

Gwen Haugen recounted the Albanian dig in an October 2001 telephone interview. The August 10, 1944, crash and efforts to find the body were related in an Associated Press story in the *Boston Globe* of June 9, 1998; and by Ann Belser, "Killed in 1944, Airman John S. McConnon May Be Coming Home," in the April 27, 1998, *Pittsburgh Post-Gazette.*

The Eugene DeBruin saga is summarized nicely in "A Light in the Black Hole," an unpublished analysis of still-unresolved MIA cases in Laos by retired air force lieutenant colonel Jeannie H. Schiff. Schiff provided me with a copy, but readers can find some of the 111-page paper's points paraphrased on a Web site maintained by a former DPMO boss at www.miafacts.org/laos.htm.

DeBruin's jungle ordeal is perhaps best understood by viewing Werner Herzog's 1997 film, *Little Dieter Needs to Fly,* which recounts Dieter Dengler's crash and capture, his imprisonment with DeBruin, their breakout, and his eventual rescue.

CHAPTER 6

My account of John Chubb's short life was informed by interviews and e-mail exchanges with his brother Clifford and by family scrapbooks, photo albums, newspaper clippings, and school yearbooks that Clifford entrusted to my care.

Flying in Laos

The discussion of the Kingsmen's trials in Laos is condensed from interviews with former Bravo Company members; former 101st Aviation Battalion commanders William N. Peachey and Bobbie Fernander; retired army colonel John Klose, who choreographed extractions along the escarpment from a command helicopter; retired lieutenant colonel Robert Clewell, who commanded the Commancheros of Alpha Company; retired army colonel Bob Bunting, CO of the 48th Assault Helicopter Company; and Jon Evans, a pilot with the Black Widows of Charlie Company.

"It was a totally different set of challenges from Vietnam," Fernander told me. "First of all, you knew you were over really hostile terrain every minute, and you knew if you went down you probably weren't getting out. Second, it was totally unfamiliar terrain. And third, the North Vietnamese weren't hesitant to shoot at you. In my two tours, I never received so much ground fire as I did during Lam Son. We had a lot more [choppers] damaged and lost in this one operation, I did, than I did for the rest of the tour."

"That was the first time in my two years of experience that the North Vietnamese stood and fought," Peachey recalled. "They came to us in that battle with the intent of destroying as many helicopters as possible, and killing as many Americans as possible. It seemed that wherever we were, they were. Every day, from daylight to dark, it was just fight-fight-fight-fight. You knew you were going to get your ass shot off every day when you crossed that border."

"None of the rules we had on 8 February stood up," Klose said. "You didn't do anything with regularity. You never did anything the same way twice, and I don't care what altitude you flew, from the surface to 8,000 feet, we still got small-arms fire and antiaircraft. We tried them all, and none of them were safe."

Kingsmen crew chief Joe Kline recalled the antiaircraft fire as "much, much worse than anything I ever saw or even heard of in Vietnam," and was made more terrifying by the high altitudes the American choppers maintained as they flew into Savannakhet. "As any hunter can tell you, if you're flying along at 100 miles per hour at 120 feet, the guy on the ground sees you for only a second. If you're poking along at 100 miles an hour at 3,000 feet, you're in sight for *minutes*. It was like target practice. The guys on the ground could practice on the first helicopter in the formation and get better as we came along."

"We had a hard time seeing anything," said Bob Clewell. "That battlefield had become a cauldron. The haze that hung over it was thick, impenetrable, and there was the smoke — plus you had cordite. It didn't dissipate. It was like flying into hell."

"And every option we had called on us to go into that LZ again and again," Klose said. "To insert. To resupply. To extract. And it got tougher every time."

Chubb's flight record is from his personnel jacket. Barker's call home on March 19 was recalled by Dee Gowin in our interview and mentioned in a letter she wrote and mailed to her husband on March 20, 1971. The letter was returned, unopened.

The summary regarding stored remains was a JCRC memo dated January 22, 1992, and is included in the Library of Congress files.

CHAPTER 7

The shootdown of Keith Brandt and Alan Boffman was described by John Klose in an article for the 101st Airborne Division's Web site entitled "Nobody Knew His Name," at www.screamingeagle.org/music16.htm. His is not the only story to ascribe those final words to a doomed aviator; Mike Sloniker, the VHPA's historian, has received several reports from other Lam Son veterans about a March 19 incident in which a CH-47 Chinook resupplying troops north of the Xepon sustained a hydraulic failure, flipped upside down and crashed into trees; that chopper's pilot also reportedly issued a radio plea that someone tell his wife and kids he loved them. No cockpit tapes of that incident or the Brandt/Boffman crash have made their way to Sloniker, who maintains an extensive tape library of Lam Son 719 flight operations.

Jim Williams, the army aviation historian, cautions against drawing too broad a conclusion from tales of South Vietnamese behavior in some of the pickup zones during the Laos extraction. He rightly points out that many of the units involved had been chopped to pieces; some had suffered 50, 60, even 75 percent casualties. Try, he says, to maintain discipline in any unit, from any army, that's undergone such trauma.

"I can tell you from dealing with a lot of vets spanning WW1 through recent events [that] what the air crews faced in the peak periods of LS 719 was way up on the scale of bad days," Williams wrote me in a July 2001 e-mail. "Their performance, as well as that of the [South Vietnamese Army] and [South Vietnamese Marines] who were on the ground, is a story that should be told with pride, regardless of the larger military/political outcomes."

Points taken. But the breakdown of order in the PZs was a recurring theme of practically every interview I undertook with veterans of the fighting in Laos. Without prompting, the helicopter crewmen I contacted almost invariably spoke of panic in the ranks, helicopters rushed and overloaded, and troops dangling from the skids. The phenomena were observed by Americans on the ground, as well. When I e-mailed retired major general Benjamin Harrison, among the top American advisors to the South Vietnamese during the operation, he noted in an October 24, 2001, reply that his orders prevented him from venturing into Laos, and that he thus "was not a direct observer except to see the troops hanging from the skids on overloaded Hueys coming back into Khe Sanh." When I e-mailed him back to ask whether he had seen that with his own eyes, he replied: "Unfortunately, I saw it many, many times."

The overloaded Huey that dropped into the crater after the Brandt/Boffman shootdown was piloted by Capt. Richard M. Johnson, a Robin Hood of the 173rd Assault Helicopter Company.

The Morning Sortie

My account of the attempted extraction at LZ Brown relies on a citation proposal lauding those involved, now on file as part of the Case 1731 records at the Library of Congress, and on telephone interviews with Gene Haag, Tom Hill, Al Fischer, Bruce Sibley, Rich Ginosky, and Joe St. John.

Chalk 2's midair explosion and crash landing were described by aircraft commander Al Fischer in interviews and in an article he wrote for the VHPA newsletter. My description of Chalk 5's shootdown and rescue relies on interviews with the aircraft commander, Bruce Sibley, and the crew chief, Rich Ginosky. The rescue of Al Fischer and crew is described in the Silver Star citations for Dillender and Chubb and in the supporting testimony, included in the Case 1731 papers at the Library of Congress, and in the soldiers' personnel records; on Al Fischer's firsthand account of the episode, included in the "Gold Book" notes for helicopter 66-16185, on file with the VHPA; and on interviews with Fischer and Joe St. John.

My account, and those of these sources, varies in an important respect from that of former Kingsman William T. "Tom" Robinson of suburban St. Louis, who in telephone interviews on July 7 and November 2, 2001, told me that he was the door gunner on Bill Singletary's Huey and that he helped rescue Al Fischer's crew from Delta One. I ran Robinson's recollection past Fischer (on November 28 and 29, 2001) and Joe St. John (on November 25, 2001); they, along with every document I've been able to dig up on the events of March 20, differ with that account.

I chose to trust the sources backed up by documentary evidence and whose memories seemed sharper on numerous points; though Robinson was adamant that he landed at Delta One, he could not recall who served as Singletary's (and his own) peter pilot that day, nor the identity of his crew chief.

CHAPTER 8

The abandoned soldier scenario is discussed at length by navy captain Douglas L. Clarke in *The Missing Man: Politics and the MIA* (Washington: National Defense University, 1979); and H. Bruce Franklin, *M.I.A., or Mythmaking in America* (Brooklyn: Lawrence Hill Books, 1992). I also consulted the Department of Defense POW-MIA Fact Book of October 1992.

The hoaxes I cite are documented on microfilm as part of the uncorrelated POW/MIA records collection at the Library of Congress: the "white tribesman" story was delivered to American officials on June 7, 1988, and was the subject of a brief JCRC report and refutation; the tale of the blind black man was the subject of an undated Stony Beach report; several memos and reports describe the February 15, 1979, interview in which a Vietnamese refugee said she saw four Americans working in a field northeast of Saigon in November 1977, and a subsequent interview, in February 1982, in which she changed her story. The tribal "John Dugan" is mentioned in a February 15, 1996, summary of Case 1731, which cites a September 25, 1992, report on the subject by U.S. officials in Bangkok; the report is also mentioned in background papers, dated April 28, 1999, prepared for conferences between U.S. officials and the survivors of the four men killed aboard 185.

My analysis of live-sighting reports relies on the Federal Research Division's Vietnam-Era Prisoner-of-War/Missing-in-Action Database, which can be found on the Library of Congress's Web site. Included in the database is a periodic statistical summary of "MIA" affairs in Southeast Asia, including live-sighting reports. My figures are from the summary of November 7, 2001.

Between Sorties

Lt. Col. Bobbie Fernander, the 101st Assault Helicopter Battalion's commander, told me any suggestion that Kingsmen refused to fly the afternoon sortie to LZ Brown "sounds like a bunch of bullshit." Fernander explained "that if it came to two aviators refusing to fly, I'd know about it. If it didn't come through the regular officers' chain, I'd certainly have heard it through the enlisted."

Just the same, Al Fischer related his refusal to return to Brown in telephone interviews on November 28 and 29, 2001. Unknown to him until years later, he said, his own rescuer refused another run, too. As I note in the text, Bill Singletary can't verify his friend's account: He died on June 25, 1989, while vacationing near Seabrook Island Resort, South Carolina. The *Richmond Times-Dispatch* reported the forty-one-year-old pilot drowned while attempting to rescue two elderly women snared in a strong undertow and calling for help. He was buried at Arlington National Cemetery. He received, posthumously, the National Guard Association's Valley Forge Cross for Heroism.

Were there others? I don't know. Fernander's views notwithstanding, it has become official that "several" pilots refused the mission: The Laos Excavation Lead Sheet supplied to Gwen Haugen by JTF analyst Bill Forsyth says that's what happened. Jon Evans told me of watching Bravo Company "come undone" on its return from the first sortie, but declined to provide details of what he saw, adding that he could "begrudge nobody anything."

Bill Peachey related his meeting with Barker at the refueling pad in an October 12, 2001, telephone interview. "I was just taken aback," he said of the exchange. "But I don't much blame him."

Jon Evans described his conversation with Barker, and his impressions of the major, in an October 31, 2001, telephone interview. John Madden shared his recollections of Barker in a November 6, 2001, telephone interview.

The Afternoon Sortie

My description of 185's return to the pickup zone relies heavily on Jon Evans, who was the closest eyewitness to the shootdown; in addition to our telephone interview, and subsequent e-mail exchanges, I referred to sworn statements he made hours after the incident.

Evans believes those written statements, which are on file at the Library of Congress and part of the personnel jacket of each of the Case 1731 missing, to have been "sanitized" at some point after he wrote them. In his originals, he told me, he commented on the circumstances that led to Barker and company returning to the PZ.

I relied, too, on the written statement of Lt. William B. Taylor Jr., who was riding in the command ship overhead, and the recollections of John Klose, the air mission commander. Klose's account of the shootdown differed from Evans's in minor respects: For one thing, he described the Huey slowing to a hover so that Barker could direct the choppers following his. The three related the rotor separating from the mast, the chopper's explosion, and its fall to earth in similar terms. Klose described the "J. C. Maneuver" and the effects of a tail boom separation.

I also consulted John Madden and the pilot of the second Black Widows helicopter, Wayne Lloyd. Madden was able to describe the RPG strike and the violence of the fuel explosion in detail. Lloyd recalled nothing specific about 185's loss.

Helicopter Losses

My figures are from a daily roster of aircraft damaged in Lam Son 719 and from the appendices to Gen. Sidney Berry's report on the airborne operations during the invasion, both of which I obtained from the Vietnam Archive at Texas Tech.

Brigadier General Cockerham noted in a March 22, 2002, e-mail that U.S. aircraft sustained combat damage for each 146 hours of flight during Lam Son and a combat loss for every 946 hours. Considering that 150-plus aircraft were often in the air at once, somebody was getting shot up pretty much all the time. A count of all damage sustained by the 214th and 223rd combat aviation battalions during a thirty-five-day portion of the operation showed that 11 percent of their aircraft were shot down and 9 percent sustained such heavy damage that they had to be shipped back to the factory. Roughly one in three were damaged but repaired in Vietnam.

Log Entries

The log entries I quote are from two separate documents. The first is the 101st Aviation Group's S-2 (Intelligence) log for March 20, 1971. The second is the 101st Aviation Battalion's S-2/S-3 (Intelligence and Operations) log. A third log, the Aviation Group S-3's, notes at 3:57 P.M.: "Maj. Klose reports one A/C disintegrated in air, thinks it was Chaulk 5 (May be Color lead?)."

"Color 6" was Barker's radio call sign.

The battalion log is on file at the National Archives. I obtained copies of the group logs from William Peachey.

PART THREE: BONE WORK

CHAPTER 1

My descriptions of Haugen's CILHI missions in July 1997 and April 2000 are based on interviews in which she consulted her excavation notes.

The improbable story of Evans F. Carlson, his famed Raiders, and the landing at Butaritari can be explored in greater detail on the official Raiders Web site (www.usmarineraiders.org) and Dan Marsh's Marine Raider Page (www.usm craiders.com), both of which feature multiple links to facets of the two battalions' histories. I also consulted Ken Ringle, "Bringing Them Home," *The Washington Post*, Nov. 26, 2000; Edward C. Whitman, "Submarine Commandos," *Undersea Warfare* 3, No. 2 (Winter 2001); Norm Maves Jr., "57 Years after Battle, the Mission Carries On," *The Oregonian* (Portland), May 31, 1999; Pat

Cataldo, "Remains of Marine Raiders Killed in 1942 Repatriated at Hickam," *The Kwajalein Hourglass,* April 11, 2000; and the Kiribati section of Jane Resture's Oceana Web site (www.janeresture.com). The Republic Pictures film *Gung Ho!* is available on VHS videocassette.

My account of Sturm's excavation is based on his account of the dig, provided me as an e-mail attachment in the fall of 2001; his official site report; and interviews with Randy Posey, Valerie McIntosh, and Bill Belcher.

CHAPTER 2

The passage on "bone work" is the product of interviews with anthropologists Gwen Haugen, Dave Rankin, Ann Bunch, and Bill Belcher; with CILHI number two Johnie Webb; and my observations while visiting the lab during the analysis of the Makin remains in July 2001.

Further reading on mtDNA can be had in Alice R. Isenberg and Jodi M. Moore, "Mitochondrial DNA Analysis at the FBI Laboratory," *Forensic Science Communications* 1, No. 2 (July 1999); Rebecca L. Cann, Mark Stoneking, and Allan C. Wilson, "Mitochondrial DNA and Human Evolution," *Nature* 235 (Jan. 1–7, 1987); Jerry E. Bishop, "Strands of Time," *Wall Street Journal,* Sept. 10, 1993; Eric A. Schon and Salvatore Dimauro, "The Other DNA: Research on Mitochondrial Diseases," one of several DNA-related articles published in the Columbia University research magazine *21stC* in 1996; and on "The Fire Within: The Unfolding Story of Human Mitochondrial DNA," an article by Brown University biology professor Kenneth R. Miller, posted on the university Web site at http://biocrs.biomed.brown.edu/Books/Essays/Mitochondrial DNA.html.

Mitochondrial Eve is discussed in Cann, Stoneking, and Wilson's 1987 *Nature* article; in Bishop's "Strands of Time"; by Tabitha M. Powledge and Mark Rose in "The Great DNA Hunt," *Archaeology* 49, No. 5 (Sept./Oct. 1996); and by Jeremy Thomson in "Humans Did Come out of Africa, Says DNA," Nature News Service, Dec. 7, 2000.

Neanderthal mtDNA is discussed by Matthias Krings, A. Stone, R. W. Schmitz, H. Krainitzki, Mark Stoneking, and Svante Paabo in "Neandertal DNA Sequences and the Origin of Modern Humans," *Cell* 90, No. 1 (July 11, 1997); by Mark Rose in "Neandertal DNA," *Archaeology* 50, No. 5 (Sept./Oct. 1997); and by Igor V. Ovchinnikov, Anders Götherström, Galina P. Romanova, Vitaliy M. Kharitonov, Kerstin Lidén, and William Goodwin, "Molecular Analysis of Neanderthal DNA from the Northern Caucasus," *Nature* 404 (March 30, 2000).

An interesting account of the Romanov case is provided by Maples and Browning in *Dead Men Do Tell Tales;* Maples, a Florida anthropologist, was part of a team of U.S. scientists tapped to conduct bone work on the recovered skeletons and describes the process in detail.

AFDIL's past work is related by Jim Garamone in "Secretary of Defense

Decides to Remove Vietnam Unknown from Tomb," Army News Service, May 8, 1998; by air force major Jason F. Kaar, "New Applications for Old DNA," *Legal Medicine* (Armed Forces Institute of Pathology, 1999); and the AFDIL Web site, at www.afip.org/Departments/oafme/dna/History.htm.

The process of extraction and typing is detailed by Isenberg and Moore in their article on the FBI lab and in numerous articles, many written for the layperson, posted at www.highveld.com.

CHAPTER 3

Barker's son, Michael, supplied copies of the major's letters home. The passages describing the families' notification are from interviews with each in the autumn of 2001. The quoted letters from officialdom were provided me by the families or are on microfilm at the Library of Congress. They include a letter to Dugan's family describing the shootdown, written by Lt. Col. Bobbie Fernander; an April 5, 1971, letter to the Chubbs from Barker's replacement, Capt. James Hennessy; and a letter to the Chubbs from Hennessy's replacement, Lynn Hooper.

Papers associated with the Court of Inquiry are part of the personnel records of the four 1731 soldiers; some are duplicated in the Library of Congress records. They include written statements from eyewitnesses Jon Evans and Lt. William B. Taylor Jr., and another from Al Fischer stating that Barker and crew left Khe Sanh at 2:30 P.M.

Former Kingsman Dave Whiteley told me via e-mail that he was the soldier ordered to collect Dillender's belongings. The inventory of Dillender's possessions is from his personnel file.

Several Kingsmen related details of the memorial service, and family members provided me with copies of the program prepared for the event. Quotes from Tom Boland's eulogy are from his notes, part of the family papers provided me by Michael Barker.

Bill Dillender's letter is part of his son's file at the Library of Congress. My description of the families' dreams and fears following the shootdown were gleaned from interviews with those mentioned; Barker's sister Eloise described their mother's nightmare.

PART FOUR: PIECES OF THE PAST

CHAPTER 1

The Library of Congress records are fat with papers pertaining to the John Chubb dog tag, including Bill Gadoury's report on the May 16, 1986, interview at which the tag and medallion were first revealed; the photocopies he made of both; a June 17, 1986, memo from Gadoury to his JCRC bosses, with which he sent the photocopies; a June 19, 1986, memo in which JCRC analysts discuss the tag's authenticity; Gadoury's January 11, 1987, report detailing his December 10, 1986, meeting with the father; and a January 1987 memo from the JCRC to the Defense Intelligence Agency, with which the recovery center submitted the tag for further analysis. I obtained later papers, in which analysts branded the story of the tag's discovery a sham, from the JTF and CILHI personnel.

CHAPTER 2

The "two missing Americans" letter, dated September 15, 1982, was written by a refugee in "Ubon camp." His or her name has been deleted from the translated, typewritten copy on file at the Library of Congress.

The quoted "thick of the fight" letter is a one-page, handwritten document dated December 9, 1982, written by an inmate at the Nakhon Phanom refugee camp. The "Lam Son area" report was documented in a September 23, 1988, message from air force lieutenant colonel James D. Spurgeon III, the chief of the JCRC Liaison Division, to his bosses in Hawaii.

As indicated in the text, the information on the attempted sale of bones purported to be Dillender's was included in the background papers the JTF supplied Gwen Haugen before the mission.

Among the mountains of MIA intelligence that the government's various investigative agencies amassed in the seventies and eighties were other nuggets they initially thought might be linked to the men aboard Jack Barker's Huey. Early in 1971, U.S. officials learned that an unidentified North Vietnamese element captured a U.S. helicopter after it mistakenly landed near their position. "It is very regrettable that the men killed the personnel already," an intercepted report read, "just the aircraft remains." On thinking it over, Pentagon analysts decided a link wasn't likely after all. "The REFNO 1731 helicopter exploded and broke apart in the air," DPMO noted in 1996. "It was not intact when it hit the ground."

In May 1971, an informant reported that a North Vietnamese unit operating in Laos supposedly shot down at least three helicopters in mid- to late April 1971, and that "one of the three crashed helicopters contained three dead Americans." Again, DPMO eventually wrote off any connection to Case 1731, noting that the time frame didn't fit.

In June 1973, a North Vietnamese turncoat told investigators that within a thirty-minute period on March 27, 1971, he'd seen eight U.S. helicopters shot down near a tall hill in Savannakhet Province and that in one of them he found one wounded and three dead Americans. He and other soldiers took the wounded man to a field hospital, but he bled to death on the way. Later, the turncoat recalled, he saw grave markers on which "O5" and "High Point 500" were written in yellow paint; a higher-up told him that "O5" meant "air pirate," local parlance for an American aviator.

Analysts from the Defense Intelligence Agency researched U.S. air losses in the region and found "no specific day during this time frame or in this location when eight U.S. helicopter losses involving unaccounted-for U.S. personnel occurred simultaneously." The agency concluded that the source "may have either exaggerated this information or possibly mistakenly identified some of the helicopters as being U.S."

CHAPTER 4

Harry Reasoner made his comment about helicopters on February 16, 1971. The *Time* commentary, by Tim Larimer, appeared in the April 23, 2001, international edition under the headline "Diminishing Remains: The Ambitious Hunt for MIAs Has Become Mortally Expensive."

Paul Wolfowitz spoke at the Fort Myer memorial service for those killed aboard the Mi-17 on April 25, 1971. He and other Defense Department officials reiterated the government's intention to continue recovery missions at the annual convention of the National League of Families of American Prisoners and Missing in Southeast Asia, held in Arlington, Virginia, June 20–23, 2001.

The Pacific Command announced the findings of its collateral inquiry on October 10, 2001. The executive summary is posted at www.vfwdc.org.

CHAPTER 5

The worm-snake was most likely a blind snake of the family Typhlopidae, which "has 200 species distributed in Africa, Madagascar, southeastern Asia and tropical America," according to *The Illustrated Encyclopedia of the Animal Kingdom*, Vol. IX (Danbury Press, 1971). "It is harmless despite its reputation of being highly poisonous," the encyclopedia notes, adding that the snake burrows underground in search of insect pupae and larvae. "It is easily confused with an earthworm."

Haugen chronicled her 1997 dig near Hanoi in telephone interviews, during which she consulted her notes from the mission.

PART FIVE: ANSWERS

CHAPTER 1

My stop in Papua New Guinea included visits to a second CILHI excavation, in the ruins of a B-17E Flying Fortress shot down after bombing a Japanese airfield at Vunakanau in June 1943. Our Huey settled in a small LZ beside a rough village road, and we trooped into the jungle, roller-coastering into creeks and over small ridges until, ten minutes into our hike, we passed a broken .50-caliber machine gun in the ferns just off the path. The grid was a few yards farther on, carefully staked into rust-colored soil where the cockpit had lain. The jungle around us — like that of Southeast Asia, far more deciduous than you might expect, its dominant hardwoods towering over smaller wild banana and palm — was noisy with the shrieks of cicadas and birds. Termite mounds jutted from the soil like black gumdrops. The two dozen local workers chewed betel nut, spitting the narcotic fruit's red juice in such abundance that the ground around them resembled the aftermath of a massacre.

Nine Americans had died in the attack and subsequent crash, which strewed pieces of the bomber over 430 yards of undulating forest floor. The machine gun was mere prelude to what waited north of the grid, down a path hacked through the forest with machetes and floored in mud and broken palm fronds. About eighty-five yards from the dig site we reached an engine driven into the ground, its prop still attached, blades still tipped in yellow paint. A stainless-steel header pipe curved from its cowling. It looked as if you could bolt it to a fresh engine.

Not far away we came across a section of wing, its army air corps insignia — white star on blue circle, red dot at its center — visible through a veneer of jungle mulch and windblown dirt. To the east, a section of the fuselage lay on its port side, its metal edges shredded, another star plain on its olive skin. Pieces of the B-17's waist guns were twisted in the wreckage; scattered about were dozens of unfired .50-caliber rounds. We slid down a steep ravine, rock-hopped the narrow creek at its base, and heaved up the far side to a massive piece of the plane's undercarriage, belly-up, its empty bomb bays ajar, one landing gear pointed skyward through an opening in the jungle canopy, a tire airless and cracked but still attached to its wheel. Uphill again, downhill again, back up. One hundred thirty yards north of the undercarriage the trail curved slightly, and I stopped cold as I rounded the bend: Just ahead was a clearing, and at its center, awash in golden morning light, stood the bomber's upright tail, a chain of painted yellow numbers — "12430" — faded but visible on its surface. We circled it slowly. The rudder was missing; shoots grew from its dirt-packed hinges. The tail gunner's small, thick-paned battle station was entwined in a confusion of twisted and torn aluminum. In places the tail's skin was ripped, and through the rents we could see metal gleaming as if the bomber had just rolled off the Boeing assembly line.

The next day I saw pieces of the plane in the New Britain museum. A slab of the nose's starboard side hung from the wall, the plane's nickname — "Naughty But Nice" — painted orange alongside a primitive rendition of a seated nude, a blue cloth draped over her lap. Her red nail polish was still bright. The plane's glassless dorsal gun turret, or "top hat," hung beside the nose art. It looked factory-fresh. Below stood the cockpit, control yokes and pedals still in place, gauges and switches still legible on the instrument panel despite their long exposure to the island's equatorial heat and rain.

CHAPTER 2

The case of Vietnamese evidence planting I cite is included in the papers associated with the October 18, 1967, loss of navy lieutenant commander John F. Barr. The papers are available at the Library of Congress.

CHAPTER 4

Bill Forsyth's faxed letter to Bell Helicopter Textron was dated September 20, 2001. He provided me with a copy, along with a print-out of Ron Cribbs's e-mailed reply, which was dated September 21, 2001.

PART SIX: PERSEVERANCE

CHAPTER 1

I conducted several interviews with Michael Barker, the longest on September 22, 2002.

CHAPTER 2

The April 16 newspaper story was written by Sgt. Matt Gryta. Headlined "Saga of 4 Who Crash-Landed in Laos," it was published on page 3 of *Southern Cross* on April 16, 1971, and is reproduced at http://www.americal.org/174/peterson.htm.

My conversation with Darold Berger took place in January 2002; my interview with Chester "Chick" Luther occurred on the afternoon of Monday, February 4, 2002.

ACKNOWLEDGMENTS

In the late 1990s I was the military editor of *The Virginian-Pilot*, the newspaper serving Norfolk and surrounding cities in Southeast Virginia and northeastern North Carolina. Among my duties was conducting an occasional class in military-media relations at the nearby Armed Forces Staff College, my students mid-career officers deeply suspicious of newsmen. As I licked my wounds after one 1999 session, a tall army lieutenant colonel with a shaved head and a guileless smile approached me with the words: "Have I got a story for you."

His name was Franklin Childress, and he was the public affairs boss at Joint Task Force–Full Accounting. I'd never heard of the outfit; until Childress started talking, I'd no idea that America dispatched recovery teams to Southeast Asia in search of soldiers who'd not returned from the war there. Our conversation prompted my first visit to the region, to Vietnam's Quang Nam Province, the following July, on assignment for *The Pilot,* and another to Laos the following March for *Parade.* A third journey, the following August and September, became the basis for this book.

If not for Childress's help, I'd not been the first journalist to accompany a recovery team on a full mission; I'd not have obtained the necessary papers from Vientiane, nor negotiated the sticky political landscape of the joint task force, the Central Identification Lab, and the Pentagon, nor found Jack Barker's case to follow. Any luck I enjoyed in putting this story together can be attributed, in large part, to his efforts on my behalf.

Others at the joint task force went out of their way to help me, too, among them its commanders, army brigadier general Harry Axson and air force brigadier general Steven Redmann; army lieutenant colonel Kevin Smith, the CO of Detachment Three in Laos; army lieutenant colonels Jerry O'Hara, Childress's successor, and Rennie L. Corey, the late CO of the Hanoi detachment; air force lieutenant Colette Ching; air force captain Renee Stockwell; and Laos analyst Bill Forsyth.

I owe a huge debt to the members of RE-1: Gwen Haugen, marine captain Patrick Reynolds, army sergeant first class Randy Posey, army staff sergeants Valerie McIntosh and David Dingman, sergeants Jessica Dean and Rula Castro, marine staff sergeant Brian Eagmin, navy chiefs Victoria Conely and Art Artillaga, air force senior airman Clint Krueger, and army privates first class Tracy Gummo and Kyna Bullock. CILHI anthropologists Dave Rankin, Bill Belcher, Pete Miller, Greg Berg, C. Elliott "Hoss" Moore II, and Brad Sturm share credit for information scattered throughout the book. I also thank CILHI's Johnie Webb and Col. Dave Pagano, who helped place me with Haugen's team and arranged my visit to the digs in Papua New Guinea.

Telling this story may have weighed most heavily on the families, friends, and comrades of the men RE-1 sought in Laos, who nevertheless were unfailingly generous with their time and memories. I also came to rely on the good graces of Frieda Powell, at the army's Casualty Affairs office; Larry Greer at DPMO; Ann Mills Griffiths, executive director of the National League of Families; retired air force lieutenant colonel Jeannie H. Schiff, who shared her unpublished research into MIA cases in Laos; Jim Williams, the army aviation historian at Fort Rucker, who asked tough questions of my early drafts; and Mike Sloniker, historian of the Vietnam Helicopter Pilots Association, a walking encyclopedia of Lam Son knowledge, who put me in touch with veterans and experts. Justin Taylan and Bruce Hoy were great help in assembling the history of the World War II wrecks I visited in New Guinea. Miriam Grier, of Civic Travel in Los Angeles, got me seats on airplanes that other travel agents told me didn't exist.

At *The Pilot*, editor Kay Tucker Addis gave me a leave of absence to research and write the book, a demonstration of faith that I'll never be able to repay. Dennis Hartig was, as he's been for years, my enthusiastic supporter, and gave the manuscript its first close look. Maria Carrillo waded through two drafts, and Richard C. Bayer, Fred Kirsch, and Dave Gulliver suffered early versions. Nelson Brown championed my initial trip to Vietnam. Peggy Deans Earle helped in my search for documents. Bob Voros took on the daunting assignment of drawing the maps that accompany the text. Photographer Vicki Cronis joined me on my first two forays to Southeast Asia, proving herself an adaptable and adventurous traveling companion and no slouch in the Beerlao department. She also volunteered her photographs and produced gorgeous prints from my own imperfect negatives. *Parade*'s Lamar Graham, who dispatched us on one of those trips, proved as good an editor as he is a writer — which is a little scary.

A host of others helped me maintain a grip during the months I spent committing the story to paper, including the fabulous Amy Walton, Mike D'Orso, Robin Russ, Laura LaFay, Lori Denney, Mark Mobley, Jennifer Peter, Ian Martin, Joe "He Gets All the Facts In" Jackson, my parents, and most especially, my sweet, smart, and beautiful daughter, Saylor.

Finally, I thank my agent and friend, Laureen Rowland, who has been my cheerleader, confidante, and caretaker throughout this project, who has listened patiently to my many long and fretful monologues, and who has shepherded me down the corridors of literary power with grace, confidence, and expertise; and Eamon Dolan, my editor at Houghton Mifflin, who has demanded that the quality of my storytelling equal that of my story, and has wielded a sharp mind and pencil to produce the book you now hold in your hands.

Eastern Savannakhet Province, Laos

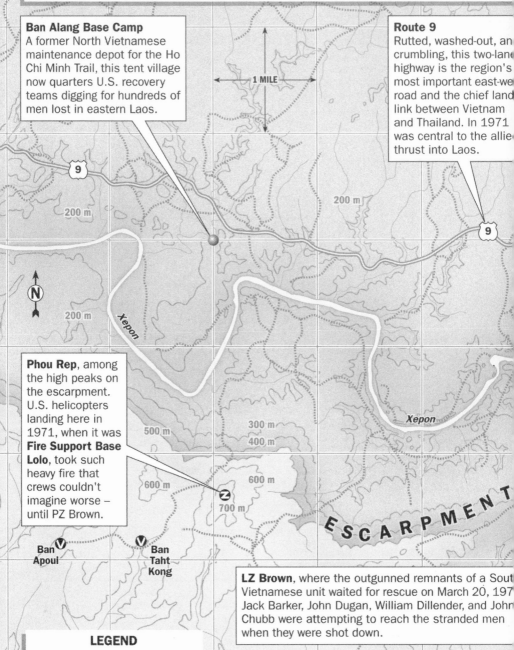

Ban Alang Base Camp
A former North Vietnamese maintenance depot for the Ho Chi Minh Trail, this tent village now quarters U.S. recovery teams digging for hundreds of men lost in eastern Laos.

Route 9
Rutted, washed-out, an crumbling, this two-lane highway is the region's most important east-we road and the chief land link between Vietnam and Thailand. In 1971 was central to the allie thrust into Laos.

1 MILE

9

200 m

200 m

9

N

200 m

Xepon

200 m

Phou Rep, among the high peaks on the escarpment. U.S. helicopters landing here in 1971, when it was **Fire Support Base Lolo**, took such heavy fire that crews couldn't imagine worse – until PZ Brown.

Xepon

500 m

300 m

400 m

600 m

600 m

700 m

Ban Apoui

Ban Taht Kong

ESCARPMENT

LZ Brown, where the outgunned remnants of a Sout Vietnamese unit waited for rescue on March 20, 197 Jack Barker, John Dugan, William Dillender, and John Chubb were attempting to reach the stranded men when they were shot down.

LEGEND

Dig Sites: ⊗ Highways: ═══════

Villages: ⊽ Cart/foot paths: ·······

Wartime Pick-up Zones (PZ) or Fire Support Bases (FSB): ⊿

Elevation: 300 m Small river or stream:

The Case 1731 excavation site, where Gwen Haugen's recovery team digs for remains of the four Americans lost aboard Jack Barker's Huey. Her expedition, more than a dozen years after th first search for the chopper, follows the purport discovery of a U.S. Army aviator's helmet here.